SALES & DISTRIBUTION MANAGEMENT

SALES & DISTRIBUTION MANAGEMENT

Amar Jyoti

genNEXT Publication

Sales & Distribution Management

Rs. 890

ISBN: 978-93-80222-15-8

Published in 2009 in India by
Gennext Publication
23 Main Ansari Road, Darya Ganj,
New Delhi-110002
E-Mail:GenNextpublication@hotmail.com
Phone: 23282060

Printed at: Singhal Print Media, Delhi

Contents

Preface *vii*

1. **Introduction** **1**
Key Approaches in Sales Management, A Management Responsibility, Searching for an ''Edge'', Summary

2. **Evolution of Sales Management** **9**
Management in the Round, Sales Management, The Last Ten Years of Sales Management, Summary

3. **The Electronic Dimension** **17**
Some Dangers, Opportunities, Best Practice, Summary

4. **The Global Dimension** **25**
International Options, A Little Local Difficulty, Best Practice, Summary

5. **The State of the Art** **31**
Planning, Organizing, Staffing, Motivating, Control, Looking Ahead, Summary

6. **Sales & Distibution in Practice** **47**
Case 1, Case 2, Case 3, Horses for Courses, An Excellent Idea

7. **Key Concepts and Thinkers** **55**
Key Terminology, Customer Categorization, Key Thinkers

8. **Resources** **65**
Research, Journals, Films, Professional Bodies, Steps for Making Sales Management to Work

9. **Significance of Communication** **83**
Listening Skills, The Theory Behind Communication Styles, The Four-Quadrant System, Roles and Situations Affecting the Style, Working With People with Different Styles, Strategies for Improving Communications, Presentation Skills

10. Sales Planning **109**
Aligning the Corporate Strategy with the Sales Team, The Sales Plan, Where Sales Fits in the Corporate Structure, The Customer-Centric Organization, Marketing's Relationship to Sales, Creating a Plan, Continuous Planning

11. Time Management, Territory Planning and Sales Forecasting **133**
Time Management, The Art of Delegating, Ranking Current and New Accounts

12. Recruiting **155**
Enhancing the Current Team, Developing Specific Criteria for the Selection Process, Optimal Sources for Recruiting, The Number One Rule in Recruiting: Constantly Recruit, Ensuring A Positive Interview Process, Other Important Interviewing Considerations, Firing is Inevitable

13. Building the Environment for Motivation **183**
Classical Motivation Theory, Aesthetic, Sales Compensation and Incentives Plans, The Sales Compensation and Incentives Plan: Where to Start, Benefits and the Total Compensation Package

14. Training, Coaching, and Counselling **209**
Methods of Training Based on Learning Styles, Multiple Learning Styles, The Core Concepts of Reinforcement, Principles of Reinforcement, Coaching and Counselling, Goal-Setting Sessions, Additional Legal Considerations

15. Steps in Becoming a True Leader **237**
The Characteristics of a Team

16. Sales Promotion **255**
Advertising, Advertising Decision, Advertisement and Sales Promotion, Advertising Aims, Advertising Agency, Measuring Advertising Effectiveness

17. Retail Selling **271**
Product Classification, Types of Buying Decision, Shopping Motives, the Buying Process, Retail Sales Roles, Retail Sales Process, Retail Selling and the Promotional Mix, Summary

Bibliography **285**

Index **293**

Preface

Sales and Distribution management decisions are at the center of marketing decisions for all companies. This feature is amplified in a country like ours where huge number of consumers, high retail activity and vast inequality between purchasing power of consumers, big infrastructure, culture etc. makes the field of sales and distribution very complex. Most of the books present in the market are from foreign authors which contains knowledge and practices more appropriate for developed countries. This volume covers the field of sales and distribution in a very lucid manner and in Indian context. This book would fulfill the need for a text that covers the concepts of sales and distribution management and their applications in day-to-day business. Integration of sales and distribution management functions is the underlying theme of the book. which recognizes the fact that today there is probably no sales manager who does not have distribution responsibilities as well.

Building on an understanding of the consumer decision process, the book defines the roles of marketing and selling strategies. Secondly, adopting a customer-centric approach to sales and distribution management, the book deals with making strategic decisions keeping the end consumer in mind and making operational decisions keeping the channel member and the sales force in focus. It highlights the importance of behavioral transactions in completing a sale and also discusses the service orientation required for selling different products.

With its unique approach, generalized frameworks, elaborate research and extensive data analysis, this book will be of immense value to sales and distribution professionals of the Indian corporate sector and marketing departments of national and multinational companies in India.

The book gives real life examples in the areas of sales and distribution to provide experience of sales and distribution environment. It covers Personal Selling Function, Managing the Sales Force, Planning for Sales Effort, Distribution System and Logistics, Distribution Planning and Control. It attempts to blend in theory with practice.

This volume is a comprehensive textbook specially designed to meet the requirements of management students specializing in sales and distribution. It highlights the major decision areas within sales and distribution and provides analytical models and approaches that will facilitate decision making. It gives an exposure to key concepts, theories and recent developments in sales and distribution and illustrates their applicability in tackling the challenges in business.

Students shall find this book extremely useful for its treatment of the sales organization, sales management, territory management, designing a distribution system and distribution management.

1

Introduction

Sales, selling and the sales force are inherently a part of the marketing mix. It must be deployed appropriately if it is to play its part and have a significant effect on the whole. That means that those people undertaking the sales task must be professional: able to communicate persuasively and create the necessary relationship with customers.

It also means that the efforts of sales staff must be properly coordinated and therefore well managed: sales management is therefore important, and can directly influence results.

The management of any group of staff is important if they are to perform well. In sales there are a number of particular factors that make it especially so, which are as follows:

- Isolation: sales people must work predominantly on their own and there is a possibility that, without supervision, they become disassociated from the overall marketing effort and that their activity is therefore incomplete.
- Geography: sales people must work away from base, sometimes far away. Apart from the isolation referred to above, this means that applying management to them is inherently more difficult, and probably more time consuming than with staff in the office.
- The nature of the task: selling is a social skill, one must be constantly fine-tuned if it is to do the desired job satisfactorily. Customer attrition can dilute such skills and management must act regularly to prompt sales people to maximize their approach in whatever way prevailing market conditions making it necessary.

KEY APPROACHES IN SALES MANAGEMENT

Sales management is not simply a supervisory process, that is, in the sense of the "policing" role of management: checking and making sure things are done. It is, or should be, a creative role, one that enhances the ongoing sales activity and ensures it achieves everything possible. So too the relationship between sales people and sales manager should be a constructive one and viewed as such by both sides. Two other factors are of key importance.

- Change and complexity: the markets of the twenty-first century are nothing if not dynamic. For example: customers are increasingly demanding and fickle, distribution patterns are ever changing (e.g. with the increasing power of large customers and the e-sales routes now possible in many industries), buying processes and responsibilities change and pressure on time means buyers may want less personal relationships with suppliers.
- Competition: competition (including global competition) seems increasing all the time. There is a direct impact here on the sales job. Customers not only have considerable choice in almost any industry and product area one cares to mention, they have choices that are very close in performance, price, service and other factors. There has come to be a powerful commodity aspect to many markets. This means that sales people have a three-tier job to do. They must:
  - Communicate (clearly and appropriately)
  - Be persuasive
  - Differentiate.

In other words it is not enough to be able to describe products and services effectively, nor even to do so persuasively - always there is the added dimension of ensuring something is described in a way that makes it more desirable than other similar products on the market.

Because of these factors the quality of selling itself can literally be a differentiating factor, giving any organization that maximizes its effectiveness an edge over competition. This is a vital factor in marketing success. The manager or managers who head up the sales function, and who work to make it effective, have a vital task. It is a complex job, and one that in future will tend to get more complex as the trends described here progress. For sales management, creatively making the sales activity work well is a challenge; for the organization an effective sales management function, now and in the future, is a must.

Despite the long currency of the word marketing, there are still sometimes questions asked about the "difference between sales and marketing." Yet there should be no confusion. The days when marketing was regularly used as a euphemism for selling, or indeed advertising, are surely long gone. Selling, and the sales people who carry it out, are as inherently part of the individual techniques of marketing as is public relations, promotion or any other.

And, to define sales management, it is the function - or person - responsible for creating and maintaining a suitable sales activity through management and supervision of the sales team (most usually the field sales team, rather than other categories of sales job), and hence achieving, through them, the required sales results.In addressing sales management - what the sales manager must do and why - it is worth noting that in some organizations the sales function can be something of a neglected area, underrated and with other more glamorous techniques claiming more than their fair share of the limelight.

That is not to say that large numbers of organizations do not pay any regard to selling. Most do - to one extent or another. Certainly sales training is now much more likely to be used than was once the case, and there is a general acceptance of the need for excellence in selling as in so many other business and management techniques.

Only through such an attitude can an organization look to thrive and prosper. Much of this concern is with the techniques of selling. These are, of course, important. Sales people must be able to deploy such techniques effectively and if they are up against a competitor that can do so better - more appropriately in whatever way - they may well lose out.

However, a broader view of selling must be taken if the overall effectiveness of the sales resource is to be maximized successfully. Specifically looking at the sales resource from a broader perspective means viewing it as essentially a marketing technique - one that needs to be regarded as a variable like any other.

The sales resource must play an appropriate part in whatever overall marketing mix an organization decides to use (something that may well vary over time). And its doing so will not just happen. It needs planning and organizing. Above all it needs regular fine-tuning if it is to act continuously to achieve planned results in the marketplace, and do so with some certainty.

A MANAGEMENT RESPONSIBILITY

It is an old saying that selling is too important to leave to the sales team. In many ways their likelihood of success is dependent upon a wide range of things from quality of product or service, to company image, technical support and after sales service and customer care. Any success the team may achieve is certainly dependent on the way the organization - and thus whatever managers this necessitates (the sales manager, marketing manager, general manager in a smaller business or others) - views the sales resource. And on how they use it innovatively to create not just an efficient final link with the market but make sales an asset that can gain real competitive advantage in markets that are doubtless also targeted by competitors. Three other factors make this overall view of the sales resource vital.

MARKET CHANGE

In recent years markets are nothing if not volatile. This has compounded increasing competitiveness, but it is an international fact of life. Everywhere all aspects of marketing are having to work harder if an organization is to hold on to, and develop, markets. It is said that sustainable competitive advantage comes only from innovation. We are in times when innovation is needed in many aspects of a company's operation: organization, product development - and that of sales is no exception.

Furthermore, one of the most pertinent changes of recent times has been with customers. They have had to react within their own organizations to protect and secure their future, and their attitudes to suppliers have changed markedly with any economic difficulty. The expectations of customers is now better defined than ever before: they know the service they want, the technical standards they want and they seek suppliers who can provide prompt and well matched answers to the problems of opportunities that initiate their purchase of anything - product or service. Not least, they want to deal with professional people representing a professional firm. And they want efficient support, response and communications throughout the relationship. Faced with any shortfall in their requirements they have absolutely no compunction about voting with their feet and going elsewhere.

In addition, buyer loyalty is less than in the past. Success on one occasion does not guarantee that people will buy again. Customers are demanding, fickle and need to be treated in just the right way. All this is not a momentary circumstance. Any lingering belief that "it will all be easier when things get back to normal" must be ruled out. Realistically circumstances are simply not likely to return to those of more straightforward or less competitive times. All organizations must all live with, and adapt to, changed circumstances.

The sales resource must be organized and must operate in a way that deals with the new realities. To do this requires more than "going through the motions," it means every detail of the process must be thought through and implemented in a way that creates the required edge.

ATTENTION TO DETAIL

In terms of detail, prevailing standards often leave something to be desired. The best way to explain this is perhaps through an example, the personal experience of the author, that shows how such details can be missed or dealt with incompletely or ineffectively.

INNOVATION

The example given above focuses on an important detail, albeit one that is hardly novel in the industry mentioned. Beyond that kind of detail other more innovative factors may be added that also create an edge (even a strengthening is worthwhile) for those doing the selling. Such may either be an individual initiative, one that is the idea of an individual sales person, or something that is adopted by management for use throughout the team. One, of course, may lead to the other, though such initiatives must be appropriate to the individual customer and may not be suitable for use slavishly with every contact (a thought we return to later).

SEARCHING FOR AN "EDGE"

Whatever aspect of the sales process one considers, it may potentially yield an examination aimed at increasing the effectiveness of the process. If so the resultant success rate will be just a little better. The process is cumulative and, unless this is too strong a word, infinite. Certainly there are many opportunities to strengthen sales activity and ensure that the sales resource plays its full part as a major component of the marketing mix. In many commercial environments marketing can be seen as somehow "better" or more sophisticated than sales. Yet there is no reason for this; sales is a vital part of the marketing mix and one that is just as likely to provide opportunities to steal a march on competitors and impress prospects and customers alike as is attention to any other technique. As such it deserves the same degree of attention and creative thought lavished on other aspects of the marketing mix.

Against this background any organization must be clear what they want to achieve through sales, and similarly any sales manager must be clear what tasks they must focus on both tactically and strategically. The key sales management tasks are normally defined as given below:

- Planning
- Organizing
- Staffing
- Developing
- Motivating
- Controlling

The classic definition of management - getting things done through other people - underpins this and the objectives towards which this is applied are the achievement of specific, measurable largely economic factors: sales revenue and profit, and within that, detailed targets such as the product mix required and overall organizational measures such as return on sales and ultimately return on capital employed.

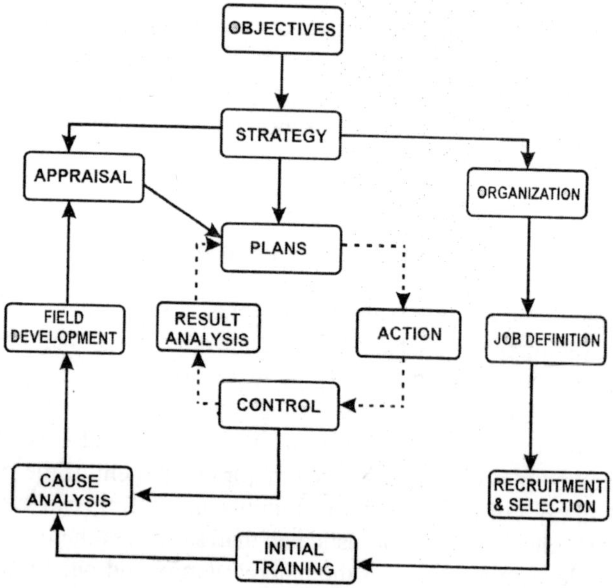

Fig: Sales management long-/short-term tasks and responsibilities.

The above figure shows in graphic form the way sales management responsibilities must be exercised and the way different tasks relate.

SUMMARY

The definition of sales management and the individual interpretation of what needs to be done are crucial for the success of sale. Successful sales management will:

- Always rate sales as a key marketing variable;
- Never underestimate the difference it can make to team performance;
- Constantly keep abreast of market changes and customer expectations, matching operational practice to the real world accordingly;
- Comprehensively define the sales job to be done, and work at ensuring that the detail that makes for sales excellence is addressed effectively and consistently; and
- Always take a creative approach: recognizing that sales management is not there just to keep things operating efficiently, but to decide what constitutes efficient operation at any particular time. They know that change is the norm.

Note: Colonial Group (Colonial) is a privately-held company. It acts as a holding company for various subsidiaries which provide storage and distribution services for liquid and dry bulk products, including bulk chemicals, motor fuels, industrial fuel oil, and retail gas. The company through its subsidiaries also provides ship bunkering, commercial shipping, and tug and barge services. It primarily operates in the US and Puerto Rico. Colonial is headquartered in Savannah, Georgia and employs about 1,100 people. For detailed information related to this chapter reader can visit www.colonialgroupinc.com

2

Evolution of Sales Management

Management is an ancient art. In this chapter we will study about the roots and development of modern sales management.

- Management in the round
- Sales management
- The last ten years of sales management

"There is no magic in management. I make sure people know what they are doing and then see that they do it."

Management as a generic activity has a long history. Modern remnants of projects such as the building of the pyramids provide ample evidence of management in action. It is not an unreasonable inference to suggest that many things before and since can be similarly regarded; without a degree of management cathedrals, canals and civilization itself would not exist.

MANAGEMENT IN THE ROUND

Yet, perhaps curiously, management, at least as a formal process worth of study, is much more modern: it is a twentieth-century concern. And it is only late in the century that we find it becoming a matter of serious focus. Consider some dates.

- 1954: This year saw the publication of what many people would regard as the original "guru" guide to management: The Practice of Management by Peter Drucker (though there have been plenty more since).
- 1959: Though Harvard Business School in Cambridge Massachusetts had been in existence since early in the century, business schools only came to Europe in this year when

INSEAD opened, and Britain lagged behind with both the London and Manchester Business Schools opening in 1965.

- 1965: From the sixties onwards management was increasingly a source of focus, indeed its study became both more formal, and increasingly also a matter of fad and fashion with a new "magic" technique seemingly arriving every week promising to be the ultimate panacea for success. Some - management by objectives (MBO) - effectively formalized common sense. Others - transactional analysis (TA) - utilized psychology in the cause of management. Some are long forgotten, though all perhaps helped focus peoples' minds and contributed to consideration of what did work best. The process continues. A few can, looking back, be viewed as milestones, for example the following.
- 1982: The book In Search of Excellence (Tom Peters and Robert Waterman) was not only a best seller and the purveyor of sound advice (and more acronyms, e.g. MBWA - management by walking about), but also a spur to the many more books, articles and a whole new consideration of the practical "best ways forward" that followed. By this time there was a general feeling that if not exactly a science, management was something that needed a considered approach and that a multitude of management techniques assisted its practice.

Certainly now as we head into the twenty-first century, things have quietened down in the sense that management is well accepted as necessary, as is the need to go about it in the right kind of way. Suppose "magic formulae" are treated with more skepticism, or viewed merely as useful - a way of prompting investigation and thought. The study of management-matters is, these days, predominantly practically based.

It should be accepted by all, however, that management does not, and never will, consist of a prescribed list of unfailingly "correct" methods and techniques. Rather it is time-dependent, that is it is something that changes over time with what is "right" being only a question of what works, today and in a particular context.

And deciding what that is exactly needs care and judgment. Remember the view of H.L. Mencken who said "There is always a well-known solution to every human problem - neat, plausible - and wrong." This is certainly the case with a specialized form of management such as sales management.

SALES MANAGEMENT

The evolution of the sales management role is not complicated. Whenever there have been teams of sales people they have needed some form of direction. There are, however, circumstances and events which have influenced the way it is regarded and the way it operates. The prime reason for dwelling on this is that as times continue to be dynamic it is important for sales managers, and others concerned, to recognize changes that may have operational implications and to resolve to spot them early and act on them.

The chronology here is not of importance in itself (and is in some instances not intended to be precise); it does however put other comments in perspective. Starting in the mid-twentieth century, we begin with the observation of major influences that operated over longer time periods.

- 1945: With the end of the Second World War, industry was left at a low ebb. The period thereafter was one of recovery in which a production orientation was pre-eminent. Making things was more important than selling them; if they could be made then, after the privations of the war, they could be easily sold.
- 1955-1965: Gradually production orientation gave way to one of marketing; it became important to ensure that what was being made would appeal to customers and that it could be sold. This was perhaps the evangelical period for marketing, a time when managers were recognizing and learning to take a market view.
- 1963: This year saw the publication of Vance Packard's seminal book The Hidden Persuaders, a message to consumers everywhere that they were being exploited, particularly that advertising influenced them in ways they did not realize (or at least that they should be aware of the "hard sell" directed at them from all parts of the marketing mix - including selling). Also becoming active at this time was the American consumer champion Ralph Nader, whose initial efforts were directed at the motor car industry (and safety issues) but which spread to many other areas. These kinds of early influence have led to others and it is from all this that selling has had to deal with increasingly well-informed customers.
- 1965-1975: As competition intensified marketing moved into a technique period. During this period, management and

marketing training expanded (aided in the United Kingdom by the way in which the Industrial Training Act of 1964 promoted training). Managers were under no illusions: they recognized that a professional approach was necessary to everything that would address competition, and produce an edge in the marketplace. Sales management was one of many marketing techniques that were viewed more and more professionally during these years as people strived to find what worked best. There was a parallel focus on the psychology of selling being developed at this time, with initiatives such as research done by David Mayer and Herbert Greenberg (e.g. What makes a good Salesman? Harvard Business Review July/August 1964) who brought the terms empathy and ego drive into considerations of selling. Alongside the development of training, more and more began to be published about management, and in an increasingly accessible how-to style.

- 1970: During this year Mike Wilson's book Managing a Sales Force (Gower) was published. This was the most successful - and the best - of the new-style books about sales management. It had little in common with the dense textbook style of much previous management writing, or with the voluminous nature of the previous "bible" - US Dartnell Publishing's Sales Managers' Handbook. Its practical format was wholly accessible; packed with forms, charts and examples - it was seminal and provided a blueprint for successful operation (and also helped change the style of management books generally thereafter). From this time onwards sales management was recognized as a significant marketing component in its own right. The current edition of this book still provides a prime reference.
- Mid 1970s: This was the starting point of SPIN. This is a trade marked term: Huthwaite International's research-based approach to sales training, which not only became a successful product (courses, packages and books are now available around the world), but was instrumental in getting selling taken much more seriously as an influential element in promoting marketing success, though much of the original premise here reflected what others already thought of as common-sense approaches. The spin (sic) this put on serious thinking about sales and sales management was important; selling - for long regarded

as something "to do to people" - gradually began to be practiced in a way that more closely reflected customer needs.

- Mid/late 1970s and beyond: A market trend began around this time that was to change sales management for evermore. Customers no longer formed one group - larger and smaller customers began to be regarded as being different in nature as well as size. The world of selling was suddenly full of people with titles such as Major Account Manager and Key Account Executive and sales management had to organize more diverse sales teams in the recognition that different customers needed differing sales approaches. Indeed customers took action to put power into their buying - for example forming the buying groups that are now common in many industries.

Similarly inflationary pressures in many markets also began to exert a pressure for change that reduced or controlled costs involved in sales forces and the way they were organized and managed. For example, the increased cost of keeping field sales people on the road led directly to experiments that resulted in the successful development of telephone selling - a development that, in turn, led directly on to the call centers of today. (These are now ubiquitous in many industries and were pioneered in some such as banking.)

THE LAST TEN YEARS OF SALES MANAGEMENT

Like so much else in business and management the IT (information technology) revolution has had a considerable effect on selling and sales management. Here we limit examples to two main areas.

- The electronic revolution has changed a great deal about the way people do business. Sales people have to deal with organizations in which the computerized stock control system has replaced "the buyer" to some degree and meetings are harder to get. The speed of transactions has increased dramatically - sales people can check details for a buyer from a mobile computer as their discussions proceed. Speed, precision and detail are the order of the day and saying: "I'll check with the office and get back to you" may be regarded as prohibitively old-fashioned and slow.
- Information has changed radically also. Sales people must file much data: sales, travels, customer details, competitive intelligence and more. For the most part this is no longer filled

in on forms and posted to the office; it is entered into some sort of electronic data collection system and is available instantly to sales management making decisions. Tactical changes should be easier.

- Buyers are increasingly professional. This means they are better, and more specifically trained, better informed (and this is increasing as buyers make use of the Internet and other developments to help with pre-purchase research). Underestimating the knowledge or ability of buyers is now not just unwise, it can be fatal.

Some developments linked more than one of these factors. The concept of Major Customers and the availability of electronic systems have given rise to new techniques of CRM - Customer Relationship Management. This is, in some respect, no more than the process good sales people used years ago - but it is formalized, systematic and comprehensive. And, in electronic form, it is fast, precise and instantly transferable. It handles the basics: reminding a sales person to renew a contact, for instance. And it does things previously impossible.

If a customer in London refers a sales person to their opposite number in Singapore, then the right person in the Singapore office can be on the telephone to them without delay - and with all the facts and figures they would expect at their fingertips. Systems are worth checking out. Their data collection role is important, and mean that sales people can operate from a base of much more precise, up to date and comprehensive information than was the case in the past. They can be customized (indeed you should never even contemplate using something that does not match your customer situation).

Essentially the changes here relate as much to selling as to sales management. Sales management is, as you would expect, influenced by the people they manage, their role, the circumstances prevailing within the organization and outside it in the market. And, if you want to nail it to one thing, then that is the fact that sales management, like selling, must be customer focused to be successful.

Two other changes are worth noting. Both are difficult to date as they have crept up on us. One is certainly significant: staff expectations of management have changed. It must be much more consultative than was the case years ago, managers must find a way of dealing with people that is both acceptable and effective. It may also be wise to keep a wary eye on such factors as employment legislation. Many would say that managing people has become more time consuming. Perhaps. If so, then the response is surely to intensify the focus on key issues and ensure that new tasks are given priority.

The second change is perhaps more frivolous. In this politically correct world, the word salesman (which used to define field sales personnel as opposed to those in other sorts of sales position) has become unacceptable. Salesperson is the order of the day - even if it seems to encompass people as diverse as the shop assistant and the major account manager - thus bringing field sales person into the vocabulary. It does illustrate in yet another way the need for everyone to keep up with changes of all sorts!

SUMMARY

The moral for today's sales managers is clear.

- Focus on three levels: your job, the sales team's job and the customers' expectations.
- Watch for change: there is no one right way of managing in this area, much less one that will be correct, as is, for ever.
- Link what is operationally possible and necessary to the organization's objectives and goals: the activity of the sales team is a means to an end - how it must be prompted to go about its job depends on the objectives and the market. So sales management solutions must be practical for the team and the organization and yet always create acceptance and satisfaction with customers, on whom all marketing success ultimately depends.

Note: Toys "R" Us (TRU) is a privately held retailer of toys, baby products and children's apparels. The company operates in the US, Australia, Austria, Canada, France, Germany, Japan, Portugal, Spain, Switzerland and the UK. It is headquartered in Wayne, New Jersey and employs about 69,000 people. Reader can visit their site www.toysrus.com for a detailed study connected to this chapter.

3

The Electronic Dimension

Information Technology affects every nook and cranny of business, this chapter shows that sales management is no exception.

Information technology in all its forms is changing the face of business. Marketing ranks high amongst those areas affected - or taking advantage of this. Some benefits come from very sophisticated systems. An example given in the book Wired Life (Charles Jonscher, Bantam Press) makes a point. A typical major airline may have ten different fares for people flying on the same flight (one of thousands of flights made each day). United Airlines have pioneered the use of computers, using probability analysis, applied statistics and econometrics, to analyze past records of bookings, cancellations and fares to formulate policy for fare setting and discounting in a way that maximizes the number of fare paying passengers and the returns made.

However, sales management and sales consist primarily of personal interactions. But it would be a mistake to believe that this leaves them untouched by the information technology and e-commerce revolution. There are already many implications and doubtless more to come; this is an area of fast change. Here we touch on key factors and some of the ways in which these affect the job of keeping a field sales team functioning effectively.

SOME DANGERS

Taking certain negative factors first, consider the customer. They are as affected by the march of technology as you are, and what technology does for them may actively make life more difficult for you. Two examples illustrate the issues which are as follows:

- Customer ordering systems are now often automated. At a supermarket checkout the till rings up the money for the customer but it also records the resulting stock level. At a particular point the computer initiates a new order to the supplier and further supplies are delivered. Much of the process in between may be automatic. Then, later, a sales person is on the supermarket's doorstep asking to see the buyer. What's the reaction? Someone might say "our computer buys your product" and a meeting is declined. The sales person has a list of things they want to discuss: product positioning, new promotion, display and merchandising opportunities - all these could be delayed or go by the board. It makes the job of selling that much more difficult and specific steps have to be taken to make the wanted meeting seem attractive - unmissable - to the buyer.

- Products are getting more and more sophisticated. Sounding good, but this probably actually means more complex. This in turn means more product information for sales people to take on board and then put over to customers, clearly and quickly (customers will not make more time for your people because they are slow, or circuitous, in explanation). This has clear implications for briefing and training - more information, more regular changes and updates. But it is an opportunity nevertheless: if sales people take all this in their stride the impression they make on people is enhanced. It is doubly useful to make sure they excel at anything competitors find difficult. Overall, in some industries e-commerce is taking over from, or being added to, other forms of distribution. So far the things sold most successfully over the internet are limited and fall into comparatively few categories. These include:
  - — Price driven purchases (often where the product is checked out elsewhere and only bought over the Internet);
  - — Enthusiast products (e.g. computer games);
  - — Convenience (e.g. buying a book that then lands on the doormat); and
  - — Niche products of various kinds.

The range may be well widen. Meantime management must ensure that where personal selling remains possible, acceptable - even wanted - it is well deployed. It is perfectly possible to persuade some customers that it is better (for them) to buy following personal, individual advice than just by scanning a computer screen. Sales people need to be aware of the environment in which they operate, and the fact that the "buying experience" that people participate in now includes a greater variety of processes than ever before.

Although there are dangers in many of the other factors now mentioned, the primary impact is positive and the moral is the same in all cases - get these things right and you add to any edge between your organization and team and their competitors.

OPPORTUNITIES

There are many ways in which technology interacts with sales. For the manager the job is to see the possibilities, and to take a broad view of them. Some of the questions that must be asked of a possible new initiative are as follows.

- What will it cost?
- What effect will it have on productivity?
- How will it affect peoples' sales power?
- Will it have a positive or negative effect on customer service and perceptions?
- Will it assist in building relationships and business?

These different factors need to be balanced carefully. Something may seem to cost too much, but there may be dangers in ruling it out and missing significant benefits. Two improvement areas must be assessed: productivity and sales effectiveness. About the first Stanley Roach, Chief Economist of Morgan Stanley, said "The productivity gains of the information age are just a myth. There is not a shred of evidence to show that people are putting out more because of investments in technology." Harsh words, and in the sales area not borne out - but careful checks are needed to make sure that a positive effect will accrue from any technological changes contemplated. Assisting productivity may make something immediately desirable, but how will customers see it and what will it do to their perception of your customer service? It is this aspect that influences sales effectiveness most.

The following examples, in no particular order of importance, illustrate the range of areas to consider here and hint at further changes to come.

- Mobile telephones: a simple one first. These are already ubiquitous and their use can certainly boost customer service and speed things up; but they should never ring and interrupt a customer meeting. They seem headed to duplicate some of what computers do, though how well they will do so remains to be seen.

- Mobile computers: these, in the form of everything from high capacity laptops to simpler handheld devices (e.g. Palm or Psion machines), can go into the customer meeting with the sales person. They allow a variety of things to be done quickly and easily:
  - Checking stock and placing an order for a customer from their own office during the visit;
  - Updating records or issuing instructions to the sales office (perhaps from the car after a meeting); and
  - Forming part of a presentation to a customer (using PowerPoint charts to explain complex figures perhaps). The net impact here should be good: saving time, adding immediacy and allowing informed decisions to be made on the spot.
- Assisted learning: a variety of skills can be put over by learning packages (e.g. programmed learning devices on CD-ROM). This may be useful for product knowledge or sales skills, though remember that teaching the interactive skills deployed during sales meetings may need other inputs too.
- Communications: methods have changed (when did you last get a telex or even a fax?) and e-mail has replaced many more complex messages. It takes time to get something written, printed out and posted, so the convenience is obvious. But it is not right for everything. An e-mail may fail to impress a customer because it is so informal, or so brief it fails to be clear. And it can be wiped out at the touch of a button (so may not produce any potentially lasting memory jogger with a customer), and it does not impress graphically in the way a company letterhead should. Horses for courses - a variety of methods must still be used, and sales people always going for the easy option may dilute the overall and cumulative impression they should be helping to build.
- Research and information: information is power it is said. Going to a meeting under-informed and showing that no trouble has been taken to find out about a new potential customer can quickly do damage. A while ago a few minutes on the

telephone, with reference books or spent getting hold of a company's annual report was worthwhile. Now the ability to access the Website of so many organizations speeds and simplifies the whole process - though more than just this may be necessary, and sales people do have to actually note information obtained and think about how it can help them sell. Some rules and guidance from management here may be valuable. Websites are similarly a good way to gather competitive intelligence.

- CRM (Customer Relationship Management) Systems: here there is considerable sophistication with many different software systems available to record, monitor and prompt action with major customers. The data available here is invaluable, but the mistake should not be made of thinking that the system will do it all. Contact is personal and whatever prompt is given to the individual sales person they must interpret it sensibly and take appropriate action. Like many areas of systems a specific element of danger here is a lack of flexibility, with the system being followed slavishly and action directed at individual customers not being sufficiently well tailored.
- Presentations: in some industries the sales process involves the regular use of formal presentations (another important personal skill), and in these and in many meetings visual aids are often very professional looking; anything ad hoc can look slapdash. Such aids are important in assisting and augmenting customers' imagination; they must support what is said, however, and not take over the process. If well used they add an important additional dimension to the sales process; if not they can lull the sales person into ceasing to think sufficiently clearly; they go through the presentation on automatic pilot led by the charts or whatever they are using.
- Your Website: sales people have always had to link precisely with other media, they must build on the image of the organization and take the customer further in terms of both information and image. The many organizations that have Websites now have an additional element to assist in informing customers, and this may mean that by the time they talk to a sales person they are better informed than in the past (and this includes the information they have about competition, competitive prices etc.). A good Website can thus make the

job easier for sales people, but even small deficiencies can cause problems (e.g. if it is difficult to navigate or manifestly not kept up to date). There are specific ways in which customer visits to Websites may be used to enhance the sales process.

- Research: information can be gathered by prompting customers or enquirers to complete information (without making it mandatory or too onerous to do). A well-designed Website can thus provide ongoing, up-to-date information about customers - their feelings, requirements and more.
- Telephone link: software (or support) is available now to link customer visits to direct contact. A customer visiting a Website and wanting to take things further can click on a box and prompt telephone contact. Systems can ensure this happens promptly - or even guarantee that it happens so quickly that a call is received while the customer is on-line: they can look at information on screen while talking to a sales person.

The possibilities here are broad and varied. Any technology used alongside sales contact must be well thought out. It must be customer oriented and enhance customer service and satisfaction rather than just improving the basis for selling and the likelihood of success (though it should do this too!).

There are other implications here also. These include: selling overseas (where immediacy and quality of contact can be improved), and demonstration of commitment (a customer may be impressed by the contact provided by a Website in the same way as they may see advertising support making their job of selling on a product easier). Further technological developments will extend such possibilities. Already smart cards are allowing information to be collected about customers and linked to future contact and promotion and sales. For example, a customer's purchase of a particular product (paid for on a card) can be followed by sending them linked promotional material - a sales pitch to the shop where this happens may include reference to this kind of process.

BEST PRACTICE

Finally, let us consider examples of the cross over between personal and technological selling, first two simple ones - good and bad - from the observations of an executive.

- Good: Recently he contacted Oberoi Hotels in India. It was easy to search for their Website and easy too to put a question to them through it. An hour later he had a call from their representative in London. They had a fresh, warm lead to follow up, but from his perspective as a customer they already knew something about me and tailored their approach well to the circumstances, making it seem like excellent service. This kind of thing now represents the simplest kind of technological enhancement; yet the effect on the customer is good, the chances of prompting business enhanced. In such circumstances if the next stage for the supplier is going to visit someone, then that meeting should be just a little easier to handle and make persuasive.

- Bad: Recently he was visited by a financial services salesman (whose organization had better remain nameless). He arrived on time and seemed very professional, yet proved so highly dependent on technology that he rather lost patience with him. He disrupted my desk with his equipment - a laptop - and took me through a seemingly endless PowerPoint presentation the bulk of which was clearly standard, when the whole purpose of the meeting was to link individually to my circumstances. The effect was the reverse of what was intended. While the charts shown looked good, their message was distanced from the customer, and the proportion of the total message that came straight off screen diluted the impression that the salesman made in a business where personalities and their expertise are crucial.
- Moral: in selling, technology must always support the personal presence.

In both these cases the implications for sales management are clear. In the first, things seem to have been well organized with the customer in their mind. The system worked and the individual sales person encountered had clearly been briefed as to how to work so that the separate effects on customers of what they did, and what the system did, enhanced one another.

In the second, technology seemed to have taken over, the salesman proceeded on automatic pilot, as it were, and the net effect made the sale less likely than it might have been. This was not because the technology could not have been organized to enhance matters, it could. Rather that insufficient thought had gone into deciding how the integration would be made; surely a sales management responsibility. The modern sales manager now has the bigger job of organizing not just people, what they do and how they do it, but also the considerable technology used in whatever way to back them up. The whole needs to work well together, and no element of it can be left "just to happen," or the customer ends up with an experience that works less well for them.

SUMMARY

These trends are set on a course. The full implications are, perhaps by definition, unclear. Writing in The Information Age Manuel Castells stated:

"The twenty-first century will not be a dark age. Neither will it deliver to most people the bounties promised by the most extraordinary technological revolution in history. Rather, it may well be characterized by informed bewilderment."

Technology may still perhaps be in its infancy. But in taking the managers must be careful to take the right view of it - and to take the right action about matters it affects. The three key rules should be to:

- Take the broad view: information technology does not effect just one, easily defined and self-contained area, it potentially affects everything;
- Seek opportunities: but remember, changing technology does not automatically mean "new = good," changes may present difficulties too and it is as well be on your guard for them; and
- Give priority to customer focus: just because something is technically possible does not mean it will create positive advantage; ultimately it is the effect on customers and on customer service that matter most. Checking things out is as important as moving ahead fast.

Note: ConocoPhillips is the third-largest integrated energy company in the US and the second-largest refiner in the country. The company is engaged in the exploration and production of petroleum, natural gas, chemicals, and polymers businesses. It has operations in over 40 countries. ConocoPhillips is headquartered in Houston, Texas and employs about 33,800 people. For a very good study of "The Electronic Dimension" *see www.conocophillips.com*

4

The Global Dimension

The world may be shrinking in some senses, but great distances are involved. This chapter looks at the "on the ground" implications for sales management of global marketing.

For many years a slogan used by the UK Chartered Institute of Marketing (which interestingly grew from the Sales Managers Association) was - The World is our Market. Certainly an organization's sales activity is necessarily going to be different if it is being directed at customers on the other side of the world; sales management reflects these differences. A business may be successful on a limited geographical scale, for instance operating only in one major city. At the other end of the scale there are multinational businesses that span the globe; witness the posters you see having landed at almost any airport in the world, names such as Coca Cola, McDonalds, Ford, Hewlett Packard, Compaq and many more appear everywhere.

The task of sales management in the context of international business is to get as close as possible to the operational situation in the home market, i.e. to maximize the effectiveness of the sales role despite the geographical differences and distance involved.

INTERNATIONAL OPTIONS

To review this we need to consider the various ways in which international business can be organized.

EXPORT MARKETING

This is selling goods to overseas customers but doing so from a base in your home market. Essentially this implies physically shipping goods across the world. This may be done by the organization themselves: for example using their own fleet of trucks to ship goods to Europe or beyond. It may dependent upon the use of shippers, whether goods are to travel by road, rail, air or sea. It can be done with no support or presence in the final market; but is an area that demands specialist knowledge of such things as export documentation, shipping, insurance, credit control etc. as well as marketing.

Sales management implications: with no people on territory, sales people must communicate with customers in a variety of ways. Continuity is important and with modern communications it should be easy to keep in touch. Almost always however, the basis of the customer relationship will be stronger if they are seen personally - visiting the territory - as well. Costs may prevent this being a frequent occurrence, but - despite the need to keep potentially high costs within bounds - visits must be organized that meet customer needs and sales staff need to be selected for this and briefed accordingly.

EXPORT WITH A LOCAL PRESENCE

The form that a local presence takes clearly affects the way a company operates and thus the nature of the operation involved. The company may have the following:

- Their own local office. This will link with the headquarters and may handle independently a range of things that have to be done locally (and maybe done differently from the way they are executed at home); local advertising or service arrangements, for instance.
- An agent or distributor, in other words a local company that undertakes the local work, and marketing, on behalf of the principal. Such a company may specialize, only selling, say, construction machinery. Or they may sell a wide range of products, sometimes across the whole range of industrial and consumer products in the way large distributors - often called trading houses in some parts of the world - do. Sometimes such arrangements are exclusive, meaning they will not sell products for competing manufacturers; sometimes not. Payment of such entities is often on a basis of results, but they cannot simply be set up and left to get on with it. Success is usually in direct proportion to the amount of liaison, support and communications that is instigated between the two parties by the principal.

Sales management implications: an active approach is necessary. For example, the distributor's sales staff must understand the product and know how to sell it. A company may well see this as an area for support: for example, they might provide training, flying trainers out onto territory and taking any other action necessary to make it work (translation of materials, perhaps). A distributor's sales staff must be influenced almost as much as a company's own sales team (though their people are not employees of the principal). Again ongoing communication needs organizing, as do regular visits.

INTERNATIONAL MARKETING

This implies a greater involvement in the overseas territories, everything from setting up subsidiaries, to joint ventures and, in some businesses, local manufacture. The complexities here can become considerable, with components, for example, being sourced from several different locations around the world, assembled in one or more main centers and then distributed to and sold in many markets. Such is common, for instance, in the motor market.

Sales management implications: whatever the nature of the local set up - its ability to field an effective sales activity is paramount. On a large scale a local sales force and all that goes with it is simply duplicated, i.e. a local force in a number of markets, and all need to be operated and therefore managed effectively. The overall marketing strategy must be reflected by sales force operations territory by territory.

LICENSING

This is an example of one of the other approaches being possible. Here nothing is done on an ongoing basis by the principal. They sell the right - the license - to produce the product to someone else. The deal may include help with a variety of set up processes (from the provision of drawings to machinery), but thereafter the local company runs their own show, and marketing, and payment is on some sort of "per product produced" basis.

Sales management implications: despite the distancing involved here revenue success will still depend upon the quality of sales involved. So the "parent" company may want to secure and agree an involvement, even if it is no more than positioning the sales manager as a technical advisor. This is especially so when the returns to the principal are calculated, even in part, on sales results.

There are other methods also: for instance franchising,well known from the likes of McDonalds and Holiday Inn, but used with a wide range of products and services. Marketing's job is to select and use methods appropriately; and maybe to originate new ones. All such may need or allow the opportunity to influence the sales activity "on the ground."

A LITTLE LOCAL DIFFICULTY

Throughout industry, some companies sell what they produce in similar form world-wide. Others tailor the product to individual markets - even something as simple as a chocolate bar may have many different recipes and flavors for each of many different markets. This applies to many aspects of a product: cars may need change to meet local safety standards, books need translating, electrical products may have to work with different voltages etc. Check major brands, Fanta will be a different colour of orange and a different taste depending on where you drink it. It can simply be arrogant to assume no change is needed, so marketing logically demands consideration of such options and that adaptations are made as necessary.

Similarly in sales, the marketing principle of "knowing your customer" is clearly paramount in overseas markets where people, culture, customs may be very different. Such differences will not only potentially affect details relating to the product, for example a number may be popular in one country and regarded as unlucky in another (as eight is regarded as auspicious by the Chinese), but also the manner of doing business. Here such things as the prevailing practice regarding negotiation, business ethics or time scale may all be different. Even a name - of a company or product - may need careful checking; what sounds catchy in English may be lewd in German or hilarious in Urdu. There is thus a prime requirement for all sales staff, and their managers, that is they strive to understand and adapt and accommodate when dealing with overseas markets. For example things will not be the same at home and overseas. At home base a manager may inhabit a large office, surrounded by staff and support services. Someone operating in or visiting a different country may be one of a handful of people there. Posting a letter may mean going to the mailbox personally. Briefing a major customer may mean a visit "up country" in a four-wheel drive vehicle on roads made treacherous by the rainy season.

There are differences that will affect people very personally. Extremes may involve sales people politely eating sheep's eyes in the Middle East or trying to remember the etiquette involved in a meeting to negotiate terms, taking place in Japan. Beyond difference, you might also like to consider discomfort or even hostility. Some countries are not an automatic choice for comfort - a range of things: climate, politics, law and order - or lack of it - or simply inaccessibility may make them unattractive either as places to visit or to live. But if such are part of your market then you must staff them with people who can cope. Management must find people right for these tasks, and manage them too, bearing in mind that they must be highly self-sufficient.

BEST PRACTICE

The example commented on below links the global nature of business and of customers with new technology. It focuses not on one company, but on a particular industry, that of publishing. Assuming you have this text in book form - where did you buy your copy? Maybe in a traditional book shop. Maybe in a specialist outlet, perhaps from a professional management institute or the direct ordering service of a newspaper or magazine. Or perhaps on line - operations such as Amazon (supposedly the best known e-business world wide) now take a significant proportion of total book sales. Traditionally publishers' sales teams have been geographically organized. A bookshop, or wholesaler (supplier to smaller retail outlets), is visited by the sales person covering the area in which it is situated. In the home market this might be one of a team of directly employed people, overseas a sales person employed by a distributor. The only variance of this has related to size, with a major chain of shops buying centrally being dealt with by a senior person (the industry's equivalent of the Major Accounts Manager).

Now there is a new breed of customer to be dealt with. Amazon are not alone, but one of many such e-tailers selling books alongside a variety of other goods (as an example, UK operators - though their customers may be located elsewhere - include BOL and The Good Book Guide). Their business is worth a good deal to many publishers. Research, carried out for the Singapore Publishers Association, shows that these kinds of organization:

- Will not see everyone and who they do see is determined by their overall image of a publisher, which is influenced in turn partly by their ongoing communications (everything from catalogues to telephone calls);
- Want advance information - and are concerned only with their own time scale;
- Depend a great deal on which individual they see from a supplier; if they rate someone as unprofessional, uncaring or simply not sufficiently efficient then they will do less business (or see someone else); knowledge and operating approach and style is important;

- May demand that one publisher liaises with a number of people their end if a range of books and topics spans their organization (e.g. different buyers for general fiction and science fiction);
- Expect accurate information and resist hype (if something is oversold, next time a different line will be taken); and
- Have mandatory criteria that form part of their negotiation (e.g. they will not buy a new book without seeing the jacket).

It is the sales manager's job to check out the specifics of such a situation and organize and then maintain the contact that these new style customers want and like. Better still to do so in a way that satisfies them more than competition. If it needs some non-traditional approaches so be it. If it needs changes to procedures (e.g. book covers available further ahead of publication than usual) again so be it. Any organization that fails to discover and respond to this sort of market change is in trouble.

Those that do may be quoted as examples of best practice today. Tomorrow? That is another matter. Anything to do with selling and customer relationships is inherently fragile. It demands flexibility and that an eye is constantly kept on the ball.

SUMMARY

The key things here are to:

- Seek opportunities widely: then organize to exploit them carefully and recognize that you must pace such development; things usually take longer when distances are involved;
- Identify and respect cultural differences: and ensure that operations are organized to cope with them; and
- Regard communications as key: overseas markets and the customers in them can easily be left feeling isolated, neglected or ignored; regular constructive contact is essential and some of it must be face to face.

Note: Unisys Corporation (Unisys) is a global information technology (IT) company. The company offers systems integration and consulting services, outsourcing services, infrastructure services, maintenance services and high-end server technology. It primarily operates in the US and the UK. The company is headquartered in Blue Bell, Pennsylvania and employs 29,000 people. For further knowledge regarding this chapter reader can visit www.unisys.com

5

The State of the Art

Sales management is a great job demanding a balanced approach and attention detail. In this chapter reviews the key tasks. Sales management is a generic skill. Its nature, importance and relationship with other activities are reviewed elsewhere in this work. Here the focus is on the day-to-day sales management process, and this in turn relates to the nature of the sales activity in a particular organization. In Sales Force Management it is said:

"Selling is important, not only because of the company's immediate need to generate revenue through the sale of products and services, nor only because sales is the largest marketing expense, but also because the future of the company depends upon sales people who can ...find more, win more, and keep more through carrying the voice of the customer throughout the firm."

It goes on:

"Managing the selling function is one of the most important management functions in any firm, not just because selling is so important, but also because managing selling is unique."

Overlong sentences apart, this is fair comment. Sales management is important, and it is unique among the all management tasks. While it is a process that must be applied differently in different organizations, industries and circumstances the key tasks are the same for all. These are:

- Planning
- Organizing
- Staffing
- Developing

- Motivating
- Control.

Each of these is reviewed in turn, with examples illustrating certain aspects of them and a link to current problems, issues or opportunities.

PLANNING

Planning is no academic nicety. Plans should drive the business, and the thinking that goes into planning is key to analysis and making sure that the activity reflects the real world. Essentially planning comes down to four key questions:

- Where are we now? (analysing the current situation);
- Where are we going? (demanding the setting of clear objectives);
- How will we get there? (this produces an action plan, setting out
- who will do what and when); and
- How will we know when we have got there? (the process of measurement and control).

These are no more than common sense, but they should prompt specific action by the manager in charge of the sales team.

SETTING SALES OBJECTIVES

This process demands looking back and forward. It is important that detailed and current information forms the basis of any extrapolation. Sales revenue will no doubt be clear, but detailed statements are needed in terms of areas which are as follows:

- Sales by product
- Sales by customer category
- Sales in different areas; and
- Sales linked to price (at different discounts and levels of profitability, for example); and more.

With this in mind, sales may be forecast, and this must be done in a way that recognizes and anticipates any changes that the forthcoming period will bring (it is not just a case of adding an attractive percentage increase). The next stage is to see how such a target can be met - this leads to the sales plan.

THE SALES PLAN

The key questions here are as follows.

- What is to be sold? (the detail, product by product as necessary): product mix is the key variable here. Depending on the product or service range, its positioning and design, direction may well be necessary for the sales force - it may be that the items to which they give priority, perhaps because they are easiest to sell, are not the company's priority - with other lines having higher profitability. Clarity is needed here, and leaving the mix sold just to "happen" should not be one of the options.
- To whom? (a statement that should reflect all categories of customer): here there may need to be plans for customers by category, or even by individual customer. Large customers may need to have strategies developed for them, especially where they have several different buying points (e.g. people, functions, geographic locations); this may be best thought of on a matrix basis.
- At what price? (recognizing the complexities of pricing policy): a logical pricing policy is necessary here, together with any discount structures that are necessary. Price is a marketing variable, but one of the places pricing policy must be implemented and work well is at the sales interface with the customer. The sales manager should be involved with decisions about pricing policy and must put the sales people in a position to work with the details effectively. Factors such as what independent authority sales people have to negotiate price and terms should be clearly understood by all.
- By what methods? (detailing how sales will be organized): the plan must specify sales actions very clearly. The mix of customers and the different levels and style of service they may want must be matched with the organization's intention to push for sales. The system must categorize customers, assign call frequencies, allow time for any necessary activity such as prospecting or telephone contact (and administration) and prompt a practical array of activity. It is little good aiming for sales results with no clear idea how they will be obtained or the scale of the effort required.

- At what cost? (and also with what cost-effectiveness): the sales plan has a cost, so budgeting is one aspect here. Sales productivity is the other concept that needs addressing here. Analysis of the ratio of sales to sales cost is just the starting point. Other measures may include: sales per territory, number of customers managed by a sales person, number of calls made per person (and on average per day), time spent face to face, average order value, strike rate - orders to call ratio, most successful sales person compared with the average (there can be a very significant gap here). There are details here worth constant vigilance and fine-tuning.

A significant part of many organizations' sales plans is the development of individual customer strategies. These sub plans can include profitability analysis, and set out details of action over a period across a complex organization with multiple buying points, matching this to internal considerations including product mix. This then becomes the basis for prompting and checking action. An example relating to this appears in the In practice section).

With the foregoing methodology in mind certain key practical points are worth emphasizing:

KEY ISSUES

- Comprehensive sales plans: plans must be active as well as results based, and targets must link to both. Thus targets must be set not just for sales figures but for the activities that potentially produce them, e.g. prospecting, calls, meetings, proposals etc. As business approaches change new activities may become important and need adding in to the planning process.
- Realistic targets: the link between forecasting and planning must be sound. Whatever objectives the organization sets, at the level of individual sales person, targets must be achievable - they can, and perhaps should be challenging - but they should be achievable. Sales managers must increasingly be involved at senior levels of marketing planning to get this right.
- Making the plan match real life: in years past sales people had a territory, period. Now plans need to reflect a number of issues beyond geography, such include: product range, markets and different kinds of customer and buyer. A matrix approach is often the answer.

ORGANIZING

Organization addresses the basic design of the sales resource. First, it must be decided how many sales staff are needed. This is best done on a workload analysis basis, looking at the level of customer service required, the number of calls that will need to be made and relating that to the number of people able to undertake this amount of work; with costs albeit often demanding a compromise.

Secondly, sales must be fitted into the organization structure. This too is dependent on size and activity. Questions such as: how many sales people can one manager manage? How many different types of sales people are necessary? How many territories or groups of customer have to be serviced? It may be that a sales director heads up the function and is supported by a sales manager with a number of area or regional managers reporting to them before the sales people appear. It may be, in a small organization, that the general manager must cope with all of this. Two factors should primarily be born in mind.

- Customer categories: for example, in the way that a building materials company might need to relate to: building firms and contractors (large and small), architects, surveyors, builders' merchants, local authorities, government departments and maybe more. In this case they might have different people calling on specifiers (architects and others) and direct purchasers. The complexities here will dictate the scale and arrangement of the organization structure.
- Number of customers: obviously if the customer base is small less sales people are needed to cover them and vice versa. Similarly if part of the job of selling is done in some way separate from a field sales operation: online or on the telephone, for instance.

In considering organization, remember:

- To review regularly: it is a variable. Many organizations hit problems because their sales organization becomes regarded as fixed, and then - over time - ceases to match the market conditions. External changes can accelerate this;
- To link with marketing: sometimes marketing innovation necessitates change. For example, Usborne who sell books for children use normal channels and sales organization, selling to book shops etc. They also sell through party style events (like

Tupperware) getting mothers with small children to organize gatherings at their homes to demonstrate and sell books. This works well, but represents a change that needs different people and organization to make this side of their operation work; and

- To prompt organization at individual territory level· the way individual sales people manage their own "patch" is also vital. They need to link intentions for call frequency and the customer mix (large and small) to a map and ensure that the way they "work" the territory is efficient and productive (e.g. minimizing travel time and cost). Again this is something they need to be reminded to review regularly.

STAFFING

One of the key issues addressed in the final chapter is staffing. The rule here is simply stated. Assemble and maintain a team of good people. There is no room for passengers, and poor performers can end up monopolizing a sales manager's time and this, in turn causes other problems as other things are delayed or neglected. Recruitment must be thorough and systematic. A systematic approach is recommended by many authorities. The following eight-stage approach is the basis of comment on this subject by Mike Wilson in his book Managing a Sales Force.

1. Writing a job description: this is worth spending some time on. It should spell out the tasks in full (it is not enough just to say it is "to sell the product"). If prospecting is necessary say so. If a successful candidate must be able to give a technical demonstration of the product, work at the bottom of a mine shaft or carry out the sale in five minutes while the buyer mans a busy cash till in a store of some sort, say so. Beyond duties and tasks this document can record such matters as reporting lines, evaluation procedures, and remuneration.
2. Writing a profile of the person: what kind of person is likely to be successful in that job? List basic characteristics (e.g. age, experience), character (e.g. persistent, self-reliant), motivations (e.g. attitudes to money, security etc.), emotional maturity (e.g. profile, capacity for self-discipline etc.). Past experience and what successes it has brought them are important here; so too are details (more than one sales person has been appointed before it was discovered they could not drive a car!).
3. Recruiting candidates: review the options. You can advertise (in local or national papers, trade magazines etc.), but do not

overlook other channels such as looking internally or asking existing staff for recommendations (and paying a reward if successful candidates are produced this way). If you use an agency it may seem expensive - but so is your time! And try to get a personal recommendation, there are agencies and agencies (and currently a look on the Internet identifies more than 5000 agencies operating that way; take care - some will not be there tomorrow).

4. Assessing application forms: a good application form (which these days may be completed on line) is invaluable. Ask for comprehensive information, match it to the job description and profile and plan to interview only those who show well at this stage. The whole process works better with more forms and less interviews rather than the reverse.

5. Checking references: not always easy, but worth doing (telephoning those a candidate gives permission to contact may be best) - and worth doing up front. If it shows up any "nasties" then you save the time of the other stages.

6. Testing: similarly this is better done before interviewing. Some things are clear: you can test someone's fluency in French, numeracy or other straightforward skills precisely - and reject them if they are inadequate. Other tests need more care, though some swear by psychometric tests that profile candidates, they need careful choosing, add time and cost - and none can measure sales ability as a specific factor.

7. Structured interviewing: this stage links your details of the job and the candidate with their personal showing. It is worth cross-checking what was said on an application form (there is a considerable temptation to lie on them) - indeed the form can provide the structure for the interview. One main interview, and perhaps a shorter second one for a shortlist works well; a second opinion might be obtained from a colleague on the second one.

8. Evaluating a shortlist and making a final decision: Check the facts, relate one candidate to another objectively - trust your judgment and experience - but beware of irrational hunches and pseudo-psychology.

This is a pivotal task and needs special care and attention.

- Assumptions: avoid making them. It is a common failing that people (especially men) believe they are a good, and worse, instant, judge of character - "I know the good candidates within five minutes of beginning the interview." Research does not bear this out. Recruitment needs a systematic approach to be successful - you skimp this process at your peril.

- Stereotypes: avoid using descriptions of sales jobs that are totally clich′e - if you say nothing in an advertisement other than asking for someone - "dynamic, self-starting, highly motivated, persistent, personable and of exceptional character" - most people reading it will say - "That's me." Be factual about the job.
- Local difficulty: as has been made clear, this is not an area for compromise. Bad selection leads, almost inevitably, to bad performance and you very rarely hear sales managers say that someone turned out better than they thought at interview stage. So if there is a particular problem (e.g. the difficulty of full employment in somewhere like Singapore) it must not be allowed to weaken resolve to make the right appointment.
- Legislation: make sure that all records, forms, contracts and processes are as they should be (check with your HR [human resources] department). In an increasingly litigious world you do not want to run foul of the law when candidates are rejected or unsuccessful people have contracts terminated.
- Experiment: and do not be hidebound by convention. For example, why do all prospective candidates have to have a degree, or have ten years experience in your industry? Maybe the place to fish is in new pools - in your own factory or amongst groups less obviously qualified. This is, without doubt, the most important element of the sales manager's job. It starts as people are recruited.
- Induction training: even if you recruit experienced sales people they need how to operate in your environment. They need to know about your organization and product, they need to understand the kind of people who will be their customers, and they need to know how - exactly how - selling skills can be appropriately and effectively deployed for you. Time spent at this stage can pay dividends. Some things can be delegated, but beware. You do not want technical product knowledge put over by someone with no understanding of customers, and much - maybe most - of what must be done is best done by the manager.

- Field training: time must be spent regularly in the field, joint calling, with people - including experienced people. Selling is dynamic and needs constant fine-tuning. A cycle of evaluation, counselling and action and advice to focus the sales person's thinking on the quality of their approach and back to evaluation is a continuous process. The most important objective here relates to the numbers involved. Working with the sales person (this is not, and must not be seen as, checking, control, or instruction) on a small, but regular and representative number of calls is a means of making all the many others they make alone go well. The most important aspect of the role is to establish the habit of self-evaluation and fine-tuning in people, making them better able to operate alone and making it more likely that they will always do so at the peak of performance. It is beyond the scope of this work to recommend specific evaluation systems on which to base this sort of process, but some formality of system may help. It must be tailor-made and seem to be clear, constructive, consistent, and fair - and above all practical, it must actually help review and improve performance.
- Group activities: field training allows the identification of common needs for development, which may then be better addressed on a group basis; one of the key reasons for having sales meetings. These must be well planned and conducted, constructive in manner, content and approach - and must make a difference. Poor meetings quickly dilute motivation. Developmental activities here can involve people in, for example, leading projects and also allow other methods to be used such as role-playing, training exercises or training films.
- Formal training: sometimes development needs more formal solution. In a larger organization help may come from an HR department or there may be a training resource center (with a library and facilities to view videos or undertake e-learning of various sorts). Sometimes the answer may be an external or internal course, the latter can be tailored; sometimes the manager may be able to conduct short sessions themselves, alternatively there may be value in having assistance from a consultant.

The ongoing need for development must never be underestimated; equally any development activity should be practically based and genuinely likely to help maintain or improve performance. At the end of the day the person most likely to be able to do this on a regular basis is the sales person themselves; but the manager should play a part and be an effective catalyst to more.

As it has been made clear the development task is probably the single most important thing sales managers can spend time on; indeed it must take up most of their time. A constructive view must always be taken of it, therefore, and thus the following need to be addressed.

- Time: in modern business, pressure on time seems to increase constantly. Managers must fight to spend an appropriate amount of time on this process. In a large organization different levels of sales management may help spread the load (regional and area managers, for instance). For others the key task is to balance overall workload - and sales managers seem inclined to have a wide range of responsibilities beyond actually managing the sales team (getting involved in everything from promotion to pricing). If sales approaches are to truly differentiate from competition, ways must be found to give this area priority.
- The personal touch: with more and more training provided through technology, and for sales people in isolation (e.g. computer based training), there is a danger that actual face to face contact declines. By all means use technology or anything else that helps, but the key activity of individuals working creatively together may achieve most and this effect must not be diluted.
- Perception of the role: the days of sales managers being regarded as primarily having a "police" role are, for the most part, long gone. Yet with control being part of the job, it is important that the relationship between sales people and their manager is, and is seen to be, constructive. Too often one hears sales people say something like "I never seem to see my manager unless there is something wrong." Managers must work with people, not just be seen as checking up on them or telling them what to do. Learning - certainly that prompts consistently different future practice - will only take place if lessons are made acceptable and people are involved in the process. New ideas, and thus new methods and approaches, will only be sparked or evolved if people work constructively and creatively together.

MOTIVATING

It is an inherent part of any manager's job to motivate. The motivational "climate," the net effect of many influences on people in their work, has a very real impact on the way they do their job. If development ensures that people are able to do what is required, then motivation ensures that they want to do so. For sales people, faced with the attrition of customer attitudes, and often working largely on their own, the way they feel about their job is especially important. The theory of motivation that provides the most practical basis for a concept that links easily to action is that of Frederick Herzberg. His description of satisfiers and dissatisfiers, provides a good analogy for balancing motivational influences: actively creating positive feeling and acting also to minimize negative feelings. For example, most sales people hate administration, but it needs to be done. It may always be an essentially negative aspect of the job, however explaining why it is necessary and creating the minimum straightforward system to get it done is appreciated, and that aspect becomes motivational.

Incentives are perhaps worth of a special word. Research over the years seems to show consistently that the best performing sales people have a reward system that includeing some element of payment on results. This is not always possible. Results need to be readily linked to individual effort (team incentives are less powerful). Such schemes need to be straightforward (it is no good if an hour needs to be spent with a calculator just to see how things are going); they must pay out regularly (for some sales people thinking about Friday-week is long-term planning); they must represent a significant proportion of total remuneration (and that means bearing in mind family income); and they should be interesting - fun - linking to published results, newsletters, and league tables all help.

Variety is also an important factor. Incentives can be linked to all sort of things, overall sales but also opening new accounts, selling in a new product or profitability of sales. Simple quarterly schemes, with regular changes work well, as do mixing financial reward with other incentives (travel is a favourite). But a simple "Well done" can be as powerful as anything - and costs nothing. Motivation is a key part of sales management and managers who are, or make themselves, instinctive motivators have a real asset in their management armory.

- Time pressure: without a doubt low motivation is more often a result of less being done than should be, than of the wrong thing being done. Motivating does take time, but it is time well spent - it needs building in as a priority.

- Resisting the magic formulae: the easiest trap to fall into is a belief that money is a panacea. Incentives, including financial incentives, have a role to play. But a mix of activities is best, and small influences are just as important in the total picture as large. To motivate successfully you must work at it; the effort is worthwhile, the process can quickly become a habit and it can be as pleasurable to motivate as to be motivated.
- Being censorious: what matters most is the people. It is easy to base motivational practice on what you would like, when sales people may have different priorities.
- Caring: if there is anything like a magic formula in this area, then it is that the simpler things - just taking an interest in people, working constructively with them, giving them authority, and recognizing achievements are probably more important than anything. But they have to be real. The manager needs to care (and the old saying that - "if you can fake the sincerity, everything else is easy" - must never be allowed to become the basis for action).

CONTROL

The word control may have connotations of "policing." In fact the concept is simple and constructive; it revolves around the following equation:

$$A - S = \pm V$$

Actual performance (A) is compared with a preset standard (S) and action is considered, and if necessary taken, by considering the variance (V) between the two. A variety of standards may be used and these may relate to everything from the number of calls made in a day to the sales of a particular product. In nature they are as follows:

- Absolute standards: these are specific targets (e.g. annual sales revenue). They are important, but only provide certain information;
- Moving standards: these look at results over time (e.g. a moving annual total) and thus highlight more about trends and likely outcome; and
- Diagnostic standards: as the name suggests these are designed to show the reasons why results are as they are.

In selling there are only four key variables: which are called on (the nature and type of customer or prospect); how many people are called on (more potential customers seen = potentially more sales); how often they are called on (call frequency); and - a whole separate area - what is done face to face with the customer (the quality and effectiveness of the sales approach).

The essence of control is change. The knowledge of what is happening allows action to be taken either aiming to bring things back on track if there is a shortfall, or to build on success. This last point is the key. Control is not simply to correct faults. It is to accentuate the positive. It is just as useful to see a positive variance, ask why this should be happening and build on the action that is creating it. While management has a duty to provide a framework and encourage discipline amongst sales people, their prime job is to act as a catalyst for the success. By viewing control as both focusing on positive and negative results and acting as a spur to change, its value will be maximized.

- A surfeit of information: the biggest problem these days may seem perverse. There is too much information. Certainly information is probably easier to collect and more up to date than was the case in the past, but key indicators can get buried. Management must focus on those factors (whatever they are from volume of sales to the number of new accounts opened) that are key; and must know what they are.
- Optimizing information collection: however information is collected, and it may be filling in a form or inputting to a computer of some sort, the process must not be over-engineered. Making sales people aware of how important it is, and making the system straightforward should get information flowing well; this must not be an area of constant hassle as this just wastes time and puts the veracity of information in doubt
- Fit internal aspects of control to the outside world: for example, if sales people man an exhibition stand at a trade show at the beginning of the financial year, high sales volume over this time may negate the effect of incentive schemes throughout the remainder of the year.

LOOKING AHEAD

It has been mentioned several times in this work that selling is a dynamic process. One of any sales manager's key tasks is to ensure their team is selling in the right way. Indeed their job takes its shape from that of those they manage. So it is a prerequisite that they are not only able to define what is necessary now, but that they are ahead of the game in spotting, better still predicting, changes that will require changes to sales practice. None of us can be sure what the future holds; however working to keep ahead can be approached systematically. The following questions flag the areas that need watching:

- What further changes will technology bring?
- How will the sales function fit in future within the organization's total marketing mix?
- With whom precisely will responsibility for individual customers (especially large ones) lie?
- How is the role of the sales force changing?
- What range of tasks will the members of the sales team need to perform in future?
- What skills - and new or changed skills - will they need to have at their command?
- What new pressures will competition bring to bear and how will that change what we need to do?
- How do we rate against competitors and on the broader stage (including international competition and market activity)? and
- What different expectations will customers have in future and what new demands will they make?

SUMMARY

Overall, sales managers have a multifaceted task. Each aspect of which is important. Some responsibilities are more occasional than others. For example, time spent on recruitment must be well organized and wisely spent, but it is not something that must be done every day (well, not in a good sales organization!). Conversely, time spent on a variety of counselling and development tasks are literally day by day tasks.

Key for being a successful sales manager is getting the right balance; and being equally effective in a disparate list of operational areas. The preceding section focused primarily on tasks, finally the following sets out a check list more in terms of the personal characteristics of the successful sales manager, who must:

- Have knowledge of marketing and an involvement in it, because sales is an inherent part of the marketing mix;

- Be an effective manager, able to direct, control and inspire a team of usually free-spirited people;
- Take the long view (directing activities, setting strategic objectives and defining a framework of targets, policies and priorities to drive towards them);
- Be a corporate team player, as liaison with many different parts of the business is mandatory and must be done effectively;
- Be productive - able to balance conflicting priorities and still spend sufficient time with the team, singly and as a group; this is something that demands problem solving and decision-making abilities;
- Sell effectively. They do not need to be the best on the team, but must understand and be able to practice the full gambit of techniques involved: sales, negotiation, presentation, numeracy etc.;
- Stay close to the market, because achieving a customer focus in sales activities is always key;
- Communicate effectively - with staff, colleagues and customers; and
- Achieve results. Managing the activity is not enough - it must work.

Perhaps in one way or another everything here comes back to customers. In the survey The Future of Selling the future role is defined as follows:

"Tomorrow's sales leaders will need to develop a clear view of the way ahead for the customers in their industries, and be able to provide their sales people with the direction and competencies to take full advantage of the opportunities available. "

Note: VeriSign is a provider of infrastructure services for the internet and communications networks. The company's offerings include authentication, validation and payment services for websites, enterprises and service providers, to conduct e-commerce and communication over IP networks. The company primarily operates in the US. It is headquartered in Mountain View, California and employs 3,297 people. For a very good case study regarding this topic, reader can visit company's website www.verisign.com

6

Sales & Distibution in Practice

How can day to day sales management be made to work out? This chapter looks at cases and ideas to see how a practical and creative approach can help. In this section, the principal tasks identified in previous chapter are exemplified by comment about how sales managers are currently operating and what makes for success. The intention here is not to focus on major strategies, still less to suggest one ideal way of operating. Rather it is to highlight approaches and thinking that is useful, and show how the right approach can help whether applied to major or, seemingly, minor matters.

CASE 1

This appears simple, but is a clear and positive example of management providing support that changes selling practice, that is realistically linked to practical issues about how the customer buys. One segment of the market of an international hotel group was for their conference business - the use of meeting rooms for everything from training seminars to wedding receptions.

THE SITUATION

The sales team aimed at, and succeeded in, meeting most prospective buyers at their properties. The hotel itself was their most valuable visual aid. A tour of the hotel was a core part of their exchange with customers, and clearly an inspection of the meeting rooms was an important part of the proceedings for conference customers. The sales staff were clearly experienced regarding the use of their own property. They were well able to offer good advice of which rooms to use for what. But, most often, of course, they were showing people around when rooms were empty. An empty conference room is not at its most impressive, particularly if it stores stacks of tables, chairs and other items ready for the next event. While staff were well informed and enthusiastic, just saying, "This is what we would recommend for your (wedding reception or whatever)" left a great deal to the imagination of the customer. Discussing a wedding, for example, a sales person could stand in the recommended room and see clearly in their mind's eye how it would be - the flowers, the sparkling glasses, the crisp white tablecloths and smiling guests. They knew such an occasion would be memorable.

But the customer just saw an empty room, and too many of them headed off to inspect somewhere else. Sometimes coincidence meant that they could be shown an event in full swing. Sometimes they could be asked back during a similar event, but they had to be made to feel it was worthwhile to do so.

THE ACTION

Imagination is always assisted by seeing something. The job was not to show them the room. Rather it was to make them believe their function would go well there and help them imagine it doing just that. The sales manager commissioned a portfolio of high quality photographs, and put them into a presentation folder that the sales people could go through with prospective customers. If they needed a business meeting then business meetings could be shown, workshops, conferences - a range of meetings, laid out in different ways and photographed (with the permission of past users) to show how well they suited people. For a wedding the flowers and everything else was there - clear, colourful and promising similar satisfaction to the next happy couple; and so on.

The organization of this, which went way beyond the shots in brochures (mainly empty of people), took a little time and cost some money. The usefulness of the material was self-apparent and, after just a short briefing, the results in use were tangible:

- Sales increased;
- Bookings made on the first visit increased;
- Sales people had more confidence (and their motivation was positively affected);
- The sales approach was easy to personalize (an important factor - being taken robot-like on what seems to be the same tour as everyone else does not impress prospects who, like all customers, want to be treated like individuals); and
- Customers liked it and commented on it (in terms of it adding to the service they were receiving).

In a service business such an initiative is clearly especially important. Sales aids are often important in many industries. The job of the sales manager is not just to chase people to use what is there (perhaps what has always been there!). It is to think about what will help, and provide everything possible - with an eye on both sales people and customers. As this example shows such ideas need not be complicated or costly, but they can certainly help boost sales.

CASE 2

The following example, paraphrasing the experience of an international financial services firm, shows the importance of getting the real facts, and of attention to detail. The sales people were involved in a classic long-term cycle in getting business. It ran from making initial contact to a meeting, a written proposal, follow up action and sometimes further meetings with formal presentations also being necessary on occasions. The success rate of each stage was closely monitored, so that management knew how many initial contacts were necessary, on average, to produce a set number of meetings - indeed all the ratios of this sort were monitored. On the success of written proposals moving things to the next stage the ratio seemed low, especially where large projects were involved.

This was bad enough, but of course anything that failed to move on at this stage had taken up a fair amount of time, effort and therefore money - all of which had to be duplicated to produce a replacement prospect. Research was conducted (formal research handled by a consultant) to ascertain how prospects viewed the quality and nature of the written proposals. This was relatively quick and easy to do as it was addressed to major recent prospects (who had declined to take things further). It showed that proposals were viewed as being different from prior discussions (which had been rated highly), as one respondent said "almost as if they had come from different people." The detail was analyzed (too long, over-formal, unclear, impersonal) and training organized to address the specific differences in writing approach that prospects found desirable.

Over a comparatively short period of time, as new - and better crafted - proposals went out the ratio of success climbed positively and significantly. The moral is clear: analysis of the sales job, real information about customer expectations, and action to get the detail right pays off. Two caveats: as customer expectations, likes, and dislikes etc. change nothing must be left unreviewed for ever on the assumption that it is now satisfactory. One aspect here was the effective tailoring of material to individual prospects - in other words, as with so much else in selling, a standardized approach risks alienating people.

CASE 3

Given the importance of training, both formal and informal, to sales management in maximizing the effectiveness of the sales team, one case here should surely touch on this topic. There are numbers of problems here, for example to:

- Provide induction training that gets people off to a good start, providing a basis for their future sales activity and helping develop good habits (not least the habit of acting on the need for self evaluation and fine-tuning of sales approaches);
- Allocate sufficient time to field evaluation and development and maintain that consistently in the face of other pressures; and
- Ring the changes, so that attention and time are focused again on key issues which might otherwise cease to be thought about, with people lapsing into an unthinking "automatic pilot" approach that fails to achieve the best possible performance.

The latter example above can be approached in many ways with the same topic being investigated through exercises, role-playing, films, projects and more - with each exposure adding to people's awareness in a fresh way. Even so, such a chain of differing approaches needs creative thought. New ideas are required, ideally of course combining novelty with practicality. The following certainly does that and, although originated by a trade body, illustrates the kind of thinking that any organization can apply.

The UK Meetings Industry Association has a membership primarily representing operators of hotel and conference venues. In many ways, including sales, this is a specialist area of business. Certainly it is one where an exclusivity is felt, thus the utilization of sales training in generic form is lower than in some industries. The education committee resolved to create something specific to assist member organizations.

The suggestion of making a film was promptly rejected. Too expensive, it was thought - a thought that many individual organizations have had. However, on reflection, a way was found. The film was to be low cost and focus on defined aspects of sales technique. Costs were kept down because, unusually, the film was shot live and the characters filmed were real. A venue was found who agreed to host the exercise, a sales situation was identified involving one of the sales team from a member company and a real client. Their permission and co-operation were obtained, and with some briefing a real meeting was filmed literally as it happened. With minimal editing, and some added commentary (and an accompanying workbook) it became as useful as many a more professionally made film - and had the merit of reflecting the exact situation of the kind of business involved.

The training input here was important (the author was involved as consultant), but so was the industry input. The main point here is that the format itself was the novelty that allowed something different to be created; something of considerable training value. Any organization could do something similar, even if a little professional assistance was needed it is a low cost option, yet provides something tailor made for what sales management must do.

HORSES FOR COURSES

Here are a few examples of practice that is designed to maximize effectiveness by reflecting the special nature of the fields in which sales people work.

" In selling pharmaceutical products sales people selling direct to doctors, either general practitioners or in hospitals, have only a limited time to sell; GPs are reported to allow an average of four minutes to someone detailing, as it is called, their products. Much effort goes into both defining what can usefully done in such a time (clearly it must be focused) and into practicing succinct yet persuasive call content that can get a worthwhile message over fast.

Other methods are also used to get to tackle the problem, for example presentations to a number of doctors at a group practice.

- In selling agricultural products sales people find that farmers, as well as expecting them to be knowledgeable about their products and applications (in what conditions precisely is a particular weed killer suitable?), want them to be participative. A pair of wellington Boots in the car is a prime piece of equipment, and many a new recruit has been taken the muddy route (or worse!) to inspect a field by a farmer regarding them as "wet behind the ears."
- In selling in financial markets the old ways of 9-5 working hours have long gone. Customers may work long, or odd hours

- to tie in with the working hours of an overseas stock exchange perhaps - and expect their suppliers to do the same.

It may seem basic, but such practices are not universally followed. By matching to the realities of markets and customers, sales people can increase the chances of a fair reception. Such factors change and thus need keeping an eye on - more evidence of the dynamic nature of sales. This is another area to look at to create differentiation.

AN EXCELLENT IDEA

Finally, in this chapter, it is worth noting that sales management is made more effective in all sorts of ways if approaches are well thought out. Seemingly simple ideas can have a considerable effect.

- Timesaving administration: sales people are not renowned for their love of administration. One idea, used now by many companies, provides an appropriate incentive to get the administrative tasks done, done right and done on time. Usually on a monthly basis sales people have to complete and return a number of reports (from call reports to competitive intelligence). These may be of no central use until everything is in and can be consolidated, and - if one is late - it sparks off a series of time wasting "chasers." The answer? To have a mandatory rule: anyone whose required reports are not in on time, complete and legible (a good many are still on paper) has their expenses claim payment delayed until the next month. It works. It is seen as fair (if explained) and, in terms of management style, can be balanced by putting the chasing time saved to use with discursive approaches to things that matter more.
- Spicing up sales meetings: it is a useful measure of sales management competence to ask a member of a sales team, "What was your last sales meeting like?" If they groan then there should probably be some changes. A key rule is to ensure that there is sufficient participation. As well as just asking questions and involving people in discussion more may be necessary. One sales manager showed a brief checklist they had developed of all the elements that could be added. They always utilized one - or more - and rang the changes to ensure variety. The elements were: role-play; demonstration; brainstorming; games, quizzes, tests or competitions; exercises (practicing or experimenting with something); formal

presentations; analysis (e.g. to produce an action plan for a major customer); films (linked to discussion or exercise); awards; debate or visitors (from another department or even a customer, though perhaps in some cases the visit should not last throughout the whole meeting).

- Heavy traffic: given the increasingly slow speed of traffic in most major cities, sales people the world over spend more and more of their time traveling - time spent in the car that is essentially non-productive. There may be comparatively little that can be done about this, though:
- Some companies have banned sales people from moving around in core city centers. They expect to see a receipt for parking the car and sales people walking from one central contact to another;
- More and more organizations use audio tape for communication (e.g. to update product information) which can be played while driving; and
- At the same time, mobile telephones can be useful, but can also be dangerous(more companies now lay down rules for this area - and perhaps more need to do so).
- Delegation: all sales managers experience the need for what are usually called PR (public relations) calls - when customers say, in whatever way, "I must see the manager." Sometimes this is necessary and useful but, while managers need to do some selling (or they may get out of touch), such calls can prove unnecessary and reduce time that should be spent on management tasks. One resolution managers might make is at least to query these requests. It is easy to be flattered and feel that no one else can deal with it - but these are prime opportunities to delegate. For example, managers can:
- Make such calls joint calls, involving one of the team;
- Use this to make sure that customers see the team as their prime contact; or
- Simply brief a sales person and delegate the call, explaining to the customer, indeed making a virtue of the change. This combines development to extend skills with added responsibilities for coping with a wider range of customers and situations.

- Major customer strategies: the fact that a customer is large can, perhaps perversely, mean that less planning takes place - a large order becomes routine and seems to negate the need to check that the full potential is being exploited. To combat this, draw attention to the need and get and keep activity moving; one sales manager set up regular lunch meetings. With the inducement of free sandwiches, he got people together in small groups that met regularly; each meeting focused on one major customer and debated the best action for say the next three months of operations. In this way each sales person had to review some of their major customers - and got the benefit of others' advice in so doing. The meetings were enjoyed, put good ideas on the table and led to positive action and recognizably additional sales.
- Just to show that even the smallest thing can bring change and improvement, we would note that banning, with attendant fuss, the use of that ubiquitous piece of sales jargon "the courtesy call" from all call reports (where it so often appears instead of anything more descriptive) can produce better planned, more effective calls and improve sales. All calls need objectives. Just calling in to say "Hi" or because the customer is always good for a cup of decent tea is not enough!

Note: Coca-Cola Enterprises (CCE) is the world's largest marketer, producer, and distributor of Coca-Cola products. The company is the sole licensed bottler for products of The Coca-Cola Company in Belgium, continental France, Great Britain, Luxembourg, Monaco, and the Netherlands. The company primarily operates in North America. It is headquartered in Atlanta, Georgia and employs 72,000 people. For detailed information & understanding more on "Sales & Distibution In Practice" reader may visit this site *www.cokecce.com*

7

Key Concepts and Thinkers

This chapter adds a glossary of key terminology and investigates ideas and concepts that can make the process of sales management easy and certain to be successful.

There is not a great deal of dedicated terminology in the specific area of sales management (though it shares much general management jargon). However, the following are important.

KEY TERMINOLOGY

- Kerbside conference - the post call "post-mortem" and development session held when a manager is accompanying sales people in the field (which may often take place in the car - hence the name). Key/major/national accounts - a variety of names are used here. First, measures vary as to what a major customer is, simplistically it is only what an individual organization finds significant. A second significant factor is the lead time involved. In industries selling, say, capital equipment it may take many months from first meeting to contract and there is an overlap here with "major sales."
- Award scheme - an incentive scheme based on non-financial rewards (such as merchandising or travel); beware - such schemes need to be carefully checked for tax implications, it is not motivational for a sales person to return from a wonderful holiday to an unexpected tax bill.
- Call frequency - the number of times in a year a customer is scheduled to receive regular calls; sometimes used to categorize customers and describe their relative importance.
- Call plan - the statement of work to be done with customers, arranged with productivity and effectiveness in mind.

- Competitor intelligence - the information collected about competitive products and services and their suppliers that may specifically be used to improve the approach taken on a call.
- Contract sales force - this refers to freelance or agency-provided sales staff who are not employed by those for whom they sell. Such teams may be used on a permanent basis or over a short period (to boost sales in a seasonal business or launch a new product, perhaps linked to a test market).
- Ego Drive/Empathy - Mayer and Goldberg's terms for, respectively: the internal motivational drive that makes the good sales person want to succeed, and the ability to see things from other peoples' (customers) point of view - and, importantly, being seen to do so.
- Field training - simply training, or development, activity away from any formal setting, undertaken out and about on territory.
- Incentive/commission - whatever the dictionary may say, the way these words need interpreting in sales is as follows: Commission rewards past performance. Incentives prompt better performance (and the addressing of particular targets) for the future. Thus commission may not act as an incentive, and incentives may involve much more than the financial payments that usually comprise commission.
- On-the-job training - field training and development activity.
- Pie system - a structured way of managing the spread of customers and prospects around a sales territory.
- Petal system - a practical way of organizing journeys for minimizing time and mileage and thus help maximize productivity.
- Remuneration - a general term, which with sales people implies the inclusion of elements of their reward package that are specific to the sales job: car, incentives etc.
- Sales audit - an, occasional, systematic review of all aspects of the sales activity and its management to identify areas needing improvement, or working well and needing extension; a process that recognizes the inherent dynamic nature of sales.
- Sales productivity - the sales equivalent of productivity in an area, the focus here is on efficiencies maximizing the amount of time spent with customers (rather than traveling, writing

reports etc.): it focuses on ratios and touches on anything that increases sales success however measured.

- SPIN - although this is a registered trademark, it is heard used generically - spin - to describe a customer focused and questioning based approach to identifying needs and selling appropriately in light of this knowledge.
- Standards - preset targets (absolute, moving or diagnostic standards are all used). This is reviewed in previous chapter "The State of the Art - Control".
- Territory - the area covered by an individual sales person. It is usually, but not always, geographic.

In addition, there is a terminology used by sales people and about selling. There is too much to list comprehensively here, the following simply provides some examples:

- Benefits - reasons to buy, specifically what a product or service does for or means to a buyer (as distinct from features, factual aspects about a product). Used in various ways, e.g. benefit selling.
- Cold calling - approaches to potential customers by any method (face to face or telephone, say) who are "cold" - have expressed no prior interest of any sort.
- Gatekeeper - someone who through their position can facilitate or deny access to a buyer (e.g. a secretary).
- Influencers - people who, while not having exclusive authority to buy, influence the buyer, through their recommendation.
- Qualifying prospects - research or action to produce information to demonstrate that cold prospects are "warm."
- Sales management is a personal - people to people - task. Its successful practice lies not so much in the adoption of key concepts (unless the conviction that sales people need managing is one such), rather in the systematic and thorough addressing of the key tasks of sales management.

Certain more conceptual factors are, however, worth of keeping in mind.

THE SALES PROFILE

Selling, and sales management along with it, have never been viewed in quite the same way as other, perhaps sexier, marketing techniques.

Selling suffers from a low status image virtually worldwide, perhaps only in the United States is this less so. Externally there is a classic suspicion of "someone with something to sell," even internally there can be a "them and us" situation of some friction, with inside people perhaps not understanding what sales people who are out of the office all day actually do.

Action: sales management has a key task to create a belief, at least in their own organization, that selling (and managing selling) is important and further that it deserves acknowledgement and should be accorded a high status. Management must also fight the sales peoples' corner on a day to day basis, and be seen to do so. If this is done and sales people themselves are made to believe that they are sincerely valued and respected, then the scene is set for them to succeed.

CUSTOMER ORIENTATION

Selling is well defined (by a character in a Video Arts training film) as "helping people to buy." Exactly so. Selling is not something to be done to people and everything about it and the way it is approached should reflect that fact.

The jargon of selling is rife with terms reflecting this: "benefit selling" has become a generic term emphasizing the need to discover what people want and why and sell accordingly. Other phrases have enjoyed some favour and emphasized the same point, for example "conceptual selling," meaning much the same or "strategic selling" which seems more vague and, anyway, would you sell unstrategically?

Action: to instill in sales people the concept of "customer first," not just as an obvious service view, but as a basis for the style of sales technique adopted.

SALES PRODUCTIVITY

This is the concept of analysis and action to "squeeze a quart out of a pint pot." It focuses on the ratios involved (for example, the number of calls made/orders taken) and examines the whole sales process to see how much more can be got from the activity and to ensure that the way things are being undertaken is correctly based.

Action: this is an area for ongoing management checking and, if possible, innovation. The productivity of every aspect of the activity should be borne in mind, for example:

- Documentation may be streamlined (or made electronic) to save time;

- Territories and journey planning investigated to ensure it maximizes time spent with customers; and
- Sales technique structured to be productive as well as effective (perhaps aiming for meetings that are shorter in duration, providing this is still effective and acceptable to customers).

CUSTOMER CATEGORIZATION

Customers are not all the same. The major way in which this is recognized is in terms of size. Big customers are not just bigger, they are different in the way they must be dealt with to make the relationship work for both parties. However this is addressed, and it may need to juggle size, potential, location, industry or type, use of product, level of technicality ... and more, every customer must be provided with the right service and the right sales resource and approach.

Action: this is a dynamic area, managers and sales people alike need to focus on how this categorization is arranged and adapt regularly, constantly almost, so that every category is related within the best possible way.

CUSTOMER PROFITABILITY

This has come to be more important as customers have polarized and the big have got bigger. As customer demands, or services offered (or both) extend, more and more margin is vulnerable to being eaten up in just getting the business. Any company that analyses the costs of obtaining business may be shocked at just how many things seemingly conspire to reduce margin.

These include: all the costs of the sales force (from recruitment to commission); discounts (and there may be many a different basis for them, e.g. quantity bought or when purchase is made); special packing, delivery (maybe to multiple locations, labeling; credit terms (and beyond), advertising and promotional support, merchandising assistance, training of customers' staff ...the list goes on. Unless this is addressed carefully profitability may well be in danger.

Action: management must address the list of possible "profit diluters," the policy involved and sales staffs' attitudes and competence. For example, it may be that policy is at fault and profit being lost because published terms need attention, or that policy is right, but that sales people are losing out due to poor negotiating skills.

CUSTOMER RELATIONSHIP

Every customer and supplier by definition presupposes a relationship. A variety of factors, not least the polarization of customer size have highlighted this and moved it from something that was taken for granted to something that should be planned. The electronic revolution has locked into this area, and for many the term CRM is synonymous with electronic records and prompt systems. As with so much else the key here is clear - it is the customer. Relationships need to reflect customer requirements and have as much in common with service as sales.

Action: the manager must make clear what is being aimed at here. Of course, the personal rapport between buyer and seller (sales person) is important here. But buyers do not now buy (if they ever did) just because they like people. They do buy, when their requirements are met by several potential suppliers, from the one who they feel goes about the process in the most acceptable and useful (and perhaps even the nicest) way.

KEY THINKERS

Management gurus abound. It is perhaps a reflection of the comments above about the profile of sales that, although there is plenty written about selling, albeit some of it in a much more evangelical style than is used for the discussion of other business skills, there have been few major sales management gurus.The following, however, are worth mentioning.

FREDERICK HERZBERG

One task relates very specifically to the work of one man, the American psychologist Frederick Herzberg, who it is not an exaggeration to describe as the father of motivational theory. His views of how motivation works also make a very practical foundation to creating positive motivation and making it work.

Briefly, he described two categories of factor affecting peoples' motivation: first, the dissatisfiers (or hygiene factors) listed as:

- Company policy and administration
- Supervision
- Working conditions
- Salary
- Relationships with peers

- Personal life (and the impact of work on it)
- Status
- Security.

All these are external factors. When things suit in these areas - all will be well motivationally. If there are problems here (e.g. sales people feel they are being asked to complete endless, bureaucratic forms and reports for which they see no purpose), then positive motivation is quickly diluted. Secondly, the satisfiers (or motivators) that act to create positive motivation. These are more personal and can be listed as:

- Achievement
- Recognition
- The work itself
- Responsibility
- Advancement
- Growth.

A good analogy here is a glasshouse, and a phrase that is often used in this context is motivational climate. Just as the plants in a greenhouse can be influenced by many factors that affect temperature, opening doors or windows, painting the glass to reflect the sun, turning on the heater, so motivation can be influenced in many different ways. The balance of factors is what matters. Managers should never underestimate the time and effort involved in getting things right here. Motivating is a continuous, time consuming process and attention to detail is vital. It is, however, very valuable, a well-motivated team will always focus better on the job and perform better as a result. It is a topic worth more study.

Herzberg's own books are now rather old and perhaps do not make good, practical references in the modern world. The workings of his theories and ideas on motivating successfully are explored in my own book How to Motivate People (Kogan Page/The Sunday Times).

DARTNELL

The Dartnell Sales managers Handbook was the earliest reference of any substance on the subject. Today the Dartnell Corporation still occupies the role of sales management guru. Probably best known for their surveys - one of which looks at trends in training methods - their Sales Force Compensation Survey is an annual publication that is the prime reference in its area; the figures may apply to the USA, but many people would find the commentary and conclusions are worth a look.

Sales

Many early exponents are now no longer the benchmark for sales excellence, though it is worth recalling people such as Heinz Goldmann whose sales and sales management seminars pulled hundreds of delegates over many years. His book Winning Sales is still worth reading, and shows the perennial nature of much to do with selling. Some, like Richard Denny who runs Leadership Development now operate in similar ways (his book, Selling to Win, Kogan Page, has a very personal style), but the most influential forces are rather different in nature.

HUTHWAITE RESEARCH GROUP

Without doubt one organization has added a whole new dimension to the way sales and selling are viewed, and thus to the practice of sales management, that is Huthwaite Research Group Limited. It is better known for its trademark, SPIN and the approach to selling this implies. Starting in the early seventies they applied new techniques to the observation of selling. Using behavior analysis, a research technique for observing and quantifying interactions between buyer and seller, it highlighted the interactive skills that seemed to best create successful sales. Key amongst them was questioning.

The main focus of their studies was on the following issues:

- How people buy and weigh up competitive offerings to help them make considered decisions;
- Reactions, particularly negative ones, that buyers tend to have to being sold to;
- Qualities that buyers regard as making a case (verbally or in writing) attractive, persuasive and credible; and
- The style of selling approach that appeared to be best regarded.

The fact that their views were based on, and validated by, research, literally thousands of interviews and observations of real sales meetings, was novel - they might say unique. In any case it was a key factor in helping make sales a profession. They offered training with sales techniques recommended by and matched to their studies, and their base of sales training has expanded to a full range of topics, including sales, negotiation, account management, major account strategies and sales management.

Though many would suggest that the Huthwaite research highlighted, at least in part, approaches that were either common sense or which had been documented by others, their success in promoting their ideas certainly gave prominence to a very practical and logical way of looking at selling.

The key to this approach is customer focus. Once selling was regarded as something "you did to people," now it is predominantly seen as a process of helping and working with the psychological process by which people make decisions to buy. Key therefore is the concept of discovering, through very specifically applied questioning techniques (this is where the patented SPIN technique comes in), exactly what is happening on the customer's side of the discussion. If sales people find out about a customer, how they think, what they need, how they operate and what their expectations are of their suppliers and those that represent them, they will more precisely be able to focus their sales approach. The concept of the sales professional and of the sales person as advisor is also key to the approach. This may seem less than novel now, but everything about selling that builds in these kind of approaches (wherever they come from) tends to work best in the real world.

If selling is not, as is sometimes imagined, a matter that may be applied largely by rote - and it is not - then the implications for the sales manager are clear. Their job is not to lay down the law, setting out the way in which selling should take place. Rather it is to give sales people the understanding of the approach that must be taken, based on customer practice and expectations, and the confidence to do it in their own way - and in a way that is always tailored to individual customers.

The practical nature of sales management means that there is a profusion of books, but your choice is very much a matter of taste as their content does not vary as much as their style and treatment. The following are chosen as a good cross section and to for illustrating different options.

Note: Foster Farms is a US based privately held company, which primarily provides poultry products such as turkey and chicken to grocery and foodservice companies. The company's product range encompasses over 750 different items, including fresh chicken and turkey, deli meats, prepared entrees and corn dogs. It is headquartered in Livingston, California and employs about 10,000 people. For a case study visit company's site www.fosterfarms.com

8

Resources

If further investigation is necessary, this section may help. It sets out sources of reference looking at sales management in a number of different ways.

- Research
- Journals
- Using training films
- Professional bodies

What external resources can add power to the sales manager's arm? The following are necessarily a disparate group and no attempt is made to reduce them to neat categories. So, with books dealt with in the previous section "Concepts and Thinkers," listed here are sources of ideas, information and inspiration varying from films to professional institutes and web sites.

A key issue throughout this work has been the question of defining the sales job realistically and usefully.

RESEARCH

The Future of Selling is a report published late in 2000 by Quest Media Ltd (the publishers of the journal Winning Business) in association with the Institute of Professional Selling and consultants Miller Heinman Inc.

This is an interesting research study, more so because the area is rarely researched. It reviews current practice and looks to the future examining: the changing sales role, customer expectations and beliefs, and the whole way sales teams are organized, staffed, rewarded and managed.

Key findings indicated that are as follows:

- Customers are becoming better informed and more organized, demanding and sharp in their dealings with sales people (with the Internet being used to a significant extent for pre-buying research);
- Technology is having, and must continue to have, an effect on sales activity: most dramatically it is replacing sales people with electronic, impersonal buying, though this is not affecting large numbers of business areas. The dynamic nature of this area is evidenced by the uncertainty respondents reflected in their forecasts of the other influences that are becoming important;
- Recruitment is a perpetual challenge as is retention;
- CRM is becoming a more widespread basis for many customer interactions, and creating a more formal basis for them;
- Training remains a constant need (and more of it is being done, and the range of ways in which it is done are also increasing) as the level of competency of sales people is seen as key to success; and
- Reporting takes a high proportion of working time - reducing sales people's time spent face to face with customers; this despite the increasing computerization of data collection and reporting systems.

Sales management, its practice, manner and style, is seen as significant to success. On the one hand the increasing professionalism of the sales role, and the broadening of sales people's responsibilities in response to market changes, heighten the role and managerial skills sales managers must have. On the other hand, there is one area where sales managers seem sometimes to be marginalized. This is in respect of new technology. For example, sales managers are often not involved in the development of e-business strategies. There are dangers here. An e-business strategy that is not made compatible with traditional sales processes may lack realism. While technology and its development are always difficult to predict, it is perhaps best done in this area with the sales manager's active involvement, or the baby might just get thrown out with the bath water.

The section of the report on the impact of e-commerce is interesting. Just to quote one statistic, 90% of respondents' organizations have a Website; but 57% of them said they were not used to assist sales. It is a valuable study that deserves to be repeated on a regular basis.

JOURNALS

Winning Business - www.quest-media.com

This is a good magazine that ranges wide across sales and sales management issues. It is the only substantial mainstream journal published for sales managers and directors in the UK and is produced in association with The Institute of Professional Sales.

Sales Director - www.saleszone.co.uk

This is also useful and has very much the style and format of something like the journal Management Today.

Sales & Marketing Management - www.salesandmarketing.com

The main US magazine on this subject, broader than solely sales management and which contains useful material.

Sales & Marketing Professional

This is the journal linked to the Institute of Sales & Marketing Management. Somehow this has always remained in the shadow of the main institutes. Its base is sales, but it seems to think marketing is more sexy and positions itself "higher."

All the above are specific, but it is worth bearing in mind that, as selling is an essential part of the marketing mix, marketing journals feature articles on selling and sales management from time to time. The Library at the Chartered Institute of Marketing will produce lists of recent articles on request, though there is a charge to non-members.

FILMS

Training films have traditionally been a good way to introduce or reinforce messages about sales technique, and the Video Arts Group - producing what will probably be forever known as the "John Cleese Films" - is a predominant producer. Though actor John Cleese has not been involved in any substantial way for a while, their own - almost always humorous - films are the core of their range. They also distribute various American products and have a range of e-learning products involving everything from CD-ROMs to DVDs available. Such films are worth using in a variety of settings - courses, conferences or sales meetings - and a good way to revisit and reinforce topics; often a number of films come at a subject in different ways keeping it fresh and avoiding repetition. It may be useful to request regular information from film producers to keep up to date with what is available. Most are available for purchase or rental.

WWW.VIDEOARTS.COM

The boxed paragraph which follows (adapted from Developing Your Staff, Patrick Forsyth, Kogan Page) is included to provide a little advice on film use, which benefits from some care and preparation.

Using Training Films

First, what not to do. Films should not be regarded as an easy option: just drag people together, stick on a film and say - look and listen. So, how do you get the most from training films?

Selecting the Right Film

Let us assume that the topic is decided. You know that you want people to develop a certain skill and want to find a film on that subject. There are not so many providers and it does not take long to check catalogs and Websites or to telephone offices and check what is available. If there is a film that seems suitable, you will want to be able to assess it - is it any good? - is it suitable for your people? Consider:

- The provider: to some degree the standard (and style) of what you will get can be gauged by the company producing or distributing the film although even films from the big, well-known operators may vary a little in standard, this is a good first measure;
- The film quality: given the standard of what people are used to seeing in the cinema and on television, a minimum standard is probably necessary. Though this is not to say that simpler things cannot be useful; one of my own "most-used" films consists of live action, real people filmed doing real things, with no script or expensive production values - but it makes some good, clear points and is a valuable training resource; and
- The message: how the film puts over its message is vital. If it tries to do too much in a short time for instance, it may not succeed. If it allows humor to submerge the message, this too may dilute its effectiveness. Not least does its style match your circumstances? Will your people be able to identify with characters and circumstances in the film? Does the message

match the kind of way the topic needs to be dealt with in your organization?

You can get some advice from catalogs or recommendations from colleagues, but there is no substitute for seeing for yourself. Most providers have systems for previewing that work well and the time this takes, and even the small cost sometimes involved, is worthwhile. You need to plan to use not just a film, but a suitable film.

The first thing to note is that using a training film is not an opportunity to train without effort. Most films are not designed to do a complete job unsupported. At the very least they need topping and tailing, more often they are most effective when incorporated into a session, albeit this can sometimes be a short one. Usually a film is supplied with training notes, a booklet or guide to its use. These should always be studied. They do not need to be followed slavishly, their suggestions for sessions can be changed, lengthened, shortened or otherwise amended. But they can be useful. For example, they may help clarify exactly why a film is being used - the role it will play. This may vary. The variation may be as follows:

- Introduce a topic;
- Summarize key issues;
- Crack through the core content, the essential principles of something;
- Spark discussion; and
- Link to a particular internal situation.

Whatever you do it must be clear. The film should help you meet your training objectives and it should be clear how it will do so and what role it will play (and this needs to be made clear too to the group). You can usefully plan film use specifically and systematically following something like the following sequence:

- Always watch the film through yourself ahead of the session;
- Read the accompanying material;
- Make notes of anything you need to mention, emphasize or explain to the group;
- Decide how the training points made in the film link to the totality of what you want to achieve;
- List ways in which the film can link to participation or exercises, classically noting questions that the group should address; and

- Link your thinking into your overall preparation of the whole session.

It is worth thinking just a little about the physical use of a film. Set things up so that everyone can see. You may want to dim the lights, but not too much if people have to make notes. Remember that some films are designed to be seen in several parts, or have a separate summary section at the end allowing you to return to key points at the end of a session.

Note: certain films are designed in a way linking to individual study. While introduction and briefing may still be necessary, subsequent solo study may sometimes work well from a time standpoint, for example allowing individual members of a department to see the film without the operational disruption of a group session. The style of the film will allow different forms of training to stem from it.

- Case study based films allow one form of discussion, for example extending the scenario or varying elements of it in discussion - what would have happened if that had not been the reaction when ...
- Behaviorally based films may allow more analysis of how people react, or even allow links to be made to real people in your own company.
- The classic wrong way/right way film style in which characters perform badly (exhibiting the dangers), learn lessons and then perform better (exhibiting the strengths of using correct technique), allow both aspects to be reviewed or discussed.

Stop/start Use

As an example of method linked to the form of a film, consider the good way/bad way film further. By showing the film in parts it can be alternated with discussion, asking:

- What went wrong and why?
- How could matters have been handled differently?
- What are the principles involved to ensure success?

Then the "right way" part can be shown and separate discussion can follow that. Role play could be organized to extrapolate the situations portrayed in the film with members of the group extending the film characters' roles.

PROFESSIONAL BODIES

CHARTERED INSTITUTE OF MARKETING

This is listed first as a prime source of reference. As an overall summary they describe themselves as:

"The Chartered Institute of Marketing (CIM) is the professional body for marketing, with over 60,000 members worldwide. "Founded in 1911, it has been instrumental in elevating marketing to a recognised, respected and chartered profession.

"It is the only marketing body able to award Individual Chartered Marketer status to eligible members. Chartered Marketer status is a professional standard which reflects an individual's commitment to developing their professional skills in an increasingly competitive marketplace.

"As an examining body for over 60 years, the Institute's Certificates and Postgraduate Diploma (DipM) are internationally recognised qualifications, available through a worldwide network of educational institutions and distance learning providers."

In context here it is worth mentioning that CIM offer various services.

" Career development services: which include a range of information in booklet form or downloadable from their Website, a Career Advice Line, a Career Counselling service (run in collaboration with Connaught Executive via a network of 25 offices around the country) and two routes for those seeking new jobs. The first is Job Focus accessed through the Institute's Website and is available to all, the second (for members only) is the Job Vacancy Database run with Quantum Consulting Group.

- The library and information service.
- The qualifications they themselves offer.
- The network of branches: these mean no one is far from a local source of information and networking (there are a number of overseas branches also and the Institute links with the European Marketing Confederation with associate bodies in 24 countries within and outside the European Union (total membership is more than 300,000).
- CIM Direct: a source of business books for purchase.

In addition the Institute is the parent body for the Institute of Sales Professionals, which undertakes a parallel role to it's parent, focusing solely on the sales function.

And CAM Foundation (Communication, Advertising and Marketing) which is the umbrella body for qualifications across the various marketing disciplines.

Note: while this is a source of value to all, you should note that some of the services listed above are available only to Members of the Institute.

THE MARKETING SOCIETY

Describes itself as, "The premier organization in the UK for senior marketing professionals and general managers of marketing oriented companies." It states its purpose as: to provide access to the best network for the leading edge ideas and practice and to inspire and support Society members by encouraging debate and contact between them. It is a long established and well respected body (with something of a bias towards FMCG companies; it has a quarterly journal Market Leader).

STEPS FOR MAKING SALES MANAGEMENT TO WORK

Some activities and approaches are more significant in creating results than others. All the given key areas are focused on creating sales management success and thus sales excellence. We begin with an area that has a great deal stemming from one word.

1. The Successful Sales Manager Must Have Vision

One aspect of the sales job is also an inherent danger. There is a necessary focus on the day to day activity. Sales people make one call at a time. They must alternate between time spent with an individual customer and time spent preparing to see the next; and the preparation must lead to a precise tailoring of approach next time with every customer needing individual treatment. It can be a rather relentless process. In one direction attention is necessary on their company and their products or services, and all the attendant detail. In the other the focus is on the market, customers and competition.

It is all too easy to get locked into a rather introspective (and, worse, repetitive) mode of operation where considered approaches are replaced by an "automatic pilot" style approach. This can become pedestrian, as well as being seen by customers as standard and losing their sympathy on those grounds alone.

The wider scale of operations should influence the day to day. Seeing the full scope of what must be achieved will enliven performance and approach, keeping it fresh and ensuring it is well tailored every time a prospect or customer is seen.

If the sales manager does not put over a clear vision, then probably no one will do so. To enthuse the team in this way, the manager must him or her self have:

- A clear overall and strategic view of the business;
- Real involvement with marketing and senior management;
- Time to spend at this level, which should be focused on key issues;
- The ability to encapsulate the current and future view of the way forward so that communicating it makes sense; and
- An ongoing commitment to keeping this view up to date and an open mind to make it possible to do so.

Sales people will always work more effectively when they see their job in the context of a broad, worthwhile and exciting intention. Making this view possible will not distract them from the day to day, it will put them in a position to undertake their day to day tasks well.

2. The Successful Sales Manager Must be Market Focused

This may sound obvious, but it is all too easy for a sales manager to become an administrator (in the worst sense of the word), with a largely introspective view of their work. Bogged down in this way they tend to adopt an attitude that sales people should be entirely self sufficient and leave them to "get on with it." All external contact is vital.

- With customers. Sales managers should not spend too much of their time selling. And further, they should not spend time selling in situations where they do so - perhaps with "difficult" or "important" customers - because "no one else on the team is up to it." What sort of team is that? But they need to keep their selling skills sharp, and they need to do enough to give sufficient first hand feedback of customers' demands, expectations and views. Only on the basis of experience and information so obtained will they be able to manage effectively, and will what they do be credible to the team?
- With competitors. Or indeed with any outside agency that can provide information about how selling should be conducted in future. This is a process of constant questioning - what is happening elsewhere in terms of product development, technological change or with competitive organizations themselves and the way they work?

All the methods of operation that managers must create and maintain in the sales area must be right externally - nothing must be done solely for internal convenience and ultimately it is the interface with the customer that is the arbiter of success; the right product, sold and supported in the right way.

3. The Successful Sales Manager Must Set Clear Guidelines

Sales people will never maximize their performance if they are not sure what they have to do. Even a smidgen of doubt is too much. Everything from job descriptions to operational guidelines must be crystal clear. Nowhere is this more important than with targets, goals, standards and any mandatory operational procedures.

These must be as follows:

- Soundly and realistically based. No sales person will bust a gut trying
- To achieve something that is manifestly unachievable or silly;
- Challenging. This is not incompatible with "sound and realistic"; it is part of what makes life at the sharp end interesting; and
- Underpinned with suitable support. If orders are delivered late, quality control is poor or necessary sales aids are either not provided or inadequate, then the challenge of targets will quickly turn into resentment of them.

First, clarity in all these areas provides a sound foundation upon which a sales team can operate. Additionally, the sales manager who is seen to be clear and well organized about such things will always command most respect - and that in turn means more of their influence will be followed.

Moving even closer to the actual management of the team, the next area is clearly a prerequisite of success.

4. The Successful Sales Manager Has a Top Flight Team

Recruitment and selection were commented on earlier. Finding the right people is crucial and often not easy. So, the successful manager must:

- Be clear about the profile of person required;
- Set high standards and stick with them; a sales team has no place for passengers or "poor relations"; and
- Link to, and sometimes fight for, the ability to give the right rewards.

It is such a clich´e but the phrase "if you pay peanuts, you get monkeys" is also a truism.

All this means a willingness to undertake any recruitment activity on a sound and thorough basis, and links back to clarity about such things as job descriptions. It takes time but attention to detail - good job advertisements, comprehensive application forms, painstaking interviewing, and a firm resolution not to resort to inappropriate, untested amateur psychology - is paramount at every stage. Then hire when you are sure and reject if you are not; people very rarely prove better than your hopes and a wrong decision in this area can be costly in many, many ways - from lost sales and muddled records to tarnished images and weakened customer relationships. It can take a long time to sort out the damage, certainly much longer than taking a little more time to make the right appointment.

5. The Successful Sales Manager Spends Time with their Team

As a category, sales managers tend to have broad responsibilities. They get involved in all sorts of things from promotion to general management duties. Yet many - most - of the core sales management tasks demand that time is spent with the sales team, both individually and as a group.

Such time is crucial for the ongoing direction of sales activity. Here we divide the tasks into two broad categories:

- A key role is development. Skills must be created and maintained at a standard of excellence. Further the precise way in which skills must be deployed changes, so a constant process of amendment, and to a degree experimentation, is necessary to ensure that selling is done in a way that matches individual customers and the moment. The evaluation, counselling, mentoring and link with other development activities all take time. But it is time well spent. Ultimately sales people must be almost entirely self-sufficient. There is no way the manager can be with everybody on their every call. Time spent on joint calling is not to improve those few calls on which this happens, it is to enable the sales person to improve all those calls when they operate alone. All the various activities that contribute to this process are key. The numbers back this up. Even a small team of say 10 people may be making some 10,000 calls each year - management's job is to create excellence in them all; or, perhaps more accurately, to help the team do this.

- The second area worth highlighting is communications. Apart from the development job mentioned above, communication should take a major part of a sales manager's time.

6. The Successful Sales Manager Actively Motivates

Fact: the sales force is more likely to perform well when they are well motivated. They will only be well motivated if attention is given to this on a regular basis. It is not a matter of throwing money at it, or having a complex incentive scheme and believing no more needs to be done. Saying "Well done" is as important as the many more complex things that are also needed (and, ask yourself - have I said "Well done" often enough lately?).

Motivation needs the following criteria:

- Consideration: unthinking or routine management will miss opportunities;
- Variety: the changes need ringing, different things doing at different times and for different people;
- Time: and this must not be skimped; enough said;
- To be ongoing: motivation is best delivered through the whole management job, not in little "motivational bursts" arranged to get it out of the way and free up time for more important things; and
- Tailoring: just as selling must be matched to customers, so motivation must be matched to the kind of sales team involved - even to the individuals. Certainly it is important for the manager not to be censorious (i.e. remember that what is important to you may not be the same as what is important to your staff).

Motivation matters. Most of what needs doing costs little beyond some thought and some time. If people see their job as important, interesting - fun - they will work harder, and more constructively and it will show in their results.

7. The Successful Sales Manager is a Good Communicator

Communication is ubiquitous to management. Motivation, above, consists largely of communication. Communication must be as follows:

- Clear: consider just how often communications problems occur in organizations. Sometimes they cause a momentary hiccup, on other occasions breakdown is the word that describes things best and serious consequences can result. The main problem is overconfidence; everyone thinks they are a good communicator, indeed often we think that communication is easy. It is not. There are principles here worthy of study, certainly communicating well needs care, consideration and time. Errors often occur in an unthinking rush. The wrong word is chosen or the right word omitted.

- Understandable: this means a little more than just clear. Things must be put in the right frame of reference for people, not assuming they know more than they do, for example, or that they have experience which in fact they do not.
- Persuasive: often it is not just a question of telling people - we need to persuade. This is simply, or perhaps not so simply, the skills of selling applied internally. As such sales managers should be good at this; though again this will not happen automatically. The old rule of "engaging the brain before the mouth" makes sense for us all.
- Not secretive: this may seem either a minor point or to go without saying, but the isolation of sales people mean any apparent unnecessary secretiveness is likely to be strongly resented. Tell people what is going on and how it affects them.

Particular activities here include the following.

- Sales meetings: the opportunity to get the team together may be infrequent, but they are important - and often their effectiveness is low, these represent a significant opportunity to inform and encourage. They deserve time being spent in preparation to get them right.
- Motivation: in all its forms. The essence of this is that it is ongoing, a matter of detail, and again takes time. The right incentive scheme may be important, but so too are the small exchanges that make up the continuity of contact between the sales manager and his team. It is clearly wrong, and something I often hear on sales courses, when a sales person says: "The only time I ever see my manager is when something is wrong."
- Appraisal: formal appraisal is mentioned as an example of something that combines a number of elements: evaluation, motivation, planning and more. Again this seems too often to be skimped. Sales people should look forward to their appraisals, finding them constructive and this should, in turn,

foster an overall constructive and productive management/sales relationship.

Communication, and you will be able to think of many other examples of how it is used and how it is important, provides the oil that lubricates the whole sales management process and with it the sales activity that it prompts.

8. The Successful Sales Manager Creates Sales Excellence

The question of development has already been mentioned, in Number 5 above, as a major example of where a sales manager must spend significant time. The process of defining what must be done, keeping that up to date, making sure that every member of the team can operate as required and putting them in a position to evaluate and fine-tune their own performance is vital. A series of activities contribute to this:

- Field training: the whole process of working with people in the field - evaluating, counselling and generally working with people to help fine-tune performance;
- Sales meetings: mentioned above, where a great deal of development work can be conducted quickly and easily with the whole group together;
- Formal training: including e-learning and other alternatives to "classroom training"; and
- Appraisals: formal appraisal systems, already mentioned, have a very direct link with development.

The above, and a whole series of other inputs, from having lunch with a sales person and talking shop to devices such as audio or video newsletters, all contribute. It is an ongoing process and the first step to making it work is clear definition of the sales job. This needs to be entirely job and organization specific, but general overviews can be helpful here too. For instance the following comes from McCormack on Selling, the book written by Mark McCormack, the American sports marketing consultant and commentator:

'The qualities that I for the making of a good salesman are as follows:

- Believe in your product
- Believe in yourself
- See a lot of people
- Pay attention to timing

- Listen to the customer - but realize that what the customer wants is not necessarily what he or she is telling you
- Develop a sense of humor
- Knock on old doors
- Ask everyone to buy
- Follow up after the sale with the same aggressiveness you demonstrated before the sale
- Use common sense

"I have no illusions that I'm breaking new ground with this list. These are essential, self-evident, universal qualities that all sales people know in their heads - if not in their hearts." Secondly, with the job clearly in mind, the team must be persuaded that development is natural, necessary, not an affront to their competence - and thus be made acceptable, indeed desirable. A sales team that recognize they need to learn and want to move their expertise ahead is always going to have the edge on people who think they know it all and see selling as something to be applied by rote.

9. The Successful Sales Manager Innovates

It cannot be said too often that sales, indeed marketing of which it is a part, is dynamic. Change is the order of the day. A quotation from management writers Robert Kriegal and David Brant puts it powerfully: "When you're through changing, you're through. Change is a process, not a goal; a journey, not a destination."

This is a philosophy any sales manager (any manager?) must take on board. Essentially it necessitates:

- Recognition of change: in all aspects of the job there is a duty to watch out for changes which impinge on you and opportunities to change for the better - better still to anticipate change. Being ahead of the trend may be a factor that helps create differentiation between you and competitors;
- An open mind: a willingness to review the options, to experiment (perhaps to make a few mistakes along the way) but one way or another to take if necessary radical or less obvious options if that is what will produce the desired effect; and
- Decisiveness: decisions need to be made. Good sales managers do not spend their life sitting on the fence, and nothing

demotivates sales people more than managers who acknowledge situations, promise to sort it out - and then do nothing.

This applies to every aspect of sales management. It is as important in a sense for making changes simply to update a reporting system (something that might improve productivity - less time to complete - and the precision of information gathering), as it is to make radical changes, perhaps to the way the sales activity is organized. Certainly small refinements in selling approach may be able to influence sales results significantly.

10. The Successful Sales Manager Actively Leads

Leadership goes beyond simple management. If management is regarded, perhaps somewhat simplistically, as organizing people and their activities, then leadership is inspiring and driving them. As management guru Tom Peters said (in a Foreword to The Leadership Challenge, James M. Kouzes and Barry Z. Posner Jossey Bass Wiley)

"Leadership, many have said, is different from management. Management is mostly about 'to do' lists - can't live without them! Leadership is about tapping the wellsprings of human motivation - and about the fundamental relations with one's fellows."

Or, as Peter Drucker put it succinctly and much earlier: "Management is doing things right; leadership is doing the right things."

Leadership comes, in part at least, from the sum total of the management tasks reviewed here being well executed. A good sales manager, giving time, consideration and attention to detail to the tasks they must address will find themselves leading. If there is a less definable "spark" beyond that which marks out those with leadership qualities then it is perhaps simply that they care: about what they do, about their organization and making it successful - and, above all, about their people.

Success here has effects inside and outside the organization. Selling is, as has been said, dynamic. Customers are demanding and fickle. The right approach - precisely the right approach - must be deployed customer by customer, meeting by meeting, day by day. Management can, and must, make a difference ensuring that sales is working effectively. When this is done it makes a difference in the marketplace; and that is the only source of all revenue and profit. From that thought a final note on which to end is struck by quoting

Mark McCormack, the American sports marketing consultant. He said in his book McCormack on Selling:

"I've never bought anything from sales people who didn't know their product and yet I have bought things I didn't know I needed from people who did." Good sales people make the difference; good managers create sales excellence.

Note: Perdue Incorporated (Perdue) is a privately held producer and distributor of poultry products. The company also provides other agricultural products. The company primarily operates in the US. It is headquartered in Salisbury, Maryland and employs about 20,000 people. The company generates $4,100 million revenue annually. For a detailed example in "Resources" visit *www.perdue.com*

9

Significance of Communication

Communication forms the basis of all of our interactions with people. Even though you are a new sales manager, you have already likely worked on improving your communication skills in order to work better with your managers, colleagues, and customers. This chapter will look at communication from all the core perspectives as it relates to your new role in management giving you many more techniques to incorporate in your daily interactions. This chapter will also help you in understanding your style of communicating, as well as that of others, in order to improve your working relationships. This involves how you communicate up, down, and across the organization, as well as with outside business associates. It is also especially important when you look at interviewing, delegating, motivation, training, coaching, counselling, and so many other facets of your interpersonal relationships with others. In fact, communication ties directly in to just about every aspect of your job and is an indispensable tool that will greatly increase your chances of success in your new career.

LISTENING SKILLS

Before delving too far into types of communicating styles and their usefulness, it is important to briefly look at what people so often neglect in skill building and personal development-the art of listening. In fact, to the novice, listening isn't even associated with communicating. In many respects, we are trained to believe that communicating involves some kind of talking, when in reality, some of the best communicators are also the best listeners. When you look back, we are all taught as children to read, write, and speak, but how often are we taught to listen? This is interesting when we think about how the best salespeople need to be great listeners when making a sales call (e.g., when trying to identify a customer's concern or conducting a needs analysis). In fact, for you as a manager, it is critical as well. How else can you truly understand and help to improve your team without the act of listening? Yet time and time again, we forget to make a conscious effort to listen. The following are some common examples of inattentive listening habits.

- Trying to finish someone else's thoughts
- Interrupting
- Talking too much without pausing or waiting for a response
- Losing your own train of thought
- Lack of eye contact
- Slouching
- Crossed arms

You will notice that many of the above examples deal with the listener actually talking (often a sign that there is a lack of listening) or other things that can cause difficulty for active listening to occur. Now look at some examples of what the attentive listener does.

- Utilizes supportive or empathetic words ("go on," "I understand," "really," etc.).
- Has an inviting posture and hand positioning (depending on the circumstance).
- Maintains solid eye contact (not staring, though).
- Smiles with regularity.

As a new manager, this is your time to shine. To show your team that you are supportive of them, the first step is to be a good listener. It is only then that you can even begin to understand how you and others communicate and how to improve working relationships. In the early goings, you need to be disciplined in order to be an attentive listener. Like any other skill, it is something that you need to work on. Some other ways to condition yourself to be a better listener include the following:

- Ask questions (open- and/or closed-ended).
- Don't rush the speaker.
- Verify or paraphrase in order to make sure you fully understand what is being said.
- Don't prejudge a person or situation.
- Limit distractions.
- Listen with your eyes and your ears.

- Try not to finish someone else's thought(s).
- Come to the table ready to listen.

The previous example is more or less a mind-set. Reminding yourself that you want to be a more active listener goes a long way.

THE THEORY BEHIND COMMUNICATION STYLES

In life, people play many roles: manager, parent, psychologist, teacher, student, friend. Each role requires a unique behaviour. At the same time, as individuals, everyone comes to their role in life with a different set of values, traits, and characteristics that have been shaped over the years, both hereditary and environmental through society.

Interestingly, psychologists have discovered that people who change as circumstances require feel their behavior is consistent, no matter what role they play. However, research has shown observable changes in behavior as the person moves from one role to the other-for example, from work to home life. Taking this idea one step further, people change not only as roles change but also as situations and circumstances change within a role. It has been evidenced that, in many cases, changes people make are done on a subconscious rather than conscious level.

You as a new sales manager will have to keep up constant communication with many different stakeholders. This will include communicating with any or all of these:

- Your sales team
- Other sales managers
- Customers
- Your manager(s)
- Senior management
- Other department personnel (finance, human resources, product managers, marketers, public relations, engineers, etc.)

Sometimes the interactions will seem effortless, and sometimes conversations will be a real challenge. The information and tools in this chapter are designed to increase your odds for successful communication with all types of people and stakeholders. In fact, while this book is meant to be a business resource, solid communication skills could of course benefit you in all areas of your life.

THE ORIGINS OF DISC THEORY

In 1928, the psychologist Dr. William M. Marston wrote a book called Emotions of Normal People. The title creates an immediate question: What is "normal"? According to Marston, "normal" did not refer to typical psychological processes, societal norms, or mores. Instead, "normal" referred to an individual's own environment. For example, if you are in your ordinary or typical environment for a particular situation, Marston considers you to be "normal." In his book he identified what he called "primary emotions," of which he highlighted four and he talked about their associated behaviors.

DISC theory got its start from some of Marston's work. The theory contends that four patterns in people emerge due to a combination of various factors. People tend to be either task-oriented or people-oriented as well as prone to either changing or accepting their environment. Today it focuses to a great extent on how people of different communication or personal styles (which we'll look at in a moment) react under different circumstances. Two of the key questions it strives to answer and improve upon are (1) How do you react in your most comfortable (friendly) environment? and (2) How do you react when out of your favourable environment (antagonistic)? Today there are many companies using different variations of DISC instruments to gauge personal styles as well as other types of measurement instruments for personal development, including listening skills, time management skills, and persuasion skills. Another important instrument used to understand and enhance communications is the Myers-Briggs Type Indicator MBTI_. Although the intended outcomes of DISC and MBTI_ overlap to some degree, they are based on a different set of principles.

Due to the proliferation of so many products and services in this area, it is difficult to try covering everything. Here the focus will be on DISC related profile instruments and the four words chosen to identify the categories of personal styles-Directing, Influencing,

Keep in mind that your company may choose to use any one of the many communication instruments with different words to describe the type of test. This ranges from Personal Style Test to Behavioral Profile to Communication Styles Indicator or some other instrument. Once an instrument style is chosen, what is critical to realize is that whatever category or categories of DISC you fall into, there is no good and no bad style or combination of styles. This model is meant to be a nonjudgmental way of looking at behaviors and communication styles. So while they are often called tests, there is no passing, failing, or grading system. They are meant to provide guidance and focus.

Also, while the tests, when taken properly, provide you with your corresponding style(s), they are not meant to delve too deeply into your internal psyche. They are intended to give you a better understanding of certain recognizable characteristics of yourself and others rather than core traits that would require a much deeper knowledge and understanding.

DISC profiles have been around for decades. Millions of people across many professions have used them. It is important that you as a sales manager utilize such an instrument, as it will aid you in three main categories: job performance, interpersonal relations, and personal satisfaction.

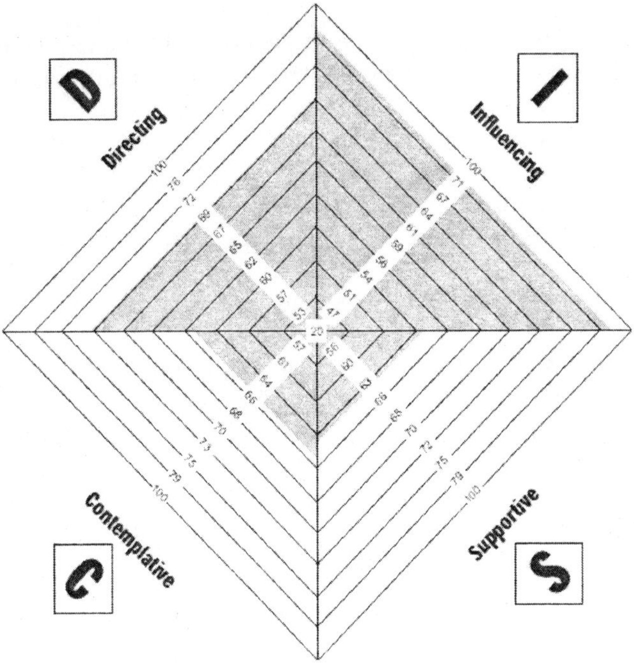

Figure: The DISC Profile.

Breaking these categories down even further, the DISC Profile can help you in the following ways:

- Determining some of your own strengths and weaknesses
- Determining certain strengths and weaknesses of team members
- Improving your communication skills (which include listening skills, as previously discussed)

- Improving the communication skills of your sales team members
- Improving team morale and respect for one another
- Enhancing customer relationships
- Reducing stress and conflict
- Working more effectively with your manager(s)
- Hiring new sales staff
- Increasing your self-awareness
- Demonstrating tolerance
- Promoting diversity
- Embracing change

A DISC profile can be taken in about thirty minutes. Through a series of forced-choice questions you then plot your results onto a four-quadrant chart. With certain DISC instruments you are able to self-assess as well as be assessed by the company or a company certified by or affiliated with the instrument's developer. Furthermore, there are often additional training resources (books, online resources, and so on) that may go along with the instruments for increasing their usefulness.

THE FOUR-QUADRANT SYSTEM

As shown above, each quadrant is defined by one of the four factors- D, I, S, or C. Remember that depending on the instrument used, the four letters can be associated with slightly different words and have other subtle differences. An example would be the word dominant in place of directing, or conscientious in place of contemplative. Notwithstanding, whether or not these four words vary, certain general themes hold true across DISC instruments; for example:

- Directing: Someone oriented toward changing his task environment.
- Influencing: Someone oriented toward changing other people.
- Supportive: Someone oriented toward understanding and accepting other people.
- Contemplative: Someone oriented toward understanding and accepting her task environment.

Also be aware that the above descriptions of each of the DISC quadrants are based on substantial characteristics in each. For example, a very high "D" would possess almost all the characteristics of the D, and this would be without regard or influence by another style. The level of scores and where you plot on the grids suggest the intensity of certain characteristics, a higher score equating to stronger characteristics. Combinations, of which there can be many, will be discussed later.

The following are some typical characteristics of each pattern-D, I, S, and C. Again, keep in mind that these are not attributable to all those who fall into a certain category and that everyone possesses at least a partial amount of the characteristics associated with each quadrant.

These examples are simply a reference point; when you and your staff complete a profile (assuming you have not done so already), you'll have a better understanding and a basis for learning and future development of both you and your staff. Also, since you will never be able to precisely know where many other people you come in contact with will plot on the DISC survey, this will give you some insights into their more likely styles and how to work best with them.

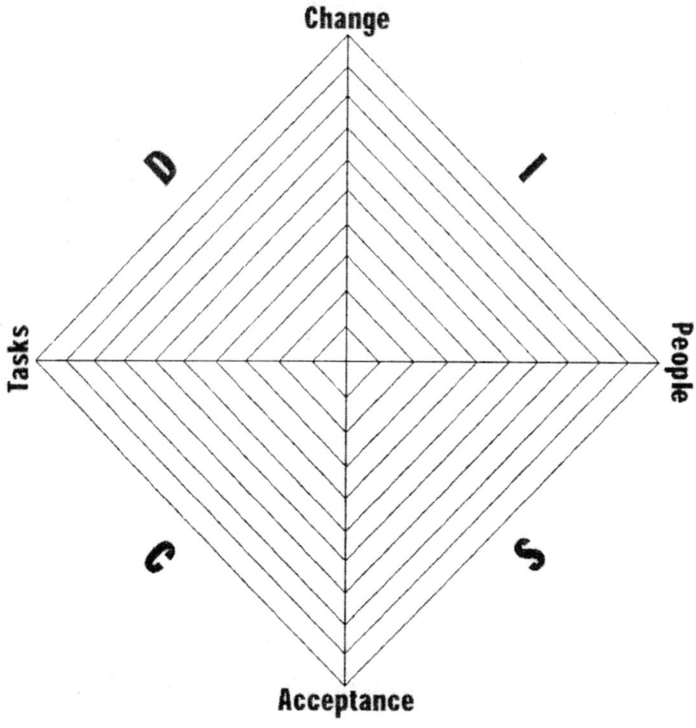

Figure: DISC Dimension

DIRECTING OR HIGH D OVERVIEW

Anyone who scores high in the D quadrant is oriented toward changing their task environment. They exhibit these characteristics as follows:

- They attack the task at hand.
- They are goal- and solution-oriented.
- They make things happen and move swiftly.
- The greater the challenge, the more active they become.
- They often works best independently.
- They thrive on competition.

Strengths:

- The Directing personalities show these strengths:
- They are assertive, efficient, and focused on results.
- Under the right circumstances, they can take direction well.
- They will exhibit strong organizational ability and operational skills in reacting to chaos.
- They are self-starters.
- They push others to succeed with the same rigor as they possess.
- They tend to be pioneering and adventurous.
- They are rather self-sufficient.
- Achieving one goal will encourage them to go after the next one.

Weaknesses:

- "Directing" people can also exhibit some less desirable traits.
- They can come across as dictatorial.
- Their focus is on getting results, not on how people feel in the process.
- They can be viewed as impatient, arrogant, or overly demanding.
- They can be perceived as cold.
- They tend to have a low tolerance for negative feelings, bad attitudes, and ineffectiveness.
- They can be hasty and blunt as well as critical of others.

HIGH DIRECTING WANTS

A Directing style wants challenge and productivity. They want to move forward constantly and make a decision. It does not really matter to them if the decision is not exactly right, because fixing a mistake is just a matter of making another decision. A person with this style wants the freedom and authority to move toward personal growth. She does not mind being tested or measured, as long as there is some associated result or reward.

HIGH DIRECTING NEEDS

These people need to have controls. Their multitasking may create mental and physical disorganization. Moderation and a balance of challenges may be helpful in relieving the continual stress.

A Directing style needs to learn patience and relaxation. Empathetic listening can help him to be a more tactful communicator. "Ready, fire, aim" is generally his motto. A person of this style needs to be more cautious and prudent in his approach to issues. Many times he will solve one problem but create two in the process.

COMMUNICATION STYLE

Because of their orientation toward changing their task environment, Directing personalities communicate assertively, with the goal of getting things done.

- Verbal Communication. Abundant verbal communication is common for the Directing style. These people tend to tell more than they ask or talk more than listen. They are usually rather blunt and get directly to the point.
- Tonality (Tone of Voice). The Directing style will tend to use a forceful tone. The volume may be high and the speech pattern fast. Directing use a variety of intonations.
- Body Language. They move with authority. They generally are fast-paced and walk with purpose. The Directing style will gesture while talking. They can also readily display boredom or impatience.

WRITING STYLE

Their writing style is abbreviated and to the point. They often leave the details for later discussion.

INFLUENCING OR HIGH OVERVIEW

These personalities are oriented toward changing other people. Here are some of their common traits:

- They see themselves in the role of persuader and motivator.
- They tend to be enthusiastic, outgoing, and interested in getting things started.
- They are people-oriented and are comfortable in both one-on-one situations and big gatherings.
- They can be very outgoing and personable.
- Social recognition and influence are key drivers.
- Their optimism can be evident since they are often very expressive.

Strengths:

- These characteristics make an Influencing personality a success:
- They are charismatic and inspiring.
- When projects involve others, they are enthusiastic and participative.
- They are idea people and get others interested in their innovations.
- They can be entertainers with a natural warmth and likeability.
- They are spontaneous with others.
- They can easily do their multitasking.
- They can adeptly manage several people at the same time by juggling priorities as needed.
- Once comfortable with the people involved, they can bring them together to achieve a goal.

Weaknesses:

- Possibly less successful traits include the following:
- They can sometimes come across as self-promoting or superficial.
- Because of their need to persuade, they can be seen as somewhat manipulative.
- They can get excited, which leads to observable impatience or potentially inappropriate behavior for the circumstances.

- At times they are perceived as overly optimistic and overly confident.
- They generally have a lower concern for facts.
- They also tend to have an opinion on most of the topics.

High Wants:

An Influencing style wants involvement. They enjoy the contact of people and their interaction. They often like "friendly" debate. They do not like to argue, but would rather express and hear opinions on a variety of subjects. They also want to be recognized. They want feedback about their accomplishments or progress toward a goal. Certificates, awards, trophies, and pins are a few ways that the Influencing style might display their successes. Also, they often want to be surrounded by optimistic people.

High I Needs:

The Influencing style often needs to become better at time management. They need to control their impulsiveness and focus on the task at hand. More time needs to be spent on checking, verifying, and general diligence. At the same time, they often need to develop a sense of urgency. The Influencing style needs to be more objective in managing different situations. They must learn not to take things personally. They can have a tendency to say things without regard for the impact their words have on others. Similarly, they need to realize that others' criticism of them is not necessarily a personal attack, but could be something constructive.

Communication Style: The Influencing style models enthusiasm and openness with people at all levels.

- Verbal Communication. They often make their points through stories and anecdotes. They enjoy sharing experiences. Some Influencing styles like to match and then "one-up" another's triumph. They might ask, "How was your vacation?" so they can proceed to tell you about theirs.
- Tonality (Tone of Voice). The Influencing style speech pattern is fast. They use a wide variance of inflection and pitch. At times, tonality is dramatic and volume is higher than normal. Their vocal style reflects their desire for active participation by others.
- Body Language. They are usually open and easy to read. Their facial expressions are animated. Hand and body movement is

lively and, at times, exaggerated. Impromptu actions are also common.

Writing Style: Their writing style is theatrical. Many adjectives, adverbs, and prepositional phrases are often used. Similar to the Directing style, the details are often left for later discussion.

SUPPORTIVE OR HIGH S OVERVIEW

- Those oriented towards the understanding and accepting others are considered Supportives. This is what they're like:
- Their major role is to be supportive and cooperative.
- They are team players.
- They can often be easygoing, relaxed, and amiable.
- They utilize systematic approaches to manage goals.
- They keep things in check by controlling the system.
- Team recognition and appreciation for a job well done are key drivers for them.
- They don't need public recognition for their efforts
- "Stay the course" would be an appropriate motto for them.
- There is security in tradition.

Strengths:

Supportives exhibit following strong points:

- They are predictable and dependable.
- Often they are even-tempered.
- They are easily able to get assistance from others because of their balance.
- They can be very loyal and tend to build long-term relationships.
- They are excellent listeners and are good at concealing their own emotions while conversing with others.
- They can often be very patient.
- They are dedicated to task completion.
- They systematically finish one task before moving to the next.

Weaknesses:

- The following may hamper the Supportive's success:
- They tend to procrastinate.

- They are slow in the process of decision making, especially if they fear that those decisions will be unpopular.
- When under stress or duress, they may withdraw and try and "let the dust settle."
- Although plodding toward project completion is considered to be a strength, they have difficulty establishing goals.
- They are slow starters, especially when the project is a directional change or lacks a systematic approach.

High S Wants:

The Supportive style wants acceptance. They enjoy belonging and group interaction. Group interaction, however, must stay on track. They want to follow the system, complete the project, and then discuss it. High S people want friendly relationships. They prefer avoiding conflict. If they disagree with an idea or decision, they will not openly debate or criticize. They will instead slow things down and gain control of the environment. The Supportive style wants to stabilize the environment. They also want to specialize. They tend to stay focused on a project from start to finish. They also like to work on repetitive projects at their own pace.

High S Needs:

The Supportive style needs to learn to say no. They often want to help and sometimes take on more than they can handle. They can be oversensitive to the needs of others to the detriment of their own position. Some High S people need to express themselves more openly. They not only control their possessions and their knowledge, they also control their emotions. It is often best for them to not hold on to or internalize comments made by others but rather to express their feelings, getting things off their chest.

Communication Style: The Supportive style is generally calm and self-controlled.

- Verbal Communication. Verbal communication is limited for the High S. They tend to ask more than they tell. They listen much better than they express their opinions. Because they want to keep the environment friendly, they thoughtfully choose and pace their words.
- Tonality (Tone of Voice). They typically demonstrate consistent or monotone delivery of a message. The volume itself is low, and the pace is slow.

- Body Language. The Supportive style exhibits their calmness through nonexpressive body language. Eye contact will vary. Their eye contact may be direct when listening, which demonstrates empathy or sympathy for what is being said. When talking, however, their eye contact could tend to wander.

Writing Style: Their writing style is friendly. Complimenting other team members for their work and support would be readily intertwined in the message.

CONTEMPLATIVE OR HIGH C OVERVIEW

Those oriented toward understanding and accepting their task environment are considered Contemplatives. Here are some of their characteristics:

- They tend to be more analytical, reserved, and focused on getting things done right.
- They attempt to avoid antagonism.
- They are accurate, precise, and attempt to remove risk from a decision.
- They are conservative and disciplined in their approach to any task.
- They do not typically need public recognition for their efforts.
- They do seek reassurance that the job is being done correctly.
- "Do it right the first time" would be a good motto for them.

Strengths: Contemplatives exhibit certain strong points:

- They are agreeably compliant.
- They are not argumentative.
- When their decision is made, however, they can be strong advocates for a position.
- Their strength comes from research, analysis, and detailed knowledge of their subject.
- Being logical, they look to eliminate emotion in a debate.
- They also tend to be good listeners and can therefore adapt their own behavior to the circumstances as they analyze conversations with others.
- They are patient during the time of dealing with facts and tasks.

- They are dedicated to task completion.
- They finish one task accurately and within the appropriate parameters before moving to the next.

Weaknesses: These traits may balance the Contemplative's strengths:

- They can become irritated with inefficiency and errors.
- Although normally diplomatic, they can be critical without enough regard to personal feelings.
- Because of their desire for accuracy, they can be seen as nitpickers.
- Their focus is on avoiding unnecessary risk, which leads others to believe that they are more interested in the method of reaching the goal than in the goal itself.
- While nonconfrontational, they can be rather critical.
- If they have a strong opinion, they are reluctant to back down, even when that might be in the best interest of the team.

High C Wants: They want assurances. They want to know that a project is being done properly and in the most efficient manner. They want others to recognize their precision. Public recognition is not as important as a long-standing reputation for thoroughness. They often opt to do something themselves, finding it the best way to get a task done right. Before jumping into a project, however, the Contemplative style wants the time to think through the process for goal achievement. They want facts, not opinions. They want specific methods, not vague ones. They want to proceed cautiously being able to check and cross-check before moving to the next phase of the project.

High C Needs: The Contemplative style needs to learn how to show sincere appreciation for others' efforts. No one can attain the high standards for accuracy that they set for themselves. They need to understand and recognize that others may be trying their best. The High C needs to be more willing to accept change. At times change includes temporary disorganization. They need to initiate solutions instead of questioning procedure. They must learn that guidelines are not laws. Compromise and win-win negotiations need to become a more significant part of their behavior.

Communication Style: The Contemplative style is very tactful, diplomatic, and thorough.

- Verbal Communication. Verbal communication is more limited to logic and facts. They express their opinions with limited emotions. Because they want to avoid antagonism, they thoughtfully plan their words, taking a formal and proper approach to communication. Their questions can sometimes seem like more of an interrogation instead of conversation because of their drive for detail.

- Tonality (Tone of Voice). The Contemplative style uses a more monotone delivery with less inflection. The volume itself is low, and the pace is slow. There is determination in their tone.
- Body Language. They disguise their emotions and limit exposure of their thoughts. Therefore, they use less facial expressions or impulsive gestures. Eye contact will vary. Their eye contact may be direct when focus is needed to analyze a situation. When interest wanes, however, their eye contact may wander, demonstrating their desire to move on.

Writing Style: Their writing style is detailed. The Contemplative style wants to make sure the message, logic behind the message, and backup detail are included.

ROLES AND SITUATIONS AFFECTING THE STYLE

As we mentioned earlier, you play different roles, and your style may vary depending on that. Furthermore, in a given role, the situation might change from anywhere from very amicable to very threatening. While we all know that we change in these situations, it is important to understand how we change and to work on ways to improve any negative signals or reactions that could be detrimental to us. For example, under pressure a Directing style might rush to judgment or become overly demanding, whereas a Contemplative style might become more defensive and, instead of making a decision, become trapped in overanalysis.

WORKING WITH PEOPLE WITH DIFFERENT STYLES

There are two key strategies that you can use when interacting with others-adapting and complementing.

- Adapting (or flexing) to other people's styles means that you are mirroring or imitating their styles. Adapting strategies are more appropriate when people are performing effectively or when you are trying to motivate or influence them. As discussed, your style or combination of styles as well as the style(s) around you each have their own more typical strengths and weaknesses. Therefore, not only is it important to recognize the types of situations and people that possess styles best suited to yours, but you must learn to flex your style in order to work with the myriad of other styles and combinations with which you will constantly come into contact.

- Complementing other people's styles means that you are exhibiting contrasting behaviors or trying to balance or enhance their style with your own behavior. Complementing strategies should be implemented when the styles of other people are either inadequate or need additional efforts to achieve the desired results. Many people already possess either similar or different styles that work together well. If that is the case, they are already in solid communication with those other styles, but if that is not the case, then being self-aware will allow you to consciously try to enhance the relationship.

Everyone Possesses Some of All Four: As previously mentioned, everyone has characteristics in all four quadrants. It is how a person is inclined to prioritize the DISC factors that will determine her personal style pattern. Furthermore, it is when all factors are considered together that a substantial pattern of characteristics is formed, giving you a more pure style. Since a pure style is not realistic, the resulting combination of styles will be many. Upon completing a DISC analysis and practicing you will become more adept at working in (adapting and complementing) all the combinations of styles.

For example, the combination of a High D and High I would typically be a very matter-of-fact person with the ability to engage others. He is astute in his ability to pick out what motivates others quickly. He might then use that insight to inspire others to move in the direction that he has decided is correct. As another example, the combination of a High S and High C is someone who is patiently analytical. She takes the time to investigate situations to determine the best direction. She forms cooperative teams that can attack the technical problems and is tenacious in moving toward task completion. Conversely, each of these two dual combination patterns has distinct potential weaknesses that, if not properly understood and compensated for, could hinder communication under certain conditions and with certain other styles and combination styles.

INTENSITY OF STYLES

Since some people possess a high degree of one, two, or even all four styles, and others possess a low degree of anywhere from one to all four, it is the intensity in a style or styles that would likely strengthen a strength and/or accentuate any weakness when particular conditions exist. In fact, it is usually easiest to identify someone that is very high in only one category and thus understand and hopefully modify behaviors as needed to enhance your working relationships.

STRATEGIES FOR IMPROVING COMMUNICATIONS

You should try to think of specific members of your sales team, your manager(s), colleagues in other departments, and your customers, with an emphasis on those with whom you would really like to better your interpersonal effectiveness. You can then separate each of them into various categories and look at the most likely DISC pattern(s) for each individual. For example:

- When resurrecting a tense yet important working relationship with another manager:
  - — If he were a High S, you could ask him about his staff and how things are going with his team.
- When selling to a customer who you previously clashed with but who still has enormous potential:
  - — If she were a High D, you would get right to the point, emphasizing direct results and outcomes if she were to implement your products and services.
- Deciding how to encourage a new salesperson who lacks confidence in closing the big deal:
  - — If she were a High I you might publicly praise her first closed deal in order to help build up her ego.
- Convincing your manager that it is time to move on from trying to land Account X because it is affecting your other major accounts:
  - — If he were a High C, you could use detailed analysis and reports to summarize your case as well, having specific answers to counter further challenges.
  - — By now you are probably thinking that some of these strategies are taking you out of your own comfort zone. The reality is that in order to communicate effectively with others, you will need to stretch yourself.

CHANGING PROFILES

Another consideration in developing your knowledge and understanding of personal style is the fact that profiles change. Because these are surface characteristics, a style can change over time. Again, these changes are neither negative nor positive-all the more reason why you should repeat the test if you have not taken it in some time. It can only benefit you to look at where you plot today. While the difference is unlikely to be dramatic, depending on the amount of time that has lapsed and the circumstances in your life, some minor changes are likely.

DIFFERENCES AMONG THE PEOPLE

There are many differences among people, some subtle and others very blatant. Attempting to use DISC Theory alone to analyze people would be saying that they can be grouped in a purely scientific sense around these styles, when in fact there are too many other factors to understand in order for that to be possible. Although in-numerable areas could be considered, a few more directly help determine and shape someone's behavior. These include a combination of influences from early childhood through today, including:

- Career path
- Culture and traditions
- Education
- Financial stability
- Health
- Intelligence
- Parents and other family members
- Spouse or significant other
- Values

How all of the people, events, and environments relate to your personal style is a more complicated subject, but it's helpful to know that although each of our personalities seem so very complicated and different, tools such as DISC profiles can be utilized to simplify and enhance our work relationships, job performance, and personal satisfaction. As a sales manager, you will come into contact with all types of communicators exhibiting a wide range of behaviors.

Now, more than ever, you will need to communicate with many individuals and groups within your organization, as well as with business professionals and customers outside of your organization. You are also now charged with being a coach, mentor, mediator, motivator, and team leader. In order to excel at all of these and other management responsibilities, you will need to apply your skills in various environments and settings, and an understanding of yourself as well as the communication of others is a solid beginning.

Also, as you know, the three major settings where you will find yourself communicating will be in person, by phone, and in written communication (e-mail, letters, etc.). Whatever your preferred style and communication vehicle, you will need to understand your audience (individual and/or group) and communicate accordingly. Keep in mind that all three ways of communicating will be necessary, at least to some extent. When feasible, the means of communication should be determined by you with the following in mind:

- Your preferred style
- The style of the recipient of the information
- The specific circumstances

How you communicate best is the starting point. For example, you might have been an English language major and feel you can write a very elaborate sales proposal (possibly a High C). However, the recipient of the information might find your style too verbose, and would prefer just a short, succinct proposal highlighting the key points (possibly a High D). To further complicate this, what if your audience was several people?

This is where you would look to try to have something for everyone: a synopsis covering all the highlights at the beginning and/or the end, and a great deal of supporting documentation in the body of the proposal addressing all of the possible questions and scenarios.

The same thinking would hold for face-to-face and phone communications. It is obviously important to know yourself and your preferred style, but it is as important to know your audience. Now that you have a solid grounding in communication styles and the theory behind it, there are two more complex settings in which both individual and group dynamics pose a challenge for many new as well as seasoned managers.

RUNNING AN EFFECTIVE MEETING

Gone are the days of "just because" or Monday morning mandatory meeting. People are too busy, and not only can it be a poor use of your time as well as your staff, but it can also be demotivating to your team.

If you do choose to have Monday morning meetings, or a weekly scheduled meeting at other times, make sure it is for good reason. Historically, weekly meetings were a time for updates. A manager would provide information on what they got from meeting with his manager, and the employees would share progress reports on their side. However, if a series of e-mails or one-off conversations can cover the information too; then the meeting is pointless-not to mention the fact that organizing a meeting is very difficult, with many salespeople either working remotely or on the road making a sales call.

It is prudent to hold a meeting when the following criteria exist:

- People seem confused as to their roles and responsibilities.
- A major change is occurring that will affect your team members- in a positive or negative way.
- Rumors are circulating that need to be addressed.
- Input is needed from the group on important business decisions.
- You need to discuss major policy changes or sensitive subjects that affect the entire group (absenteeism, business ethics, new hours of operation, etc.).

Once you have determined that a meeting is necessary, it is then incumbent upon you to make it productive. Follow these tried-and-true rules when planning meetings in order to make them a good use of everyone's time:

- Keep it on time (beginning and end time). There is nothing worse than stating a time and people feel they can show up later or that the meeting will run past the scheduled time.
- When possible, rotate the meeting facilitator-people like to get involved, and since a meeting is really for the benefit of everyone at the table, let others run the meeting or at least certain parts of the meeting.
- Have an agenda in advance-no one likes to go to a meeting and always wonder, what's next? Every meeting should be defined. Even if it is just for brainstorming ideas in a roundable setting, you should specify that in advance.
- Make the environment as comfortable as possible. While you might not have abundant space for meetings, be sure that everyone is accounted for with proper seating, lighting, and a comfortable room temperature.
- Include remote team members. Today there are a myriad of ways to get remote staff involved, including phone conference calls as well as Web and video conferencing. Depending on

the objectives of the meeting and the regularity, it might be well worth your time to have a process in place for remote staff to access meetings on an ongoing basis.

- Invite the key stakeholders-make sure you include those who do or will play a part in subject matter being addressed in the meeting. It can be very unproductive to discuss plans that would need the time and resources of another department and not include them in the meeting. At the same time, limit the meeting to only those necessary so as not to misuse the time of nonessential participants.
- Always provide next steps. Whether it is an idea generation meeting or a more formal planning session, summarize the meeting at the end as well as provide next steps both there and in writing afterwards. This could then set the stage for any possible follow-up meetings.

When leading a meeting, you should do the following:

- Keep an outline of the meeting, marking topics off as they are discussed or addressed.
- Use flipcharts, PowerPoint, white boards, and other resources as necessary-using various forms of communication keeps people engaged. Also, if there are numerous details that need to be either seen or captured, you might wish to appoint a scribe or someone to flipchart the key discussion points, and have someone type them up afterwards.
- Avoid wordsmithing and being too detailed. There is no point in getting caught up in semantics and minutiae when everyone is pressed for time. Stick to the key points and topics of the meeting, and parking-lot other subjects that can be addressed at a later date.
- Be inclusive. Some people tend to participate more than others. The atmosphere should be cooperative, where everyone has her share of input. In fact, the quiet ones could have some of the best ideas.
- Confirm the conclusions. Make sure everyone really is on board with any conclusions or next steps that are determined. While you might be charged with running the meeting, you are really acting more as a facilitator, keeping everything on track and conversations productive. In certain circumstances you might

need to play arbiter or the deciding vote, but when at all possible let the team decide.

- Practice your listening skills and then paraphrase or repeat what is said so that the points others make are clear to the group. You can then weed out non-related information and help to keep discussions on target.

PRESENTATION SKILLS

It is common knowledge that making a presentation is one of Americans' (and likely that of many others around the globe as well) biggest fears. It has it roots in the fact that, growing up, we are not necessarily taught to present to a large audience. Sure, there are exceptions, especially those who grew up involved in the performing arts, but for the most part it is an uncultivated skill. At the same time, as your career progresses, you will find the ability to give a solid presentation more and more critical. Whether it is leading a meeting or presenting to a large audience, by having sound presentation skills you can stand out from the pack. In fact, many have found that it has opened new doors for them, as a good presenter commands respect and recognition from others. Clearly, certain areas and tips will help you to become a more confident presenter. Some of the basics include:

- Maintain good eye contact. Pick some friendly faces in the audience until you get more versed at this.
- Keep a nice even pace. Remember, human nature is to speed up when nervous. When presenting, err on the side of a little too slow, and you will find that it is just right for the audience.
- Avoid distracting the audience. Hand gestures or fidgeting with papers tends to focus the audience's eyes on these areas and away from the message you are trying to convey.
- Use different tones, inflections, and pauses to accentuate key points. Nothing will tune out an audience faster than a monotone presenter. Remember, no matter what the topic of your presentation, no one wants to be bored.
- Dress appropriately. This usually means being a bit more formal than the audience. The only exception is when you are trying to really fit in with the group and want to therefore dress just like them.
- Know your topic, objective, and audience. Before making any presentation, make sure you are up to speed with what it is

you are trying to convey; only then can you develop a presentation to match this. You also need to tie it into the knowledge level of your audience, and then speak to their interests.

- Don't worry about seeming a little nervous. Those who are too comfortable presenting often come across as arrogant.
- Prepare. Probably the best piece of advice for a novice presenter is to practice. Until you get more versed at presenting, this could initially mean starting off with an outline, then fully writing out a first draft and then turning that back into an outline. Keep in mind that you're probably not delivering a speech, so avoid trying to read something word for word. You can also practice with a colleague or by yourself in front of the mirror. By actually hearing yourself, you can get more and more comfortable with everything.
- Don't apologize. If you show signs of being nervous, you don't have to tell everyone. The audience understands and really wants you to succeed. They will understand if you lose track somewhere or accidentally skip a point.
- Less is more. Don't try and convey every thought. This is a common mistake of inexperienced presenters, trying to tell the audience everything. Remember, they don't know what you have left out. Stick to the pertinent facts and not all of the minor details.
- Engage with audiovisuals. Audiovisuals are meant to stimulate the audience, not to overwhelm or confuse them. Try to mix things up to keep them involved, but always keeping in mind your message and objective. You can also use the visuals in place of your notes; they can be your guide in and of themselves.
- Stay on time-here again is where preparation is key. Only by practicing will you know how long your presentation should take. In fact, the pressure of running out of time can compound itself, further increasing your nerves. Plan to end a little early rather than going the full time allotted.

Most important, develop your own style. Remember, there is not one perfect way to present. Learn from others, but in the end your personality plays a good part in what your style is, and this should come across in your presentation.

Keep in mind that often Q&A is an integral part of a presentation. In fact, it can make a good presentation great or turn a solid performance sour. Some tips for handling the Q&A period are:

- Solicit questions from the audience. Far too often, the inexperienced presenter forgets to even ask.
- Think of all the possibilities of questions that might come from the audience and prepare for them.
- Paraphrase or restate the question to be sure that you, as well as the rest of the audience, has heard it properly.
- After you have responded, always verify with the person that you have answered the question at hand.
- If you do not know the answer, say you are not sure and that you will get back to them, and be sure to do so.
- Finally, not only should you expect questions, but you should look forward to fielding them. It means your audience is engaged, and it allows you to clarify points made.

Remember, almost everyone fears making presentations, so you are far from alone. That said, if you practice, practice, and then practice some more, you will be one step ahead of your peers. The only way that people really are able to judge and work productively with one another is by the way they communicate.

By recognizing your likely areas of weakness, you at the minimum have the ability to compensate for them, and hopefully turn them into a strength. If you are able to grasp the fundamentals of communication styles, realize that we are all very complex, and accept that there is no "silver bullet" that works under every circumstance, nor with the same person all the time, you will be that much further along to being a well-respected sales manager by your sales team, peers, managers, and customers.

As we progress through this book, it is important to be aware that your personal style and how you communicate becomes key in just about every aspect of your job. Also, realize that while awareness is a good beginning, practice is what will improve you as a person as well as help in the advancement of your career. As you delve into the next chapter on planning, you will continue to see how key that solid communication skills are to all of us.

Note: Rich Products Corporation (Rich's) is a US-based privately held manufacturer of frozen foods. The company manufactures and markets products, including toppings and icings, breads and rolls, finished desserts and cakes, pizza dough and sweet goods, beverages, Italian specialties, barbeque, seafood and appetizers. The company primarily operates in the US. It is headquartered in Buffalo, New York and employs 7,200 people. For detailed information related to this chapter reader can visit www.rich.com

10

Sales Planning

Planning is one of the first functions in the process of sales management. Before you undertake any other managerial function, having a good plan is imperative. The reality is often that certain aspects of a plan are carried over from the prior quarter, half, year, and so on. As is true with many of the areas of management, you do not often have the chance to start with a clean slate. However, just as you likely already possess some star salespeople, your current plan likely has certain very useful aspects. This chapter is meant to complement what is already in place and possibly challenge what your company is currently doing with the intent of improving the plan so that everyone will benefit.

ALIGNING THE CORPORATE STRATEGY WITH THE SALES TEAM

Plans exist at all levels within an organization. Typically senior management deals with long-range plans, that is, where the organization is heading, what changes may be necessary to generate more profits, what new products will be introduced, and other strategic issues that may occur over the next three to five years or longer. On a departmental level, planning is just as crucial. While you will incorporate some long-term strategies, the majority of the plan deals with the short and medium term (up to one year and between one and three years).

MEDIUM-TERM PLANNING

This part of the sales plan deals with the means by which longer-range objectives are to be met. The focus is on defining road-blocks to success and then planning solutions.

SHORT-TERM PLANNING

This is probably the most important focus for the sales manager. Short-term plans concern goals that need to be met over a period of ninety days to one year. These are most often very tactical in nature, having specific objectives that exist within the framework of higher-level plans. Whatever the time period associated with each part of the plan, nothing can operate in a vacuum. Corporate planning needs to take into account departmental plans, and each plan needs to consider the period of time.

THE SALES PLAN

The sales planning process deals with numerous constituents. However, the key ones to focus on are: Customers (industry and markets), Employees (the sales team), Your products/services (R&D, finance, engineering, manufacturing, operations, suppliers, etc.), Competition

Of course, you will need to ask many questions when preparing the sales plan that will fit into one of these four categories. Depending on your industry, the questions you will need to answer could be as follows:

- What is the length of a typical sales cycle (one week, one month, one year, etc.)?
- How do you segment your customers (industry, regions, etc.)?
- Do you have major, key, or strategic accounts, and does a separate structure exist to manage different types of accounts?
- Do you have global customers?
- At what level will your sale people be selling (multilevel, senior level, team selling, etc.)?
- Do you have many competitors or are you involved in hyper competition (a few major players controlling and competing in the market)?
- How do you match up to your competition in terms of products, reputation, etc.?
- How does the sales team tie into the new product/service development process?
- How is research conducted on products, markets, competition, etc.?

Depending on your business, you will need to answer these and many other questions, sometimes in great detail. However, before taking a look at some of these questions in more depth, you should understand your corporate structure and how sales fits into this structure, and also how sales touches the customer.

WHERE SALES FITS IN THE CORPORATE STRUCTURE

It is critical that your department's planning process ties in with the overall corporate plan. The corporate plan should also be one where you have some influence, meaning not only does the plan filter down to you from the top, but this bigger plan should also be developed taking into account your guidance in the sales plan and sales forecasting for the future. If not, the corporate expectations are out of touch with your part of the business. This could mean that your team is working toward something that does not match the goals and expectations of the overall business. As importantly, this can have a major effect on the resources and budget you are allocated to generate the desired results.

In order to be an integral player in the corporate-wide planning effort, you need to know the key areas that could affect your team both directly and indirectly. One way to look at the overall role that sales plays in your organization is by looking at your corporate structure.

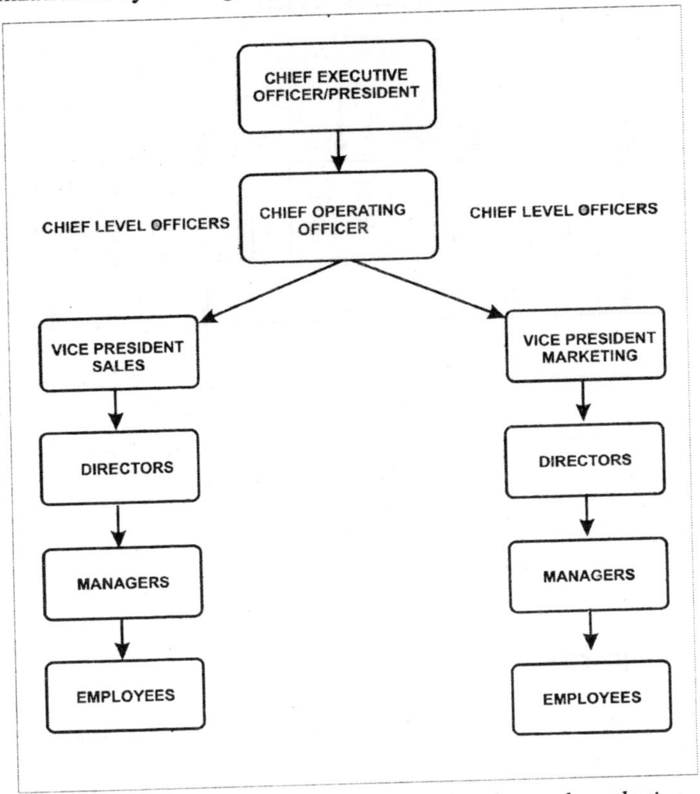

Figure: A corporate structure in which sales and marketing report separately tothe COO.

There has been a long-standing debate about the best fit and reporting structure for sales. Some believe that it is a part of the marketing function, while others say it belongs as a stand-alone unit.

The answer is that it really does not matter. What is key is that they collaborate well with one another. Below are a couple of sample corporate reporting structures, one with sales reporting directly to a very senior officer and the other with a senior executive heading up both sales and marketing (Figure 3-2).

Of course, sales not only needs to tie closely in to marketing but also needs to work in tandem with the entire organization. This includes R&D, finance, human resources, manufacturing, customer service, and so on. Most important, whatever corporate structure you are in, the goal is to serve the customer.

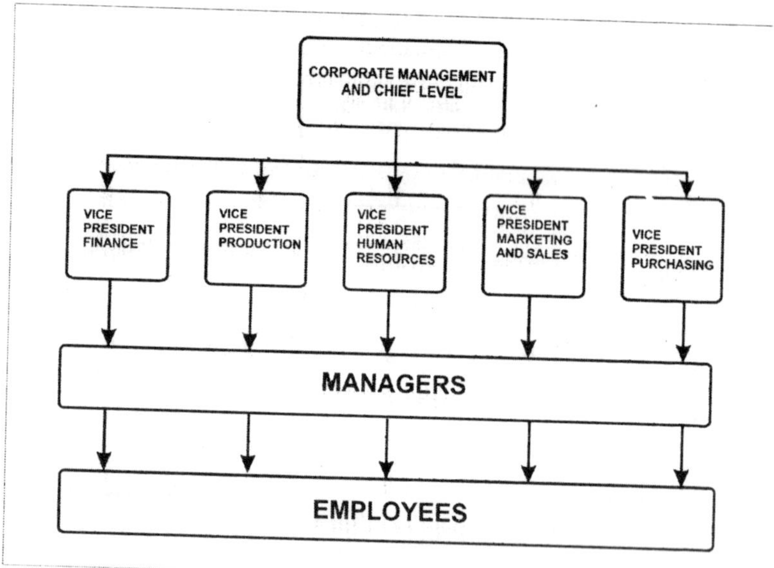

Figure: A corporate structure in which a senior executive heads up both sales and marketing.

THE CUSTOMER-CENTRIC ORGANIZATION

There are two critical questions that everyone involved in the organization should be able to answer:

- What does your company define as a successful customer?
- What is the desired customer experience?

There has been a great deal of talk over the past couple of decades on how to develop a structure whereby the entire organization is focused on the customer and the customer experience.

This is in contrast to the old days, when marketing, sales, and customer service's main focus was in creating demand, selling to, and then satisfying the customers, and others had very little involvement in the process; the back office, with human resources and accounting, was merely there to help ensure that the daily activities and processes were functioning, and they did not readily see any direct or indirect link to the customer. This type of straighforward department layout would look something like the one in figure below.

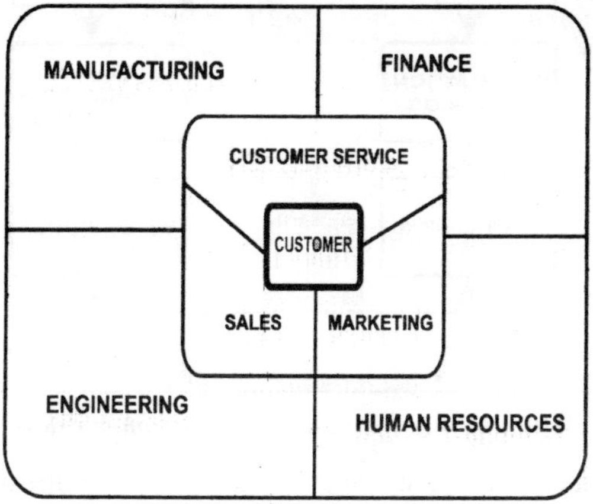

Figure: A common approach to the customers.

While this still has validity and does depict the customer as the central focus of the organization, today a truly customer-focused organization is that much more complex and intertwined with the customer, and all parts of the organization are thinking in terms of customer value.

This would mean that there are many areas of the organization that do not necessarily have regular direct contact with the customer but are still developing strategies and processes that enhance the customer experience. For example, instead of accounts receivable concentrating on just billing and collections, they might be looking to integrate their information technology systems with that of their counterparts at the customer organization (accounts payable).

Therefore, a more complete view of an integrated supplier and customer relationship would look something like Figure below.

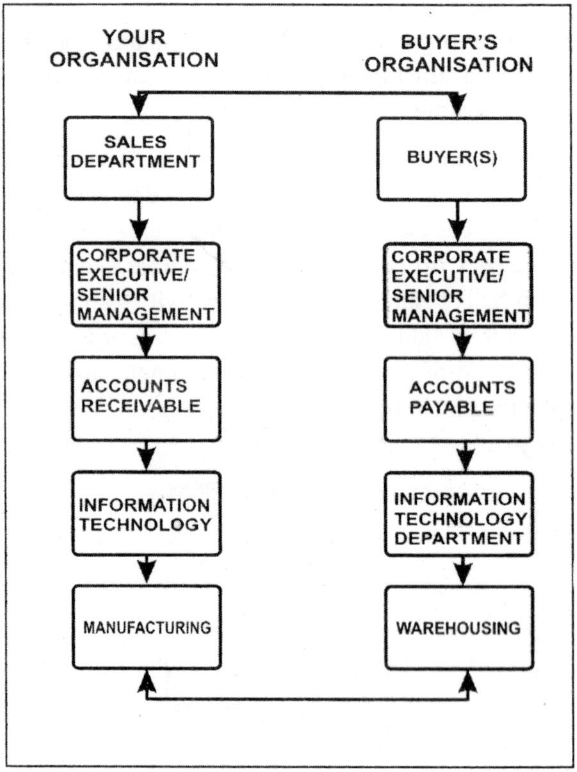

Figure: An integrated supplier and customer relationship.

Furthermore, since your team is not likely selling directly to the final end-user (business to consumer sales), you could have any number of layers involved in the supply chain that ultimately delivers the final product/ service to the consumer. This more stepped approach common to business-to-business sales opens the door to an array of areas in which to integrate your processes.

Some major companies, for example, have their processes so refined that everyone involved in the supply chain meets certain standards of quality, communications, technology, and so on. Some of the key benefits to these companies are everything from cost savings to higher profit margins, improved quality, and increased customer satisfaction. When you think of it in terms of your sales team, there are many ways that a customer-centric organization will have a direct benefit:

- Better Efficiencies. Members of both the selling and buying organizations are working in conjunction with one another, communicating and collaborating in the most efficient ways possible.

- Barriers to Entry. The better your company's processes are working with your customers, the more difficult it is for one of your competitors to come and take away that business.
- Competing on Overall Value (not just price). You are able to compete on many more levels than just price, which then becomes just one factor in the sale as opposed to the main driver.
- Benefits to End-Users. Whoever the final end users are of your product/service, they will benefit from better value, quality, and service from you and those in your supply chain. They will therefore remain more loyal and become long-term customers.
- Benefits to You and Your Staff. All of this will culminate in more sales and profits for your team.

With this understanding of a customer-focused organization and departmental synergies, it is now time to see more definitely how other departments work, and their importance in the sales planning process. Furthermore, you will realize the extent to which they affect your team and its ability to sell.

MARKETING'S RELATIONSHIP TO SALES

Marketing is one such department to understand more in depth. As you saw in the corporate structure, marketing has, or should have, a great deal of interaction with sales. In fact, in order to get a clearer picture of the customer and how to best approach him, you will find that some understanding of marketing is essential. Marketing probably has a greater impact on how your sales team performs and the ability to maximize your team's efforts than any other single department.

Today marketing is much more than just one-way messaging through advertising and direct marketing. In some companies the line between sales and marketing is quite blurred. For example, business development is at times a sales function and other times falls into marketing. Again, it is important to understand each other's roles because the information that you can provide one another is critical toward building each of your department's business plans. Here are some common similarities as well as differences between sales and marketing (as adapted from AMA's

Advanced Course in Strategic Marketing) along with some useful integration strategies that can enhance both departments.

The Role of Sales

- Front line with customers.
- Generate orders.
- Short- and medium-range (primary focus).
- Identify and set up key accounts and other account management strategies.
- Build one-to-one business relationships.

The Role of Marketing

- Creates leads for the sales team.
- Develops messaging and brand image.
- Short-, medium-, and long-range.
- Informational and educational.

Of course, this will vary, depending on the organization and types of products/services. For example, a company that sells credit cards will be largely marketing-focused and would probably rely not on field sales representatives, but rather on inside sales and customer service representatives. The marketing department is therefore set up primarily to generate leads for transactional sales. On the other hand, a niche high-end supplier of business software might be very sales-focused. The message might not be as impactful through marketing tools such as direct mail, TV and print ads, the radio, and so on, so the focus and higher departmental budgets would be with the direct sales channels.

Another way to look at this is how some companies are considered either "sales organizations" or "marketing organizations." This is typically due to how large the budget is for sales versus the size of the budget for marketing. Some examples that commonly fall under each category are:

Sales Organizations

- Pharmaceuticals
- Consulting
- Auto
- Financial services

Marketing Organizations

- Consumer products

- Travel and leisure
- Retailers
- Entertainment

No matter the structure and emphasis, the key again is that sales and marketing must work collaboratively with one another. The information and capabilities that each possess are so important to the other that it's foolish for the two departments to act independently. In companies where the integration is weak, salespeople often find that marketing is sending out messages that do not tie in to what they have to sell, or the key benefits are not highlighted properly. At the same time, while sales believes problems or issues exist within marketing, the marketing department likely has its own set of challenges and difficulties when working with sales. For example, it is not uncommon for marketing to feel that many of the leads they acquire through their various campaigns are not properly followed up on.

Therefore, it is incumbent on you now as a manager to try to move everyone toward a more collaborative work environment. Again, most of this can be done by accomplishing one major task- sharing of information. This could mean having your sales force report what customers are saying back to marketing as well as providing competitive information regarding what the sales force is seeing or coming up against in the field. Sales could also provide some of those customer "pain points," or what the customer is really looking for in a product/ service or overall buyer/ vendor relationship that is not currently being addressed. Marketing could then more accurately focus its messaging and highlight certain key benefits more clearly.

At the same time, marketing can try to engage the sales force more and reach out to them for ideas for marketing campaigns, bringing them into the creative process early on in its development. Additionally, marketing can be sure to work with sales on all special promotions and keep them apprised of all of the details on any new offerings. Without this information a salesperson can be at a great disadvantage with a new or potential customer.

Furthermore, whether or not your department is structurally intertwined with marketing, you as a sales manager can adapt some core tools from marketing for the planning process. One tool that you are likely familiar with in some form is a SWOT analysis. SWOT stands for Strengths, Weaknesses, Opportunities, and Threats. A SWOT analysis is a basic tool for planning that a sales manager can utilize in many ways:

By filling in what falls into each of the four areas, you can gauge in broad terms where you stand in whatever category you choose to analyze. You can conduct this type of analysis on many areas that relate to both your company and sales team.

Things to consider for a SWOT analysis include:

- Current products and services
- Potential new products and services
- Brand image
- Pricing strategy
- Competition
- Experience of sales team members
- Reputation in the industry
- Market share
- Training needs
- Service/maintenance capabilities

It is also helpful when plotting the above to think of internal factors such as new products and services as either a strength or weakness, whereas external factors such as competition and regulation fit into the categories of either opportunities or threats. Furthermore, the phrase environmental scan is a concept similar to the external factors piece of a SWOT analysis (i.e., you scan the external environment and see what is affecting your business). This type of analysis can be as general or detailed as necessary. For example, you can look at the competition even more precisely through an analysis from the perspective of each of your competitors; or you can analyze the strengths and weaknesses of each individual team member at a very granular level.

Another tool you could adapt from marketing would relate to ways to more precisely look at your products and markets. For example, you would look at each of your product lines, and determine its relative strength in the industry. Then you can compare that to the markets you are currently in along with what markets it might pay to try to break into.

Product/Market Analysis			
Product Line	***A***	***B***	***C***
Penetration (Existing Markets):	8	4	6
Potential (Existing Markets):	5	6	2
Potential (New Markets):	2	3	9
Total:	**15**	**13**	**17**

In the above example, on a scale of 1 to 10 (1 being weak and 10 being strong), Product A has a high level of penetration in its existing markets, a medium level of upside potential in existing markets, and very little potential to spread out this product line into new markets. Of course, you can get into more and more detail with something like this; for example, looking separately at each product within a product line. Another tool adapted from marketing would be something to help you to analyze your competitive landscape. Here you could look at all of your products and services and then score them versus your competition, in order to see how you stack up.

Competitive Product/Service Analysis:

Product/Service	***Your Company***	***Competitor X***	***Competitor Y***
A	8	2	3
B	6	3	2
C	0*	8	3
D	1	7	8
E	5	3	6
F	10	8	0
Total:	**30**	**31**	**22**

*A zero would mean that you do not currently carry or compete with this product/service.

You can then analyze where you rank with each product against each competitor. For example, you are strong in Product A and weak in Product D. Here again you can get more detailed and might even wish to weight each product based on one or more factors

(e.g., revenues, profits, core competency, etc.). Another result that could come out of these kinds of analyses is that you might find that there are certain markets not worth competing in or products that you do not wish to carry. This might be the case in product lines where you have almost no presence (Products C and D), and it would be too costly or out of your core compentency to truly compete. A better strategy might be to partner with certain competitors in order to stengthen both of your positions against other competition.

Another function that typically falls into marketing is market research. You likely have some familiarity with market research through surveys or questionnaires (at least from having taken them over the years). However, market research is much broader and is a responsibility of every sales manager, whether you conduct the research directly or others provide you with this service.

Besides surveys, other typical market research techniques are focus groups and observational research. Focus groups are a group of participants that share a common element that will enable the selling organization to gauge their interest in the company itself, an existing product, a new product idea, and so on. Observational research is just like it sounds-researchers observe a customer using a product or service and see how they react with it (e.g., how they open the product, how they use/interact with the product, etc.). These three techniques (surveys, focus groups, and observational research) are what many think of as the main tools to conduct research. But these techniques are only one form, called Primary Research. These three types of primary research involve collecting new information from the customer in some way. Secondary research is the other major form of market research. This type of research includes all of the information you already possess but that has not yet been formulated. Once it is, however, a great deal of analysis can be done. Some areas that fit into the category of secondary research are:

- Sales growth (or decline)
- Customer geographic distribution
- Percentage of sales of newly launched products versus core products
- Industry growth
- Product or service growth

This is information that you either can readily get or can utilize others to help put together. You can then interpret it and incorporate the findings as needed in your planning process. The range of resources for secondary research is anything from your own records to departmental and company (internal) records, as well as through external resources (e.g., D&B, industry trade associations, Department of Commerce, etc.). Of course the key is to get the information in such a way that it can be analyzed. Another useful research component is other researchers' reports or survey findings that you are able to purchase or get for free.

The next two areas to understand, which are very intertwined with marketing (as well as other departments), are new product/ service development and pricing strategies.

Depending on the organization, new product/service development could be closely tied to sales, marketing, R&D, engineering, manufacturing, or any combination of these. The idea is to bring about new products/services or new features that will generate increased sales and profits. Since you are a sales manager, your input as well as that of your team is invaluable. After all, who has their ear closer to the customer than the sales force? It is imperative that you have some processes in place to funnel this information. Whether it be a structured, rigorous one or more ad hoc, it needs to get done. This helps to avoid finger pointing later on as to why a product was developed in a certain way.

A typical new product development process encompasses everything from generating ideas for new products to the launching and postlaunch refining or changes. To put into perspective the process and how it further relates to your sales department, your team's input will be not only important in the idea stage but also in the testing of the products. After all, before the launch the products will need to get tested, and who else are they tested on but your customers?

Pricing decisions are also tied in closely to new products and services, and can reside in any one or more department(s). Pricing strategies can therefore greatly vary from organization to organization and industry to industry. Of course, they should always keep in mind the end-user. As it relates to your sales department process, the pricing strategy will be very instrumental in helping you achieve your goals. Pricing often includes very senior-level officers who help to set the big-picture pricing strategy (price structure), and then individual pricing decisions can be made to fit within the structure. Furthermore, a great number of factors, both internal and external, will impact how your company makes pricing decisions. Here are some key areas that will play a role in pricing decisions (adapted from AMA's Advanced Course in Strategic Marketing).

External

- The economy.
- Demand for your types of products and services.
- Competitions-are you the only game in town or do you have many competitors with similar products and services?
- Are you in a commodity or premium products type of business/ industry?
- Government and other regulations.

Internal

- Pricing structure-what is your cost of goods sold, fixed costs, variable costs, etc.?

- Are you a public or private company (i.e., who are your shareholders, and what is your strategy for increasing their value)?
- What is your company's brand recognition and reputation?
- What are your channels of distribution (manufacturer, distributor or wholesaler, direct to consumer, etc.)?
- What is your mix of sales vehicles (field sales, inside sales, telemarketing, on-line sales, etc.)?
- What types of sales do you do (transactional, long-term, reorder/ replenish)?
- Do you deal with government contracts and bidding, requests for proposals (RFPs), global sales (letters of credit, foreign exchange risk, etc.)?

You will need to take into account many of the above questions when making pricing decisions. Here again the internal players and their input in the process will vary depending on many of the answers to these questions. For example, in the credit card example given previously, the pricing decisions might be primarily driven by the marketing department. However, in the niche high-end software example, pricing might be more determined by the sales department, with others such as marketing, finance, and R&D giving their necessary contributions.

Now that you have some of the foundational elements and tools to consider when initiating the planning process as well as an understanding of the key players and departments involved, it is time to take a look at the structure of a plan.

CREATING A PLAN

A reassuring thought when beginning the process is that for every hour spent planning, many hours of inefficient activity can be avoided. Furthermore, taking this time and initiative to develop and implement a well-thought-out plan will have a great deal of other benefits for you as a sales manager. It will allow you to:

Set priorities and allocate resources, ensuring that time and resources are spent on accomplishing goals that are agreed upon and shared by all necessary stakeholders.

Develop strong internal and external partnerships for sharing information and resources, and promoting new and improved business practices.

Have a predictable budgeting process, whereby expenses, revenues, and income are planned for in advance, and adjusted as necessary.

Create team stability allowing for continuous and progressive growth of your staff.

CHARACTERISTICS OF A GOOD PLAN

A good plan requires the following elements:

- Vision
- Mission
- Goals and objectives
- Strategies and tactics

This is a very common-type structure that is used in strategic planning. Your company is likely already involved at the higher levels in planning and therefore utilizes this type of planning framework or something similar. Other types of building blocks for strategic planning include issues-based planning, by which the planning process begins by looking at issues that the organization faces and then develops strategies to resolve these issues and ways to improve the organization. Whatever the specific planning model looks like, the key is that you work with all the necessary stakeholders to build from the corporate plan a sales plan, with the end result being improved corporate, departmental, and individual performance. Also, your company likely has a schedule for their strategic planning and some sort of process, be it formal or more ad hoc, in place. Typically it is a historical practice and one that is often determined by the industry you are in. For example, in some slower-growth, mature industries the corporate planning process can take place annually. However, with fast-moving high-growth industries, corporate planning can take place two times a year. Your sales department will need to tie into this large plan as well, but keep in mind that you might have many more specifics that relate to much shorter time periods, such as quarterly, monthly, and so on.

THE VISION STATEMENT

Long-range corporate plans require a target called a vision statement. In most cases, you will find that your company has a thoughtout vision and might even communicate this internally and possibly externally through any number of vehicles (intranet, Web site, newsletters, press releases, annual reports, etc.). A vision statement answers the question, "How is the company's mission [to be looked at in a moment] to be served in the future?" A vision statement should both inspire and guide. It must balance aspiration with realistic insights into future potential. In order to guide, the vision statement must capture what is unique about the company and what will continue to be unique about it in the future.

Some like to look at the vision as the "stretch" goal for the organization. For example, what is possible if all aspects of the corporate plan come together consistently and all goals are reached over a sustained period of time (e.g., at least three years)? If this happens would you be satisfied achieving the vision you have in place? If so, then your vision is likely on target. If not, you likely have not aspired enough in your vision. One very simple way to think of it is "No pain, no gain!"

The irony is that despite all its importance, the vision should be summed up in only a very short statement-usually one quick succinct sentence.

THE MISSION STATEMENT

The mission is the main purpose for conducting business activities. It is a compass that gives the direction to stay the course. Like the vision statement, it is likely already communicated to various stakeholders through any number of methods. It is a tool frequently used for corporate, departmental, and individual motivation. The mission statement, more so even than the vision statement, is written not only for employees, but also for customers and often stockholders. Since it is a core, rallying cry used to unite a company, it is often printed on business cards, posted about the offices, and used in marketing literature.

Also, while the mission statement should carry a great deal of weight, and receive buy-in across the organization, like the vision statement, it is also a short precise statement, typically one sentence in length. The company's mission statement can then be broken down by department. The mission statement for each department within the corporate structure needs to be personalized by the manager for that area of responsibility. By reframing the definition of a mission statement, the process becomes definable.

CORPORATE-LEVEL MISSION

A corporate mission statement should answer the following types of broader questions:

- Why does this entity exist?
- What is the company's impact on society (local, national, international)?

As a sales manager, you will not likely play a large role in developing a corporate mission. In fact, it is probably already in place and only changes if there is a major corporate directional shift. Most companies, for example, have the same mission for ten years are more. However, on a departmental and team level, you can have some or even a great deal of input.

DIVISION- OR DEPARTMENT-LEVEL MISSION

Of course the mission for a division or department needs to align with the larger corporate mission. This more specific mission is what others would ideally say about the people in the division and the manner in which business is conducted.

It would answer the following types of questions:

- Why does this department exist?
- What is the department's impact on the company?
- What is the department's impact on customers?
- Who (in general terms) are its customers?
- What (in general terms) are the products/services it provides?

It is also a good idea to include something about the employees, answering the question, how does the department take its employees into account? After all, it is the employees who need to buy into the mission.

You should find that everything in the plan needs to tie back into the corporate and departmental mission statements.

GOALS

The mission statement is the overall direction. Goals are the mandatory, shorter-term direction to move toward the mission. In its most basic sense, the goals are what needs to be accomplished. A plan should take into account three main types of goals. Some goals are corporate goals, which will be driven by the corporate mandate such as the dollar volume.

A departmental goal, on the other hand, might deal with targeting a new market or introducing a new product/service to specific accounts. The third type of goal is a personal business goal. Personal goals include activities that go beyond the corporate and departmental dictates. A personal business goal might have to do with learning a new computer program for making presentations. Some would even include a fourth type of goal, personal goals. When thinking of this in business terms, it might include working toward an advanced degree or a certification that might not tie in directly to your business responsibilities but is still something that you value, and at the same time, your company sees as something that helps you to build your character. Regardless of the types of goals you are establishing, the goals must always be SMART:

- Specific
- Measurable
- Attainable
- Relevant
- Timely

While this is a very common acronym, it is a very important one. In some descriptions, some of the letters represent different words, but the meaning is still similar. (Achievable is sometimes used instead of Attainable, or Realistic instead of Relevant.) Specific goals are definable. There are no gray areas or room for interpretation. All words used are concrete in nature; for example, a specific goal is a 25 percent increase in telesales calls this quarter over the same quarter last year. Relative terminology cannot be used in goal setting; "make more productive prospecting calls" is a goal that uses relative terms. What is more productive to you is not necessarily more productive to someone else.

Measurable goals have a beginning and an end. Therefore, at the end of a specific time, it will be obvious whether the goal has been reached. If the goal was missed, you will know the shortfall. If the goal was exceeded, the measurement will indicate the exact overage.

Attainable goals are real-world goals that push the comfort zone outward. Some people set goals too high and actually set themselves up for failure. Other people set goals too low because they do not want to overextend or necessarily push themselves. Attainable goals are balanced and meant to be challenging.

Relevant goals are directly related to the mission and have meaning. If the goal does not mean anything, the intensity may be low and the dedication to the goal lacking. Also, if certain goals are relevant and others are not, the associated work will be scattered and not necessarily benefit the company as a whole.

Timely goals could be measured at checkpoints along the way (say every thirty or sixty days) or have one fixed time for completion (by the end of the third quarter). This will vary depending on many factors, including the fact that "importance" should greatly affect timeliness. For example, if a project needs to be done in the next ninety days in order to secure a contract that will increase profitability by 6 percent, then the timeline should reflect this. What priorities you have set up will be key to making the plan effective.

Objectives in many cases are a subset of goals-your goals broken down into more specifics. Some like to use goals as something that all departments are working toward, whereas objectives are more department-specific. Like goals, objectives need to have the SMART elements. Also, certain objectives can apply to more than one goal. Typically they work in tandem with outcomes-those results, or lack of, that tell you whether or not you achieved your objective(s). For example, after you list a goal and then the associated objectives for the goal, at some point in time you need to verify the outcome that was either obtained or not and when.

STRATEGIES AND TACTICS

In order to achieve your goals and objectives a plan must incorporate the necessary strategies and tactics. Specific activities will always be necessary to move you forward. In this section you identify the strategies necessary and then the specific tactics or tasks for which to accomplish your identified SMART goals and objectives.

The specifics areas to include in this part of the plan are:

- Action Items: This is your road map for how you are going to get something achieved.
- List the actions that need to happen. By listing every action item, focus can be maintained, and productive communications can be established. Keeping a list also allows you the opportunity to have a log that you can see and check items off as they are completed.
- Responsibilities: This should answer the question of who is required to carry out a certain part of the plan. After overall responsibilities have been identified, determine who needs to do which task. Think about what assistance is required from others within the company to fulfill the necessary steps. Make sure the people in the other departments involved are fully aware of their part in the plan. Once people have committed to certain responsibilities, follow up to make sure they have the resources needed to accomplish their part.

- Tracking: This tells you when parts of the plan are to be completed. Establish a realistic forecast. Think of a time frame that allows all involved parties enough time to complete their responsibilities. Keep company deadlines in mind. Set scheduled start and completion dates. Define checkpoints that will determine progress. Make sure the plan stays on track. If the schedule gets off track, the plan may also.
- Flexibility: Allowing for some flexibility will better your chances of not getting caught off guard when there are minor changes or challenges to the set plan. It is important to allow your plan to be flexible. Allow for juggling people or responsibilities if necessary. Try to stay on track as best as possible, but don't be surprised when unexpected things happen.

CONTINUOUS PLANNING

Continuous planning takes into account not only the need for day-to-day flexibility but the fact that in today's extremely competitive and fast-moving environment, trying to adhere too strictly to a plan, whether short-, medium-, or long-term, can often lead to dissappointment. For example, no matter how much competitive research and intelligence you have conducted, there is always the unknown. Who would have guessed ten years ago that the Internet and e-mail would have been what they are today? Only a few of the pioneers in this category, and not even they could have foreseen the explosive growth.

It is therefore imperative that, whether your planning process takes place one or more times a year, your team (and hopefully others in your organization) recognize that planning is meant to focus and give direction and should not be so rigid as to hold you back.

In essence, what you should really be asking during the planning process is the following:

- Who?
- What?
- When?
- Where?
- Why?
- How?

If you are able to answer these, you will have a successful plan that takes into account the realities of your business and the environment in which it operates.

ASSESSING THE BUSINESS

The planning process described above still needs a starting point. You can't just start off planning without having a baseline. This is where assessing the business, again bridging corporate and departmental areas, comes into play. In other words, what is the business environment today in which your company and your team are operating? While you are not involved in all aspects of the corporate assessment, certain key information undoubtedly will affect your department, and the knowledge of this will be helpful in developing your own strategies.

For example:

- If it is a public company, how is it faring in the markets?
- Are you meeting the numbers projected for the shareholders and other stakeholders?
- Is your company in a hiring mode, hiring freeze, or downsizing?
- Are you and/or any of your competitors involved in a merger or acquisition?
- What types of information is your company sharing with you regarding future planning?

In the absence of strict facts you might also need to make certain assumptions. For example:

- A defective product line has created a media frenzy and will continue to challenge your company's reputation for an unspecified period of time.
- X competitor just announced a new CEO, and, judging by her prior track record, she will likely initiate a pricing war.
- Interest rate hikes could likely benefit your overall business in the coming months.

As we mentioned earlier, planning can be initiated in various ways. Before you are able to fully conduct an assessment of your business, you should also understand the basics of decision making. Decision making typically follows a logical model or sequence of events. This includes:

- Defining the problem(s)
- Gathering and analyzing the pertinent facts
- Looking at the options available and weighing those options against one another

- Selecting the appropriate option based on the information at hand
- Implementing that option
- Evaluating the results (a final step would be to use that feedback as input for subsequent decisions).

Brainstorming is one way to get discussions going and gather information for decision making. There are many types of brainstorming, some more formal and others more ad hoc. Some of the keys to productive brainstorming sessions include these:

- Let all voices be heard.
- Don't get bogged down in minor details.
- Use a facilitator if necessary.
- Make sure all necessary stakeholders are present.

Most important in decision making is to have an atmosphere whereby you arrive at a true consensus. This means that the highest-ranking officer in the room does not make the decision for everyone. Of course, it is often the responsibility of the most senior-level person to have the final say, but it should be based on information that has been carefully analyzed first. In some group settings a voting process can help to eliminate this concern.

Thus far you have seen tools like the SWOT analysis, product/market analysis, competitive product/service analysis, and market research. These are all tools that could give you needed input for your plan. Also, as you saw, these are often cross-functional tools or ones that reside in another department altogether. It is therefore important to identify all of these other stakeholders and departments to be sure the necessary players are involved to help make accurate business assessments.

Some of the key categories of stakeholders are:

- Your company management-CEO, president, SVP, COO, VP of sales and marketing, etc.
- Other sales managers (your peers)
- Your sales team-those you manage such as sales representatives (in-house and/or independent), field and/or telesales people, customer service representatives, sales coordinators, etc.
- Other department managers and key personnel-marketers, engineers, call center managers, accountants, human resources professionals, etc.

- Customers at all levels, including the senior managers, buyers, purchasing agents, buying assistants, etc.

BENCHMARKING

Another useful tool in assessing your business is benchmarking. Benchmarking is really a tool for making comparisons of any sort. Benchmarking can be conducted on anything from internal processes to the competition or the industry. It is a great tool for looking at current or past results and being able to compare them with the future. Benchmarking allows you to measure and then analyze the appropriate data to make decisions for improvements going forward. The areas you can benchmark are endless.

Internal benchmarking is used to measure against other departments or to get a baseline to then compare progress. It could include:

- Product and/or service satisfaction levels
- Number of complaints
- Number of defects
- Employee satisfaction

External benchmarking would look at similar processes or departments within your competitors' organizations as well as best practices in the industry. Some examples are:

- Customer service levels
- Market share
- Return on investment
- The sales process
- New product development process

Each of these could of course be broken down in smaller parts. For example, employee satisfaction could break down into morale, job security, and opportunities for advancement. Once again, many of these categories for which you can engage in benchmarking will not reside fully in your department. However, they could be of enormous benefit to you and your sales team as you set strategies going forward. For example, your sales team could be out selling a new product that offers first-of-its-kind features, yet production is way behind. Benchmarking can help you and your organization see what processes internally are working best and to then transfer that knowledge to other departments. You can also look to the outside for best practices in different industries as well as processes within companies in such areas as new product development or supply chain management.

This knowledge would help to give direction to those involved so that production times can improve and customer satisfaction increases. Conducting business planning is a complex area. The types of tools that are used and the process it can follow vary greatly. By utilizing your enhanced communication skills you can more effectively work with your team, others in the organization, and outside stakeholders to gather the necessary information in order to plan for today and tomorrow. In the next chapter, you will look at one of the most challenging areas for the new and veteran sales manager alike. It is also a key factor in the success of you and your team. While in many respects it is a specific piece of sales planning, it also has many more implications and carries with it other long- and short-term implications. It is the area of territory planning and sales forecasting. However, before delving into this critical topic, you will first need to fully grasp the importance of managing your time.

Note: Sheetz is a privately held family owned business that operates convenience stores and gasoline stations. The company operates more than 350 convenience locations throughout Pennsylvania, West Virginia, Maryland, Virginia, Ohio and North Carolina. The company primarily operates in the US. It is headquartered in Altoona, Pennsylvania and employs about 11,000 people. Reader can visit their site www.sheetz.com for a detailed study connected to this chapter.

11

Time Management, Territory Planning, and Sales Forecasting

In order to truly gauge your sales team today and where it is heading tomorrow, you will need to have a full understanding of your sales staff and their accounts. Territory planning is a critical area for your team as well as for you in order to manage for the right results. Here, once again, many skills will be necessary for both you and your staff. None is more important than time management.

TIME MANAGEMENT

Since account planning plays such an important role in sales, it must only be with the right skills and mind-set that the team goes into this process. Time management is most critical. Think of time management as being to territory planning what listening skills are to communication. In other words, you cannot even attempt to realistically, let alone strategically, analyze your accounts without understanding the value of time. What also makes time management so important is that it so often ranks as one of the poorest skills of not only salespeople but also managers. In order to best maximize your use of time, there is a critical starting point-desire. By wanting to manage your time more effectively, you will be able to bring many of the tools and techniques to follow into your repertoire. The good news is that since you are embarking on a new journey as a sales manager, you are in the position to have a fresh start.

Your time is affected by the following influences:

- Corporate demands (senior management)
- Your manager's demands
- Your sales team's demands
- Other departments' demands

- Customers' demands
- Your family and friends' demands
- Other personal demands

What you should notice is that these are all based on the demands from others of you. This is commonly how we think of the forces that affect our time. However, if you look at them differently, in terms of your demands of others and your demands of yourself, you could begin to see time in a different way. In a moment you will see more relating to "Your Demands of Others." The latter, "Your Demands of Yourself," relate to where you are today and where do you want go tomorrow.

Looking back at the influences on your time, you will see that values come into the picture. For example, values can range from very "big picture" lifestyle areas such as, are you the type of person who values work above all else? Or is it family? Or is it a combination of the two, etc.? Values can also be as specific as do you value eating a sit-down lunch versus working right through lunch? Some people like to relate values to attitude. What is your attitude toward time? What is important to you might not be important to someone else. Typically a value is something that is more of a belief that you possess about something and whether or not it is right or wrong, at least as it relates to you and your life. A good exercise to help you to sort through some of these questions would be to have a basic personal strategic plan done for yourself. This could include areas such as-Where are you today? Where do you want to be in the next three months, two years, five years, etc.? You could break down the categories into work, family and friends, sports and recreation, hobbies, volunteering, etc. How detailed you get is entirely up to you. While this seems like a very basic exercise, it is helpful to put into words some of the thoughts you have circulating about. Also, you will be surprised to see how this can change over the years due to age and circumstances, so this is something you should look at periodically.

Once you have a better understanding of what value you place on time and how you would like to spend it, you are able to work on some techniques to improve your time management. Below are some basics that you need to be comfortable with first:

- Make a daily to-do list.
- Organize your paperwork and projects and rank them by priority (A, B, C, or 1, 2, 3).
- Break down large projects into smaller parts.

- Set aside certain times during the day to check e-mail and phone messages.
- Set aside time for just yourself (quiet time).

If you are not versed and comfortable with all of these or have questions as to how to implement them, you might want to look at any number of time management articles, books, or training out there that cover a lot of these fundamental skills. As a manager, you now have a whole new complex set of time management challenges. This is where that whole notion of "demands" from others of you could start to become all-consuming.

When you were in sales, those "others" were a different set of people than you now face as a manager. Now you have a team of people who are looking to you for answers. And you can't just tell them, sorry, but I don't have the time. You should first look at breaking your time down into the appropriate categories that match your new responsibilities and priorities, which could include:

- Customer visits (joint calls or your own customers)
- Time for your staff
- Time to write your reports for your manager(s)
- Time to review reports from your team
- Time for planning
- Time for yourself

You could then estimate how much of your time each day should be dedicated to each. Of course, exceptions can be made-for example, when you are on an extended business trip. However, you will find that even on the road you can keep to some of the time frames you have identified. A good exercise is to, over the course of a week, keep a log or journal of where and on what your time is spent doing. Then you can see how close to plan you actually are or how much help and practice you need in this area.

After you have identified where your time is currently being spent and where you want to be, it is time to close any gaps. Before getting into some additional time management tools that relate to your new job as a manager, you should understand that any problem or political situation is that much more delicate as you move up the corporate ladder. Also, realize that such issues as customer emergencies, corporate infighting, and a whining staff member comes with the position-to a point.

Drop-Ins

There are many types of office drop-ins. Some examples are:

1. Your manager needs you for something.
2. One of your salespeople is having a customer crisis.
3. One of your colleagues is looking to talk about the game or TV show last night.

While your initial reaction might be that one and two require your immediate attention and that number three is the only unproductive use of your time, the reality is that all three might be unproductive at this moment. Remember, you have set up goals and objectives in the planning process, and you need to make sure you are doing the appropriate activities to meet or exceed them.

This is not to say that at times your manager and staff do not require your immediate attention; they very well might. Just make sure you are asking yourself the question, how important is this versus what you are currently working on? And if you are practicing sound time management principles, what you are already working on might be of too high a priority. If that is the case, you need to be honest and then set up a mutually agreeable time to discuss the issue with them.

A useful way of thinking of this is that if you put too many things into the funnel, you create a bottleneck, where nothing can get done. When that happens, everyone loses, including you, your manager, your staff, and the customer. This thinking holds true for those so-called fires that need to be put out and what can be termed "Project of the Week." Both usually start off small and then seem to take on a life of their own. Some call this "Scope Creep," where the scope of your work seems to keep creeping up, or getting larger.

PUTTING OUT FIRES

This could involve anyone from an employee to your managers to a customer or other stakeholder. This is likely not a real fire nor or anything close to it. Assuming it is not a real emergency, remember, just because others are overreacting, you do not have to do the same.

Panic can be contagious, and therefore counterproductive to all those involved. In fact, if others see you as too excitable, it usually will tarnish rather than build up your reputation. And remember, so-called fires can be thought of in terms of your plan and where they fit into it.

OTHER PROJECTS

Often other projects will come up that don't take into account your time and priorities. Even if they are worthwhile, you may need to give some pushback. Again, the key here is to be truthful. Express to those involved that while it might have its merits, it will be setting you back in your other work. When these projects come up, you should talk to your manager and others involved to see what takes priority. Then you will hopefully be able to reduce the scope of work to something that is more manageable.

With all of this knowledge, keeping everything in perspective is still key. There will always be strategic projects outside of the realm of everyday that you will need to work on. You need to determine how each challenge and opportunity fits into your personal strategic plan. And when you do get more involved, especially in high-visibility assignments, look at them as exciting opportunities to let yourself shine as a new manager. Remember that similar to you, others have their own plans and certain priorities that, while not as blatantly evident to you, could be very important to someone else.

THE ART OF DELEGATING

So far you have looked at many of the responsibilities of a manager and ways to manage time more effectively to succeed at your new role. So much is expected of you, yet how can one person possibly fulfill the functions of a manager and still develop new ideas for growth? This is where the need to delegate becomes vital to your new career. Delegation is something that you need to embrace. At first, many fear using it, believing that it creates tension between you and others. However, if done correctly, not only is it a tool to manage your time, but it can also help you to forge better working relationships and build up your staff as well as your own career. Delegation is in many ways synonymous with Time Management. However, it is really a part or subset of time management a great deal of attention. The following are some typical warning signs of someone who lacks sound delegation skills:

- Regularly taking work home
- Regularly working overtime
- Work not getting done when you are away
- Major aspects of the operation known only to you
- Your staff and others coming to you for most decisions, even on minor things

Now some of these are not always an accurate sign of lack of delegation skills. For example, working overtime could be something that you would like to do regardless (i.e., favouring work over personal time). However, whether or not you choose to bring work home or to spend your weekends playing tennis, there is always more of the "appropriate" or strategic type of delegating that can be done.

A major mistake of new, and even veteran, managers is to try and hold on to as many job-related functions as possible. This could be out of insecurity, believing that the more you have on your plate, the more job security you have. The other reason for this is that many managers feel that it is either too difficult to explain or that others are not as qualified or lack the competencies to get it done. Well, the reality is that you are only as good as your team. If you feel that the team members are not able to perform a wide array of tasks, then there is in inherent problem-either in your thinking or that of the staff. Since the staff is not changing overnight, and you likely have some very talented team members, you should challenge yourself to not hold on to the reins too tightly. The objective is to get the team functioning well and producing results. Your job is to get roadblocks out of the way of the salespeople. Delegation has several benefits, of course, one being that it gets the task complete. However, the other key benefit is that it helps both you and others grow. All in all, when done properly, delegating can:

- Lighten the manager's workload.
- Develop organizational efficiency.
- Provide a growth environment.
- Allow the manager to focus on other strategies.

Delegation benefits your employees as well, especially in terms of job enlargement and job enrichment.

JOB ENLARGEMENT

The objective of job enlargement is to extend the duties that the employee handles. Keep in mind the limits that one person can do without feeling over worked. Once the person becomes proficient at these new tasks, you can expand their duties into other areas.

JOB ENRICHMENT

Assigning new responsibilities is the key to job enrichment. This should mean not just tedious work, but work where there is a defined purpose. If done well, self-esteem and confidence will build as people take on more responsibility and are successful at completing this work.

In previous chapter, on communication, you saw the four types of communication styles. You have your main style(s), and certain characteristics are present to varying degrees. As a delegator, you need to think in terms of your style as well as others', to be sure that you use delegating properly, so something that should be a positive does not become a negative for those involved. For example, as a Directing-style manager, you might have the tendency not to delegate because of how you view time. It is easier to just do it than explain it. Also, when delegating, this type of manager might be rushed and even vague in explaining the task, leaving the employee to fill in too many gaps.

Couple this with the need to think in terms of the style(s) of the salesperson or other staff member to whom you are delegating. For example, when delegating to a Directing style, you might want to start with the goal. If they have questions, they are typically not afraid to ask. Also, be sure to establish boundaries with the delegation. Directing styles might want to take authority beyond the boundaries of what is being delegated to then.

Another example would be that of a Supportive-style manager. This is the type of manager who tends to be a team player and might feel uncomfortable delegating too much. She will therefore hold back on a great deal of the necessary information. The employee will then need to check in more often than would be needed, eventually getting enough information to complete the task. At the same time, a Supportive style employee will want to see how the task being delegated fits into the overall strategy. They want to know how their efforts are supporting the team or company. They might actually prefer getting the tasks piece by piece instead of all at once. This way they feel more connected to the work and the outcomes.

Of course, there are things to keep in mind for each of the DISC patterns. Odds are that it will not be a Directing style delegating to another Directing style. It could be any combination of patterns and intensity of styles. So the more practice you have in communication styles in general, the better you can become at delegating.

TASKS THAT CAN BE DELEGATED

The general rule is that any goal that is SMART can be delegated. Some additional considerations for delegating are:

- Those which are closely related to tasks that your team is already performing

- Tasks that are clearly defined through procedures and end results
- Tasks that are repetitive and that could be made a part of the normal work flow
- Tasks that enable your team members to develop personally or professionally

TASKS THAT MAY NOT BE DELEGATED

Any goal requiring a judgment call on the manager's part cannot be delegated.

- Tasks of a highly sensitive nature (e.g., salary reviews, discipline)
- Tasks involving the settling of conflicts among workers
- Tasks involving confidential data (e.g., payroll)
- Tasks that are not clearly defined, or about which uncertainty exists

SOME GENERAL DO'S AND DON'TS OF DELEGATION

- Accept the concept of delegation.
- Delegation is not merely desirable; it is necessary for successful sales operations.
- Specify goals and objectives.
- Besides SMART, you can think of this in terms of the 5 W's and "How." Once specified, everyone involved knows their responsibilities.
- Know your staff 's capabilities.
- If you have an understanding of your workload as well as that of your staff, you can delegate accordingly. Do not overload them.

AGREEMENT UPON PERFORMANCE STANDARDS

It is important that you and your staff agree on the standards against which their performance will be measured.

PROVIDING TRAINING

Delegating is more than simply turning tasks over to others. Coaching or training may be needed to ensure success.

TAKE AN INTEREST

A manager who really cares about the delegated tasks will take the trouble to find out how the task is progressing, without looking over someone else's shoulders.

GIVE APPROPRIATE REWARDS

An employee who successfully completes a delegated assignment deserves recognition and praise. What if you get pushback? If you are getting resistance it could require addressing the task being delegated and either modifying or reconsidering it. Pushback can also be indicative of a larger problem. For example, a staff member with great computer skills might feel that you are asking him to develop more and more reports and spreadsheets, and not balancing the workload with other team members. Falling into this trap is common when someone possesses a certain skill that is important to the task. Think before you delegate; you don't want to take make a star performer resentful and feel like you are taking his time away from generating more business.

Also, keep in mind that speaking the truth about the task you are delegating is important. For example, if it is an administrative activity that simply needs to get done, then say so. If it is something that could help the team overall (i.e. with morale, a new process, streamlining, etc.), then let them know that. If it is something that is asked of you from your managers, let them know that as well. When there is a lack of communication, or details left out between you and your staff, they are likely already picking up on that. Also, always try to remember that the same challenges that you have when being delegated to by others, your sales staff could be facing as well, so be understanding and empathize.

DELEGATING UP

Just like you need to manage your manager's expectations and work well with him or her, there are times that you will need to delegate up. This could mean delegating something to your direct manager or to someone in senior management, including even your CEO. While this may seem awkward at first, it is not much different than any other type of delegating. Of course, you can only delegate things that fall primarily in their domain, and they should not be administrative tasks. That said, if you do not have your own administrative person and can utilize the administrative skills of others to some extent, then more power to you. This, of course, needs to be approached with caution, but if done correctly, it could actually raise your visibility and enable you a chance to interact more with various high-level officers in your company.

You are likely being demanded of and delegated to by your manager, your peers, your sales team members, and customers. The time management tips provided in this chapter will have provided you with some ways to cope with unnecessary tasks and burdens placed on you as well as determining what is appropriate to take on and to what extent. Remember, the goal is to be able to properly manage your time in order to increase the productivity of yourself and your team. And again be conscious of your staff and make sure you are making the delegated task as achievable as possible for them. They, like you, have their own attitudes and values as it relates to the use of their time.

The other major reason to understand and improve time management skills is that it has been found to be one of the major differentiators between top-producing and low-producing sales professionals. Since one of your core responsibilities as a sales manager is to increase the productivity of your sales team, then by helping them manage their own time you have a great head start. As we look at territory planning, you should see many ways to tie in time management with the managing of accounts. This might include anything from identifying sound prospects early on in the process, before too much time is expended on them, to looking at low-producing accounts and limiting your time with them, and possibly even dropping them.

SALES TERRITORY PLANNING

You could be in any number of industries and have a wide array of sales channels that you use. This might range anywhere from field and inside sales (telesales) to distributors and independent reps (those who do not work directly for your company and are typically paid on a commission-only basis). Furthermore, your customer service personnel might be more engaged in upselling rather than just handling transactions and troubleshooting.

Next, your accounts could vary from small mom-and-pops to global 100 companies. You could also be selling to different business units within the same company or to different locations or buying offices. Finally, you might be selling to multinationals or global accounts. As such, there could be any number of ways to combine and integrate the different sales channels. Furthermore, determining who sells what to who (commonly called the sales territory) can be done in various ways. Some of the more common forms are by:

- Geography: By state, Zip code, region of the country, etc.

- Industry: Selling to telecoms, pharmaceuticals, financial services, etc.
- Product Lines: Selling X, Y, or Z products
- Alphabetical: Assigning specific letters (A-F, G-L, etc.) to salespeople (not very common)
- First to Initiate: Once you begin contacting an account, they are assigned to you (also not very common and difficult to manage)

Other unique situations:

Major Accounts: Separating accounts over X size or revenue potential into a separate account management structure Global Accounts: Separating those global accounts into a separate structure

TEAM SELLING

Most companies, especially midsize to large, will opt to use a combination of sales territory and account management strategies. Whatever the scenario, your role as a manager could again also vary from pure managing of your sales staff to actively managing your own set of accounts.

Team selling is very common today. Many salespeople are not expected to handle every part of the sales process, from initiating the sale to implementing a solution, training, and account maintenance. Therefore, team selling could be configured in many different ways depending upon the industry, sales organization, and customer. For example, in many highly technical industries there are likely technical salespeople (some might even be engineers) who are part of the sales team. In other industries, such as consulting, it is common to have a sales representative who cultivated the business, and then an account manager, who takes over the ongoing day-to-day business with the account.

RANKING CURRENT AND NEW ACCOUNTS

Most salespeople, along with their managers, use some type of a system to analyze their current accounts and prospects for new business. In trying to identify and categorize accounts, it would be too cumbersome to constantly use words like "current business account" and "potential new customers." What you are looking to do is rank customer and prospects based on their value moving forward. This way, time, money, and resources can be dedicated to accounts with the greatest value to your organization. Furthermore, it puts everyone on the same page (you, the salesperson, your managers, other sales-related personnel, etc.) so that salespeople are not out there haphazardly calling on customers without the right direction and support of others.

You have the option to use any one of several types of ranking systems to determine where to maintain your focus. You likely have been exposed to or created some type of system that uses numbers (level 1,2,3), letters (A, B, C), words (Diamond, Gold, Silver,

Bronze), and so on. However, the important question is not what symbolizes their rank, but how to decide who belongs where. After all, depending on your industry, you could have in your territory anywhere from one account to hundreds of customers and/or prospects. The reassuring news is that it is really not all that difficult to prioritize accounts, assuming you follow a few simple steps. First, you need to consider some of the following:

- The industry that you are in-have a limited number of large (major) accounts, many smaller ones, or a combination?
- How are your territories divided up-by geography, regions, product lines, etc.?
- How are your competitors covering their accounts?
- Who is involved in the sales process-your team as well as your customer's?
- What is the risk associated with your type of sales-very consistent or volatile sales?
- Are your sales cyclical-e.g., based on season, weather conditions, trends, etc.

As no two sales strategies and the factors that go into them will be the same for any two companies, it is incumbent upon you to determine what the relevant ones are for you to be considered. Once you have some of this basic analysis, one of the main goals of analyzing existing customers and new prospects is to determine their "overall value."

Then, it will be in your domain to manage your time as well as that of your staff so that time is spent on those opportunities with the "greatest overall value." For purposes of simplification, let's break down accounts into the categories of "High Value," "Medium Value," and "Low Value." With this as a baseline, you will need to set up your own thresholds. For example:

Accounts greater than Rs. 1,000,000 _ High Value

Accounts between Rs. 500,000 and Rs. 1,000,000 _ Medium Value

Accounts less than Rs. 500,000 _ Low Value

(Note: Numbers are used for demonstration purposes only and will vary greatly depending on your business.)

Yet what these numbers are really referring to is still uncertain. For example, does Rs. 1,000,000 mean past business (e.g., for the prior year), current business (orders in progress), or future business (over the next six months, year, etc.)? Therefore, when determining the thresholds right for your accounts, you will need to keep in mind both revenue (or other measurement unit) and when it can be accomplished. Also, remember that while past business is important and can give you some indicators and insights into the future, for some types of sales, it is almost irrelevant. An example would be if you were selling an enterprise-wide software system to a company. Once you have completed the sale, the customer might not be in the market for a new system for many years to come. Sure, they will require servicing, maintenance, software upgrades, etc., but the bulk of the sale is complete. This type of an account, even though they might have accounted for one of your largest recent purchases, would not be a very high-value account, because additionally, business opportunities are limited. This is not to say that the company is not a very important customer to service and get referrals from, etc., but it might not require as much time and resource commitment as other accounts going forward.

Also, you may have everything from "core" customers (the day-in-and-day-out buyers of your products and services) to "wish" prospects (those who you are eager to sell to, but who might never buy from you). Therefore, it is important to be realistic when prioritizing. Similarly, you could have two customers (both with growth opportunity of up to Rs. 1.5 million over the next year) that could be ranked High Value and Low Value, respectively, because the first company has a much better track record or chance of success. As you have seen, ranking accounts relates to both customers and prospects. If it were an existing customer, then it is referring to additional business, whereas if it were a prospect, then, of course, it is relating purely to new business. With respect to new business prospects, you can either meld them into the High, Medium, or Low rankings or they can be tracked separately as High P (for Prospect), Medium P, and Low P. This often depends on the amount of prospecting your company or a specific salesperson does versus working with mostly pre-established accounts. A good reason to include them is so that you can see more directly where to prioritize and devote your time. For example, a High P could be as important as a Medium Value or even a High Value existing account. While this is not likely-because as the age-old adage goes, it is ten times more expensive to acquire a new customer than keep an existing one-you could still have some prospects that are poised for accelerated growth.

The following is an example of where a prospect could fit into the account mix:

Account Revenues (over the next year)	
Customer X (High Value)	Rs. 1,500,000
Prospect Q (High P)	Rs. 1,250,000
Customer Y (Medium Value)	Rs. 750,000
Customer Z (Low Value)	Rs. 250,000

You will also notice that we are mostly ranking customers and prospects in terms of revenues. While revenues are often an important factor, they are not always the only nor necessarily the critical ones. Remember, business goals may vary from anything from profits and revenues to market share, quantity sold, brand recognition, and so on. Also, even within an account, the measurement might vary. For example, you might use revenues or profits for current product lines versus quantity of test orders for new products. As evidenced, account value is not something that can be simply made at random. Some additional factors to consider that can affect new business opportunities are:

- A new buyer has taken over, who could either slow down or speed up the buying process.
- Lack of customer budget to implement your solution until at least XX/XX/20XX.
- Prospect is under contract with another supplier until XX/ XX/ 20XX date.
- Customer is involved in a merger and/or acquisition, and new purchases are delayed.
- Multiple decision makers in the selling or buying organization who all need to approve the deal.

You will notice that a common theme here is that they all have something to do with the sales cycle or the sales pipeline. You will need to determine where accounts are in the cycle in order to ensure that the opportunities are prioritized. You and your salespeople can together determine where in the sales process you are. For example, has the salesperson gotten through the "discovery" (needs assessment) stage, and moved into making a sales presentation?

Conversely, if she is in the discovery stage, the buyer is likely in the "evaluation stage." This could be determined because the customer has requested a sample of the product or asked her to come in for a demonstration.

Taking the idea of High, Medium, and Low Value one step further, you can break down these three levels into some more detail, as not every group of accounts will be a the same level either. The benefit would be that you can more precisely prioritize. Similar to A, B, and C tasks in basic time management, you can further rank the A's (beginning with the High A's), then the B's, and finally the C's (the lowest C's, of course, having the least amount of time and resources dedicated to it then).

It is even prudent to add another level "Exit" or "Drop" accounts to the mix. Putting exit accounts into the analysis is a way to force you to focus on the right opportunities. You are likely aware of the 80/20 rule-80 percent of the sales time should be with the best accounts and 20 percent with the balance. However, as we all too often see, it is usually the reverse, where the lowest priority accounts are eating up the majority of our time and energy.

This is, of course, a discipline and time management issue, and it can be managed more strategically by ensuring that you and your team stick to the account plans you have put in place. By incorporating the exit account, you and your team are consciously choosing to find an exit strategy for certain accounts the effort expended to maintain them at such a low, unprofitable level. By intentionally moving your weakest accounts into this category, you are setting a stake in the ground, not to mention the fact that this can actually be measured during performance reviews. The strategy would then be to either discontinue selling to them or move them over to someone who specifically handles smaller accounts-for example, from a field salesperson to an internal one or even to Web-only status.

Of course, with certain accounts, it might not be appropriate to drop them entirely without a safety net. If your company supplies them with replacement parts that only you carry, it would be at a minimum unethical and possibly illegal to no longer provide them. way to get the process under way though is to no longer take new product orders, but rather only reorders, or just continue to supply the disposables or component parts. Reviewing and adjusting the company policy on minimum orders might help to accomplish this fairly. Again, the intent is to not eat up the salesperson's valuable time with accounts of least benefit to both you and them.

Your time then begins to free up so you can give more attention to the High Value and some of the stronger medium value accounts. This will also become critical when you make in-person sales calls. Whether your sales territories are set up by region, product line, national accounts, or other strategy, your staff will have accounts dispersed in such a way that they either form a geographic pattern or it ends up being more piecemeal (scattered). Working with your salespeople, you need to ensure that they make customer/prospect visits in priority order. This would mean that a lower-value accounts really a "nice to visit" or time-permitting account, whereas the higher-value customers/prospects are the "must-visit" accounts. Again, the specific pattern or sequence will depend on the territory, the amount of time needed for the visit, etc., but a sensible sales strategy needs to be made. Last-minute changes (e.g., a major customer cancels the meeting) and extenuating circumstances (e.g., a core product launch becomes delayed) could affect the strategy. Yet without a plan, you are operating in the dark.

Furthermore, account values can change at any point. This can be to your benefit or detriment. Some reasons for this to occur could be:

- A major prospect's supplier has just gone out of business, opening the door for you and your company.
- A regulatory change is now enabling you to compete in a new market where you have a great deal of products/services to offer.
- A prospect has been given a major grant or funding that will enable it to consider your company as a new supplier.
- Your customer has a new CEO who wants to get out of (or into) a certain line of business, thus divesting of (or demanding) your products.

It is important to note here that account management techniques will need to be adapted in a way that fits your business environment. For example, sales strategies will vary not only due to customer versus prospect status, but also the quantity of existing versus new customers. Your sales team's accounts may range from anywhere from hundreds to dozens to just a few. Also, the balance between existing and new could range from an even split of customers and prospects to all of one or the other. And this could vary from salesperson to salesperson as well. Of course, much of this will have to do with your industry, corporate, and departmental strategies.

For instance, your company may have decided to enter into a new market from the ground up. In this case, a great deal of prospects will need to occur in that particular market. Alternatively, the customer base may be so consolidated that focus is on a very limited amount of existing high-level accounts. Therefore, time and resources would need to be dedicated accordingly (e.g., via a high degree of team selling). Whatever the case, it will be incumbent upon you and your management team to align your people, time, and resources top fit the determined business goals.

Your salespeople, along with your input and direction, will need to determine the best use of their time. As a manager, you will also need to keep track and jointly agree on each member of your team's course of action, so having a solid understanding of their accounts and territory are critical. Furthermore, you will likely be making a percentage of sales calls with your staff, and quite possibly have some of your own accounts to visit-all the more reason to understand how to budget your time effectively. As you can see, time management is a critical skill as it relates to territory planning and account prioritization strategies.

SALES REPORTS

These are a great way to keep track of the progress or your team members and help them make any adjustments along the way. However, gone are the days of lengthy sales reports with detailed information that in actuality told you nothing. Today, reports should take your salespeople very little time (less than thirty minutes per week). After all, by reducing unnecessary paperwork, the salesperson can spend more time actually selling.

The following are some areas to consider for these reports:

- Progress on existing accounts (updates against quota)
- Progress on prospects (where they stand in the sales cycle, e.g., requested a proposal, samples or demonstration requested, etc.)
- Until what date a prospect is under contract with a competitor (date for when the contract is up for renewal or expires)

CONTACT LOG

This is usually a different report that is managed by the salesperson and that you can review periodically. Keep in mind that the volume of customer contacts is only as good as the outcome of these calls or visits. It has some specifics, like initial contact made, next phone appointment made, in person sales call scheduled, and so on. Remember, just making a large quantity of phone calls or sending out lots of e-mails or letters is not following SMART principles and might just be consuming valuable time.

SALES FORECASTING

In actuality, sales territory planning lays the foundation for sales forecasting. However, sales forecasting typically refers to a corporate exercise by which target numbers are used and then budgets and resources are tied into them. The problem with many business sales forecasts is that they are typically guided from the top down, with little input from the sales manager and salesperson. For example, often a goal trickles down to you through the various corporate layers. The goal is Rs. 115 million in revenue and Rs. 17.25 million in profit for your department. How did upper management come to this figure? Well, last year you did Rs. 100 million in revenue and Rs. 15 million in profit, so forecasters merely marked each one up by 15 percent. This is far from the ideal, as it often is missing one of the core elements of SMART planning-realistic.

When taking part in forecasting, you need to answer both corporate and departmental questions. The first step is to understand what is directly within your domain as a sales manager. This generally relates to your sales team, customers, and prospects.

Some of the many questions to be considered are as follows:

- Should a good salesperson be able to land an account in one, five, or fifty touches (touches being marketing outreach, phone calls, field sales calls, or any combination)?
- Approximately what is the value of each touch?
- What is the time frame for each of these prospecting activities (daily, weekly, monthly activity)?
- What is the typical time frame to arrive at X amount of business with each type of existing account (High Value, Medium Value, etc.)?
- How much time needs to be dedicated to maintaining accounts, and who, if more than one person, makes up the sales group-

the salesperson, a technical sales support person, a sales coordinator, or any combination of people?

- Does the account have multiple customer contacts (purchasing agent, buyer, manager, senior-level officer, etc.)?
- Is there team selling involved (e.g., account manager, engineer, researcher, sales manager, senior-level officer, etc.)?
- What are your department/team costs associated with each type of sale (overhead, travel, samples, etc.)?
- What "special circumstances" are in progress or have tremendous growth potential-e.g., are there any major orders pending that could increase the entire department's sales by over 10 percent once finalized?
- Are there any new markets you will be tapping into with a new product launch with tremendous growth opportunities?
- What is your role in a typical sale? How much will it vary depending on the salesperson, account, etc.?
- How many, if any, accounts do you currently manage? Are you the sole contact or do you have any sales support staff ?
- To what extent is your manager and any senior managers involved in selling?

Next you need an understanding of the role of other departments and how internal stakeholders will take part in business sales forecasting:

- What new products are in the pipeline (production, R&D, engineering, etc.)?
- What marketing campaigns are in place to drive demand? Is the marketing budget expected to be increased or decreased, and by how much?
- What is the financial stability of the business? Public or private company? Who are the investors? What is the guidance from your financial executives?
- What are the human resource requirements in progress? What is the company's hiring status (bringing on new employees, on hold, etc.)?

The crux of this is that forecasting cannot be done in a vacuum. There is no magic formula except the combination of past performance and future predictions that end up being "very educated guesses." Some try to make it an actual science, utilizing predictive models that look at historical data and many of these other factors. This can be beneficial, but it is still incumbent upon you to ensure that you have some involvement. What you are really trying to avoid once a forecast is set are major surprises (at least of the negative kind). Here is where you also need to take into account the direction you are given by each of the following key areas:

- Direction from the Top. For example, an initial mandate to grow your sales by 15 percent, sometimes based on outside investors, and stockholders as well.
- Direction from Your Manager. Likely tied into direction from the top but could be somewhat more conservative.
- Direction from Your Sales Team. For example, grow by 5 percent, based on management's figure of 15 percent; this more conservative figure might be given in order to increase their chances of beating forecast.
- Direction from Other Departments Involved in Forecasting. Marketing, HR, finance, manufacturing, etc.
- Direction from You. How do you interpret what all of these factors are telling you?

Finally, external factors play a pivotal role in what the future holds. They include:

- Competition. What are they doing in terms of market share, new products, brand recognition, sales force expansion/contraction, etc.? Are there any new players in the market or are some bowing out?
- Mergers and Acquisitions. Are you or any of your competitors involved in any partnerships, buyouts, etc.?
- Regulatory. Are there any major changes in the horizon that could positively or adversely affect your plan?
- Economy. What is the economic environment? Growth, recession, etc.? Will interest rate hikes, commodity pricing, the unemployment rate, dollar fluctuations, and so on greatly affect your business?

Some say that you as a manager should adopt a philosophy closer to that of your salespeople-that "beating the numbers" is the name of the game. They are, after all, your front line to the customer, and their buy-in is certainly a key factor. A great deal of this has to do with the corporate culture that we discussed earlier. It might at first seem like a very good idea to try to "downward revise" any forecasts put before you in order to better your chances of coming in at the higher end, allowing you and your team to shine. However, other factors are at play here, since not only aren't you forecasting in isolation, but others are involved in their own forecasting as well, and ultimately everyone reports to the top. So you must be realistic. The important part is that you strive for as much say and collaboration as possible when forecasting so that all parties can accomplish what they need to satisfy their key stakeholders and constituents.

After all, the best way for a company to be succeessful is through building stronger teams across the organization. This is where motivation and incentives comes into play. No matter what the numbers are telling you or what numbers you are being told to reach, one of your core responsibilities is to make sure your salespeople feel rewarded for their efforts. You can help bridge the gaps by ensuring that there is a connection between the forecast and the incentives to then make or surpass the plan. Always keep in mind as well that incentives can come in the form of both monetary as well as nonmonetary compensation. The theory behind motivation and how to best implement compensation and other incentive and rewards programs will give you some greater insights into how to inspire your team going forward. This is how you can get the best out of everyone in order to achieve the results that you, your team, and your company are seeking to do so.

Note: Novelis, a subsidiary of Hindalco (the metals flagship company of India-based Aditya Birla Group), is engaged in the production of aluminum rolled products. Novelis operates in North America, South America, Europe, and Asia. It is headquartered in Atlanta, Georgia and employs about 12,700 people. For further knowledge regarding this chapter reader can visit www.novelis.com

12

Recruiting

This chapter will guide you through the maze that ultimately leads to hiring the best candidate for the job. In this chapter you will see the process from finding sources for new recruits to the interview itself, extending the offer, and then signing on a new sales team member. In your own career, you have likely only been on the outside working your way in; here you will be on the inside looking out, identifying and incorporating new sales professionals to strengthen your current team.

ENHANCING THE CURRENT TEAM

You might think that in order to build the perfect sales force, you need to build your team from scratch. Unfortunately, you probably won't have that kind of luxury unless you work for a new business or a new sales unit within a larger one. The reality probably is that you already have a team in place and will need to enhance or adjust the current team. Firing the entire team is rarely an option, nor a good idea. Your recruiting realities may include a combination of hiring and firing; they may be done in a short time frame or in a longer, more gradual way. The good news is that while you might be inheriting difficult personalities or marginal or low performers, you are likely also getting some very talented sales professionals. Whatever the case, what is best for your team from this time forward will vary based on many factors. The following are some of the core areas to consider:

- Existing competence level of team members
- Changes in business direction (introducing new products/ services or expanding into new markets)
- Regulatory changes (possible need for a new skill set)
- Corporate mandate (due to increased or decreased budget)

- Corporate culture (how the sales force fits in with the overall corporation)
- Economy (recession or growth)
- Major industry changes (mergers, acquisitions, expansion, contraction, etc.)

Add to this list by thinking about the areas that affect your sales team and what might cause the need for minor shifts or broad changes in your current staff.

DEVELOPING SPECIFIC CRITERIA FOR THE SELECTION PROCESS

You have heard the advice to "think before you act." When it comes to the recruiting process, this especially rings true. Too often sales managers post job descriptions based on the requirements of the position but then just select the candidate whom they feel they can get along with best. This is a selection based on emotion rather than reason. While it might have its place in your social life, you really need to remove the emotion and base your decision to hire someone on specific criteria that you have set up and that the candidate then meets.

Before searching for a candidate, managers must know whom they want for the position. A starting point would be to consider the characteristics best suited for the position, and how the person in the position needs to fit with the team. In analyzing the territory, the sales manager must look at both functional skills and other requirements for the job. For example, the sales manager must consider the territory itself and the strengths and weaknesses of the team as a whole. It is only by having goals and objectives and sticking to the plan that you will hire the right person for the job, and as a bonus, you will also avoid turnover, which is just as important due to all the costs in money and time associated with hiring and training.

Some core questions to ask are:

- Is this a new territory?
- If so, is it similar to any other territory?
- Is the territory open due to either turnover, termination, or promotion?
- What worked with the person who represented the territory?
- What areas need improvement?

- What personality styles would best fit this territory?
- Will it require a significant amount of prospecting or will it require more servicing and relationship building?
- What technical expertise, if any, is required?
- Is this an isolated territory where the salesperson needs to be an independent self-starter?
- Is this a territory that requires teamwork?
- Has the candidate already offset any potential weakness?
- What training will be necessary (immediate and long-term)?

By proper planning, these and other questions can be addressed early on in the recruiting process. Sales managers with no plan usually make the mistake of hiring in their own image. This is only successful when it matches what is needed for the territory. So odds are that you are not getting the right candidate when you hire in this fashion. One way to help you with this is to make a list of your specific criteria. Once you have this, it is critical to stick to it (assuming no major changes in the sales environment are taking place). Of course, you will never find someone who fits every single criterion to perfection. One way to help keep you on track is to rank criteria and to correctly weight the categories. For example, if you are looking for someone who has specific technical knowledge, you can rank each candidate (1-10, with 1 being very weak and 10 being very strong). You could then give a weight to technical knowledge (for example, 3) whereby it is 3 times as important as something with a weight of 1.

You would end up with something like this for a candidate:

Criteria	*Rank (1–10) x*	*Weight (1–3) =*	*Total*
Ability to Read Financial Statements	7	2	14
Ease at Cold Calling	8	3	24
Industry Contacts	6	3	18
Total:			**56**

This means that candidate X got a ranking of a 7 (out of a total of 10) for her ability to read financial statements, a job requirement. Of a total of 3, it is considered a 2 (of medium importance). When you run the numbers, you get a total of 56 for candidate X. Then you can see how she stacks up against the other candidates. We will look at the interview process more in a moment. You will also notice that this criteria fits in nicely with the sales skills model (technical knowledge, business acumen, communication skills, market experience). This ties in to the fact that the exceptional salesperson is what you inherited, are training someone toward, and/or are looking to bring on board.

In fact, those companies that excel at hiring today are more and more hiring to plan. So if a candidate does not have X years' experience doing Y, then he would not be a strong candidate. While this may seem overly stringent and could keep some potentially strong applicants, it helps you to maintain focus and hopefully bring to the top of the list those with the highest degree of matching skills and background, thus lowering the burden on training, coaching, and other areas. At the same time, remember that in most cases you are legally required to allow anyone interested the chance to apply, and always be sure that each candidate is properly and fairly considered.

Before getting the posting out into the marketplace for candidates to see, the sales manager needs to take the time to ensure that she is familiar with all of the key elements of the position. Ideally you should have some part in writing the job description. Fortunately this serves you as a sales manager as well as the candidate, because the job description sets the stage for many things, including delegating, motivating, and counselling, among other areas. Below are some of the questions you should be asking to ensure an accurate job description that will be useful in the interview itself.

EDUCATION AND EXPERIENCE

- What formal skills and knowledge are needed to function well in this job?
- Why are these skills and sets of knowledge important?
- Could someone without these skills do the job well?
- Are there parallel skills that would substitute for what is listed?
- Do the requirements coincide with the job description?
- Are the requirements fair to all applicants?
- What is most important of all of them?

REPORTING RELATIONSHIPS

- Where is the position on the organizational chart?
- Who will the candidate report to, and will the candidate supervise anyone?
- What compatibility is needed?
- Are there also informal or dotted-line reporting relationships?

Work Environment

- What will the working conditions be?
- Is this job permanent? Will the description be changing soon?
- Is there travel involved? How often? What is the duration?
- Are there specific work hours? Do they rotate? Is there regular overtime?

Salary

- What is the starting salary? Any flexibility or room for negotiation?
- What is the commission structure? Is there a bonus plan? Merit versus across-the-board increases?
- When is the salary review period? Are there opportunities for raises before the standard review?

Benefits

- Is there health insurance, life insurance, dental insurance, auto insurance, etc.?
- Is there a profit sharing, 401(k), retirement, or pension plan?
- What is the vacation, holiday, sick day, and long- /short-term disability policy?
- Do we offer specific training or other education programs as well as tuition reimbursement?

Growth Opportunities

- What is the company policy on promotions, and are there interdepartmental promotions and/or lateral transfers?
- Can a promotion be turned down? Will that impact future offers?

Special Requirements

What else is expected and/or provided-for example, company car, tools, uniforms, dress code?

Behavioral Analysis

- What communication style did the previous person to hold this position exhibit? What were the strengths and weaknesses?
- What type of communication style would work best for the opening? with the territory? with the existing sales team?
- What are the probable strengths associated with this pattern?

- Will this pattern help compensate and/or offset any weaknesses on the team?

Internal Motivators

- What is the ideal internal motivator for a person in this job?
- What is a secondary motivator?
- What are the internal motivators of others on the team?
- Will they be compatible and/or complement one another?

Of course, the job posting will not need all the answers to these questions, only those most pertinent to the job. Think of them as the need to know versus the nice to know. For example, if travel is a large percentage of the time and requires a car (that the company will not provide), then this should be stipulated in order to be able to focus on the appropriate candidates. After all, omitting pertinent facts or responsibilities on the job description, while not always purposeful or misleading, could prove to be a waste of the candidates' time as well as yours.

OPTIMAL SOURCES FOR RECRUITING

The recruiting process is an ongoing effort and responsibility of most sales managers. Though a corporate structure may be in place vis-a`-vis human resources to generate candidates and to conduct the initial screening, being aware of exceptional people is part of a manager's ongoing function. Successful sales managers will take a proactive stance when recruiting to support the larger corporate effort. That being said, there is no greater misuse of time than sorting through pages of unqualified candidates because the initial screens were not in place. Hopefully you have a human resources department that can help with this process. Either way, there should be some involvement on your part, so having a plan and maintaining the discipline to stick to it will be up to you.

Below are some of the major sources to be considered for the recruitment process.

- Campus recruiting
- Contingent staff
- On-line job sites
- Company Web site
- Job fairs
- Newspaper ads

- Recruiting firms
- Trade associations and magazines
- Referrals by company employees
- Internal candidates

CAMPUS RECRUITING

The advantage of campus recruiting is that the candidate pool is wide and enthusiastic. A great opportunity exists for the hiring of potential winners at entry-level salaries. The disadvantage is the risk of early turnover because the candidate cannot do the job or discovers that the job is not what they anticipated.

Maximizing Campus Recruiting

- The Internet. Many online job sites provide a specific category for posting jobs for college students or recently passed graduates. Here you can fine-tune your search and post a position only with the schools you preselect. Also, you do not have to spend the time going from campus to campus posting a position, as it can be disseminated centrally to all the chosen schools via the site. It may also be a good idea to go directly to some of these schools, as they sometimes have a specific area where they post opportunities.
- CD-ROM Presentations. Most all campuses give students access to computers for job searches. A CD will give the candidate an overview of the company history, products, services, work environment, and frequently asked questions. CDs are excellent substitutes for the expense of a campus visit.
- Video Conferencing. Certain campuses today have facilities to interview candidates through closed-circuit video. The advantages are time and money savings, that several managers can observe the interview, and that the interview can be taped (with permission) for managers in remote locations to observe. One disadvantage is a lack of the human element. Students report being uneasy about the scrutiny on camera and feel anxious about being taped.

CONTINGENT STAFF

Certain staffing firms specialize in contingent staff or employees who work on temporary assignment. They are similar to more traditional temporary (temp) agencies, except that the candidate profile is often more specialized. Lawyers, teachers, accountants, and specialized consultants are a few examples. The employee works for the staffing firm, not your company. This type of firm may also provide a complete sales force for special one-off projects. A company will use this option when adjusting for seasonal trends, national launches of products, trade shows, or spikes in business. The advantage is that there is no need to hire people and get them registered for employee benefits when it is a short-term project. Companies turn to such outsourced workers to control the ebb and flow without the hassle and expense. The major disadvantage when working with contingent staff is training. Although the jobs that fall into this category might not require significant job training, there is likely still certain procedural and product training. Lack of employee loyalty can also be an issue. As you will see later, the motivation level of different types of sales staff can vary, and it is up to management to come up with a plan to address all types of employees.

Maximizing Contingent Staff

It is important that the staffing firm's representative(s) understand as much as possible about your company's business and customers. It is necessary to provide honest estimates as to the length of the employment or assignment. A sudden or abrupt cutoff can cause significant morale problems. Make advanced arrangements with the firm for potential hire of a contingent worker. If someone is compatible and a full-time position opens, "stealing" the firm's employee could cause ethical and/ or even legal issues. Waiting until the opportunity arises is never the best approach, as it limits options and can only cause more problems.

ONLINE JOB SITES

This is where the "volume" of re´sume´s comes from today. Limitless sites are available for the advertisement of job openings. HotJobs.com, Monster .com, and Careerbuilder.com are some of the major ones, but they only scratch the surface of what could be out there for you to take advantage of in your industry and/or job function. Many industries have specific online job sites (i.e., those that specialize in financial services, the entertainment industry, etc.). Glocap.com is one example of a site that offers jobs with a special emphasis on the financial services industry. You are probably already familiar with those that are in your industry and just need to decide where is the best place to expend your time and money. There is also an array of job Web sites that are based on functional areas (e.g., specific for marketers, human resources professionals, project managers, accountants, etc.). Sales Ladder_ (sales.theladders.com) is a job site that specializes in opportunities for high-level salespeople as well as sales executives.

Advantages

- The cost is low.
- The cost for job seekers is typically nothing, or a very low cost. A job seeker can send out an infinite number of re´sume´s.
- Job postings are easily categorized. This is convenient for the recruiting company and the candidate.
- Electronic transfer eliminates the waiting time for a response to a newspaper ad via regular mail.
- Paperwork is dramatically reduced. Many government agencies require that companies hold re´sume´s for a certain period of time. Storage of paperless re´sume´s is obviously more convenient.
- The target market is extraordinarily large.
- On these sites you can take one of two approaches. You can either post a job, then see who responds, or search for candidates yourself, selecting your own determined criteria and then browsing through re´sume´s that are posted.

Disadvantages

- While almost everyone in the workforce today works to some extent on a computer, it is possible that a great candidate does not feel comfortable searching for hours through Web sites applying for positions of interest.
- A disproportionate number of unqualified candidates respond due to the ease of re´sume´ submission. A job posting can get hundreds of responses.
- There is typically a cost to companies to post positions and to search for candidates (this can vary greatly from service to service).

COMPANY WEB SITE

Companies that utilize their own Web site and include a job opportunity section can dramatically increase their chances to find qualified and motivated candidates. Also, you can utilize your own Web site as well as linking your career opportunities page to online job sites, getting both those who seek you out directly and those who do not. The great thing about having jobs located on your Web site is that candidates that already have an interest in your company have direct access to apply for any open positions. They can also readily search your site for more information, company background, etc.

It is likely that your human resources department will have certain information to provide and also that needs to be filled in for all candidates. It is a great way to keep track of them and maintain the information for future reference (e.g., should a more appropriate position become available). Some of the information typically requested is about the candidates' educational background, current and former employers, references, salary history, special skills, and so on.

Maximizing Company Web Sites

- Making searching for jobs easy. An "employment" button in a prominent place on the home page should be available. Offer a re´sume´ builder or a form that is compatible with the database management system.
- Making the site navigable. Speed and easy access are crucial. Slow loads and dead ends are frustrating and will lose even an experienced browser.
- Responding quickly to the applicant. A confirmation of receipt, a rejection due to lack of qualifications, or a "next step" response should happen right away.
- Continually updating the Web page. Leaving already filled jobs online creates a series of unnecessary problems.
- Screening out unqualified applicants. Utilize a candidate profiler so that you can automatically help to identify those candidates who most closely match the criteria.

JOB FAIRS

One of the most proactive methods of recruiting is the use of job fairs. Companies can interview numerous candidates over the course of a few days. Generally the candidates are specialized and motivated. Often, companies sponsor their own job fairs. Most companies participate in fairs hosted by others. In this case the company pays a flat fee to participate. Job fairs are often sponsored by colleges and universities.

Maximizing Job Fairs

Limit the time with each candidate. The objective is to use the fair for screening interviews as opposed to hiring interviews. Limiting time allows the recruiter to see more people. When applicable, have full job descriptions made available. If you have set up a schedule to meet with people (in advance or onsite), be sure to stick to it. This demonstrates professionalism to the candidate, and a follow-up can always be scheduled if a mutual interest is evident.

NEWSPAPER ADS

The main advantage of a newspaper ad is that it can get a fast and large response. But a newspaper ad can be expensive and, depending on the state of the economy, could elicit varying results. For certain positions they are more useful. But, for highly technical jobs they are not usually the best resource. Blind ads, ads where the company name is absent, generally generate the poorest results.

Maximizing Newspaper Ads (Advertising Costs)

- Use a headline to get the job-hunter's attention.
- Select a prime location for the ad.
- Use graphics where possible.
- Allow for "white space" in the ad so that it is not too cluttered.
- Display the company logo.
- Use colour if the newspaper provides that service.
- Put in enough information to dissuade the unqualified candidate and to stimulate the interest of the qualified candidates.

The main categories are duties, responsibilities, and requirements.

RECRUITING FIRMS, EMPLOYMENT AGENCIES, AND SEARCH FIRMS

The main advantage of using an outside firm is the ability to fill a position quickly and from a labor pool that would otherwise be inaccessible. They can also provide a service for which your company does not have the internal resources to adequately handle. Costs can vary depending if they are on retainer (retained search firm), or they are paid on a commission by the employer when the right candidate is located (contingency search firm). Retained firms generally work with an exclusive agreement, whereas employers often use more than one contingent firm. Some companies choose to work almost entirely with outside firms like this, and others use a mix of their own hiring function complemented with one or more of these additional resources.

Maximizing Recruiting Firms

Develop explicit guidelines for the job requirements. The recruiting firm can screen to very specific criteria or be more open to exceptions based on your guidance. A long-term relationship with a recruiting firm allows the firm to get a good understanding of the company operations and environment. Invite agency representatives to tour the company facility and meet people from different departments.

Note: Retained firms are generally used to fill higher-level positions or more intricate roles that require more research, which a contingent firm would not have the time and resources to handle.

TRADE ASSOCIATIONS AND MAGAZINES

You are likely already familiar with the publications and associations that relate to your industry. Sometimes the field is very specialized, and other times it is a very broad community made up of buyers, sellers, vendors, dealers, and so on. Assuming you have a relevant association for your industry it is always a good idea to stay involved with it.

An association should be able to provide you with insights into what is happening in the field and can serve as a resource for finding talent. In fact, many associations are starting to have their own online job resource centers. The National Automated Merchandising Association (NAMA) is one example of a resource that serves the vending, coffee service, and food service industries. Trade publications fit into this category as well, and many have either a print and/or online version of their magazine with a career section. The Hollywood Reporter, serving the entertainment industry, is an example of this. Other magazine resources are Selling Power and Sales and Marketing Management. Both serve the sales professional and have online resources as well.

REFERRALS BY COMPANY EMPLOYEES

Employee referral programs are used to recruit prime employees. The program can have the added benefit of boosting morale and increasing employee loyalty, as employees feel their suggestions are valued by the organization. In fact, many firms go as far as offering a reward or monetary compensation for referring an employee who is ultimately hired. Typically the new hire must stay for at least a prespecified amount of time (e.g., three months) before the compensation can be paid. The sales force itself is one great place to get referrals, but this could also include those in other departments as well. A salesperson who makes a referral is in the unique position of actually knowing the positives and negatives of working in the sales department. The main challenge with employee referrals is that it can be awkward if you do not hire that person. Not to worry, though; most people understand if the referral does not pan out. If you stick to your criteria, the right candidates will rise to the top of the list.

INTERNAL CANDIDATES

The potential for internal candidates is of course dependent on the type of sales position and whether or not there are well-qualified candidates in other sales roles looking to make the change or other department members looking to get into sales. However, it is also a corporate culture question. Does your company prefer to promote or reassign from within or does it more often than not look to the outside? If the latter is true, you might want to challenge this policy. It is usually a smart idea, not to mention a morale booster for employees in general, to know that additional opportunities are available within the company should their current position not be optimal for them. Your company will likely have requirements around timing for how to post jobs both internally and externally in order to accommodate corporate strategy and the law. That said, depending on whether you are looking for a high-level sales representative for national or key account sales or just someone eager to hit the pavement selling, your strategy for recruiting will vary greatly. For example, in some instances the person might need to be so specialized that you have only one or two places to really look for solid candidates. At other times you can utilize a broad mix of resources for new candidates.

A note about posting the salary range: This is often a sticky point for many companies. You will find examples of both out there. If industry and title in that industry already dictate a range, then it is not necessary to post but still an option. Also, your company might not want to invite attention to what you are paying for everyone to see, including competitors, vendors to your industry, customers, and other stakeholders. Also, if the range may vary dramatically based on experience, then you might opt to leave it out. Furthermore, your company might have a policy about this, or the requirement to post or not may be governed by law.

In the absence of these situations or mandates, you might want to consider including the salary range. Furthermore, you can also identify the base and potential commission. This could help either attract or reduce the amount of inappropriate candidates. After all, it is tough enough narrowing down the search already, so why add one more challenge to the process?

If you do choose to include salary information, be sure to be accurate in your wording, so as not to mislead. Also, make sure you have some standards in place as to what you mean by experience. There is also the question of whether or not you ask for the salary history from the candidate right away. If you do post the salary and choose to ask for their salary requirements up front, you will likely find candidates who state that based on their experience they are entertaining positions in a specific range (this will more often than not be on the high side, if not slightly above your range). If you do not post the salary range yet still ask for their salary requirements, you will at least be able to match this with the reality of the job. There is no exact science to this, as human nature often has both parties trying to maximize their negotiating position. Always remember to be as fair, up-front, and consistent as possible, and everyone will benefit in the end.

THE NUMBER ONE RULE IN RECRUITING: CONSTANTLY RECRUIT

Managers should not rely on knee-jerk reactions to fill an unexpected vacancy. Good managers already have a list of people in their database to call. These may be people they have met on a plane, on a train, or through a casual conversation. You might have found their background and experience to be well suited, but there were no openings at the time. They may not be interested in your position for themselves, but there is a chance they know someone of equal caliber who does. These can be some of the best referrals you will receive.

Also, when networking at industry events like conference and trade shows, make a mental note of anyone who is visible and impresses you. You may hear a speaker in your industry who possesses great public-speaking skills, something that is part of your criteria. You might wish to either approach her at the event or follow up with her afterward. At the same time, keep in mind any noncompetes she may have or other legal/ethical considerations if she works in the same or a related industry.

ENSURING A POSITIVE INTERVIEW PROCESS

A well-run interview benefits everyone involved-you, the candidates, your team, the organization, and the customer. The number of highly qualified recruits will only increase if your company has a good reputation, as you find more and more candidates will be seeking out your organization as their desired place to work.

REVIEWING THE RESUME

Depending on your human resources department, you may or may not have an active role in the selection of candidates. If you are a part of the first screen phone interview in conjunction with human resources, you will likely eliminate certain candidates even before the actual interview. In either case, reviewing the resume prior to both the first screen and actual interview is very important. The review might just be a refresher to the candidate's background and qualifications or it can help you to prepare for questions to ask during the interview.

In a way, resumes are like a sales pitch sheet on behalf of the applicant. It is important that you take them very seriously. Someone who cannot sell himself well on a resume has a lesser chance of stellar selling for your company. That said, be careful not to judge certain nonessential elements of the resume. For example, style and layout will vary from applicant to applicant, so don't think there is one best approach. When screening resumes, you will certainly find red flags. These will not necessarily rule out a candidate but can cause some concern or at least trigger the need to question. The following is a basic list of what to look for in a resume:

- Overall appearance
- Typos or unprofessional use of language
- Blanks or omissions (e.g., missing dates or education information)
- Gaps or overlaps in time
- Frequency of job changes
- Job titles and responsibilities (lack of progression)
- Consistency or inconsistency between career experiences
- Vague job description

Again, it is common that either you, your human resources department, or both conduct an initial screening interview by phone. This is typically not the time for in-depth interview questions. The purpose of the telephone screening interview is typically to:

- Determine if the candidate's qualifications match job requirements.
- Establish the interest level of the candidate.
- Set up a face-to-face interview.

If it is determined that an in-person interview is warranted, this is where your more elaborate preparation and interviewing skills will be required.

CONDUCTING AN IN-PERSON INTERVIEW

There are typically three parts to interviewing: finding out about the person and how they react to certain situations; going over their background (as it relates to the position); and making the offer. All three parts could be handled in the same interview; however, this is rare. For example, with higher-visibility positions, the interview process will more likely require several meetings and could spread out over days, weeks, or even months. Also, depending on the position, it could require that anywhere from one to numerous people in the company meet with the candidate to give their feedback and/ or approval. Of course, this could be for a new sales position or an existing one where the territory has been left open and the customer could suffer, so timing and urgency may vary.

The interview is not just a method of hiring; it's an important tool that managers utilize to build an effective organization. It also further establishes the corporate image. The first part, finding out about the person, is probably the most important. It allows sales managers the opportunity to learn about the individual in terms of judgment calls, internal motivators, and her behavioral style.

Interview Styles to be avoided are as follows:

- Sticking to the Resumeand Nothing Else. Typically, an interviewer will take the application or resume and start asking questions that relate to that information. The applicant then repeats the same information on the resume, and the interviewer discovers that the interviewee knows or seems to convey only what relates to the application. This offers a 180-degree understanding of the candidate at best.
- Giving Away All of the Answers. Another style that managers often use is to first describe the intricacies of the position, the work environment, and the corporate/department culture to the applicant. However, in this case, the interviewee will likely pick up on what the interviewer expects him to match up to, and will then try and become that person. Then the manager is surprised to later find that the person she hired is quite different from the person she envisioned, and his performance is not at all what she expected.

Boring and Canned Interviewing Questions. You have likely heard of questions like these:

— Can you tell me a little about yourself ?

— If you came to work for us, what assets would you bring to our organization?

— What is a weakness that you have that you would like to change?

While these questions will elicit some helpful information, they are not going to get to some of the nuances and potential concerns, nor will they necessarily help in getting to the behaviors you are looking for in the ideal candidate. This is where the idea of "behavioral interviewing" comes to be so important.

The premise behind this style of interviewing is that past performance in similar situations is the most common predictor of future performance. Behavioral interviewing is a way to delve deeper into the candidate's decision-making process. The style of questions probes in a way to elicit a far greater amount of useful information than a traditional interview would. Not only is it important to become better at this approach, but keep in mind that many candidates have likely practiced this as well.

The good news is that it is difficult for the interviewee to practice, and if an interviewer uses this approach correctly, no amount of practice can help certain weaknesses or areas of concern from coming to the forefront. Below are sample behavioral interviewing questions. They should, of course, be modified for your organization, but they will give you a very good idea of the types of questions that you should be looking to use.

- Tell me about a situation when you had to sell an idea internally to your coworkers.
- Describe a time when you disagreed with your boss and how you handled the situation.
- Tell me about a time when you had to think creatively in order to get a job done.
- Tell me about a time when you were overloaded with responsibilities and how you prioritized the work.
- Describe a situation when you tried to achieve something and it failed.
- Tell me about a time when you had to conform to a corporate policy that you did not agree with.

It is also beneficial to relate some interviewing questions to the criteria you are seeking in an exceptional sales professional (one who posseses strong technical knowledge, communication skills, business acumen, and market experience). For example, you can try and gauge the interviewee's communication skills through questions such as:

- Tell me about a time when you had to make a presentation to multiple buyers.
- Describe a time when you had an objection from the buyer and you found it to be unreasonable.

The other key to this interviewing technique is to utilize the information you received to probe even further. For example, if the question is, "Describe a time when you tried to achieve something and it failed," and the candidate says that her boss was a roadblock to achieving the goal, you could ask why, how, and so on. As mentioned, though candidates might have had some training in answering these types of questions, the main benefit to this technique is that it is very difficult to practice. Questions are unpredictable in nature, so the answers are difficult to have prepared. That said, you will find that some candidates attempt to use a similar answer to different questions because it is within their comfort level. Here is where having a list of questions in different categories will be helpful.

One other category of questions that is very important is motivational questions. While the overall style of behavioral interviewing will lend itself to identifying what motivates a sales candidate, there are certain more specific questions you could ask as well. The following are some examples:

- Tell me about a situation when you outperformed your peers.
- Describe a time when you were able to make a difference within your company.

Here you will find out how important pure monetary compensation is versus status, public recognition, or other motivators. Some additional considerations to be aware of and practice (or avoid) during the interview are:

- Make sure that the environment is very professional and not distracting. There has been some debate over the type of environment in which to an interview is to be conducted. Some have even suggested trying to catch the candidate off guard by using tricky tactics like making an interviewee uncomfortable.

While some useful information could come of this, it is not recommended. The interviewer should try his best to set a favourable environment for the interviewing process. There is no need to create any unnecessary stress or uneasiness on the part of the interviewee. Also, by acting professional, you enhance your own as well as your company's reputation.

- Don't react too quickly. The answers that the interviewee gives may not be the same answers that you would give to the questions. However, that does not make the applicant wrong-it makes her different from you. That difference may be exactly what you need to offset a weakness that you may have and to fill a gap on your current team or a particular territory. Remember, you are trying to hire based on the preestablished criteria. You are not looking for your mirror image; falling into that trap almost always backfires.
- Avoid prejudging or stereotyping. Similarly, trying to categorize or lump people together too early is a surefire way to damage the integrity of the process. For example, because applicant A is neatly dressed and well groomed, it cannot be concluded that this person is a detail-oriented, careful worker. Similarly, because applicant B is a football star, we cannot conclude that he is aggressive or competitive in a work setting. In both cases, more information is needed in order to reach such conclusions. Again, sticking to the plan is what will help you get past any preconceived notions you may have. You will find that you will often be way off base and pleasantly surprised by taking the more disciplined approach.
- Always seek sufficient information. Frequently, interviewers reach conclusions about people's abilities based on insufficient or invalid information. For example, many managers make false assumptions related to the interviewee's current salary. At first it might appear that the candidate is earning 15 percent more than the company is willing to pay. The candidate, however, may be paying personally for benefits that your company would be covering. Conversely, the candidate might be earning a significant percentage less than you are willing to pay. In this case, many hiring professionals might discredit this person or value them less. Keep in mind that while salary history and current compensation have some weight as to an applicant's current market potential, it is not necessarily an accurate

indicator of future success. In fact, a candidate might possess all of the qualities you are looking for and is in looking to move out of his industry into yours specifically for this reason, to increase his earning potential.

- The interviewee should do most of the talking. This is perhaps the most frequent interviewing error. When the interviewer does most or even half of the talking, the interviewer cannot be effective in gathering pertinent information, observing the interviewee, and truly learning about them. Otherwise, as the majority of people who lack sound interviewing skills find, there will not be enough information to draw valid conclusions and then not enough time to accurately interpret and evaluate the candidate. You will then feel pressured and make impulsive decisions.

Keep in mind that this is similar to the "discovery" or "needs assessment stage" in the sales process, where you should be listening a great deal more than speaking. This still requires discipline because many people have a tendency to comment on every response and then go off on a tangent from there. You can counteract the tendency to talk too much simply by asking a great deal more open versus closed-ended questions. This should automatically get the interviewee to do most of the talking. Also, as you saw in the behavioral interviewing examples, you will get more information out of open-ended questions.

Limitations of Resume

While having a list of questions to begin a dialogue is important, reading directly from it is very limiting. In fact, you will likely skip right over important need-to-know information or other clues or red flags that you should have picked up on. Furthermore, by asking too many questions directly relating to the resume you are getting a minimal amount of new information and likely playing right into the strengths of the candidate. After all, he wrote or worked with someone to write it in that way. Furthermore, it tells the interviewee that you have not done your homework and are not interviewing based on a plan. So while you might have specific questions that you must ask based on corporate policy or the resume at hand, don't get so caught up in routine that you forget the true goal: to find the best candidate for the job.

Avoid "Leading" the Candidate

It doesn't take the smartest of candidates to realize that you are looking for a certain response. Asking a question like "Tell me about a time when something was really going wrong with a sales call and how you handled it" is fine; however, if you continue with the question by saying: "And did you need to think out of the box to handle it?" you are giving up the right answer. To further clarify, in the first instance, you will be able to determine how organized the candidates are and what they consider to be most important, and you will likely get responses that go well beyond what is provided on the resume. In the second example, the interviewer has in essence told the interviewee to discuss a certain topic (in this case out-of-the-box thinking) that may be important to the interviewer but not necessarily a strength of the candidate. However, now the candidate knows to make it a priority. Remember, you are trying to hire a sharp salesperson, yet the irony is that almost anyone can catch on to this.

Rushing the Final Decision

Of course, the opposite holds true with. You might have the urge to immediately dismiss someone you feel is different from you. This is something of great concern. For example, it might be something as simple as someone who worked in a certain industry or for a certain company that you were not very fond of, and for that reason you are more apt to discredit the candidate. However, at the far end of the spectrum, this practice is either subconscious or overt bias or discrimination. I do not have to tell you here how wrong this is, morally, and it is very possibly illegal as well. On the other hand, you might find that the interviewee has something in her background that you really appreciate or can identify with, and this seems to resonate with you even before you have gone through the full interview process. This is a tendency that must be brought to a conscious level and guarded against.

There are many examples of interviewers saying, "I liked this guy the instant I met him. I think we should hire him." Odds are, their behavior patterns were exactly the same. People like people who are similar to themselves. This is where the expression "hiring in one's own image" comes from. Another example is when the job vacancy might just seem so important to fill that you feel pressured to move quickly. Remember: A hasty decision is rarely a good one. Rather, we must continually remind ourselves that effective personnel selection is in the best interest of both the applicant and the company. In fact, harm can be done both to the individual and the company when an unqualified person is hired and set up for failure. It is simply not in the best interest of anyone involved to place someone in a position for which they are poorly suited and that will ultimately end in failure.

The purpose of this part of the interview is twofold:

- To observe obvious discrepancies in the candidate's image or personality, according to the intended plan and criteria.
- To determine what areas might be needed in order to further train, develop, and motivate the individual once hired. Unless there is an obvious mismatch, managers should, at this point, avoid either hiring or not hiring.

The other area to explore relates to specifics about the individual in terms of work, school, and any other pertinent information that could relate to the position. Here you can use the re´sume´ or application to ask about certain specifics, for example:

- Clarify those "red flags": gaps between jobs, horizontal moves, several moves, major salary changes, etc.
- Clarify positions held: job description, duties, accomplishments, etc.
- Some useful questions to ask that relate to his job (if currently employed) are:
- What do you like about your job?
- What do you dislike about your job?
- In what areas do you know you excel and how?
- What is the greatest challenge for you, and how do you try and overcome it?
- How do you think your coworkers would describe you?

Answers to these questions could further help to expose the concerns, strengths, weaknesses, and motivational factors of that individual. Of course, while a candidate should feel comfortable asking a question at any time, it is at this stage that you would more formally solicit questions from the interviewee. Keep in mind that her list of questions might very well shed even more light on her. For example, an interviewee might ask questions such as:

- Does the company have and contribute to the employees' 401(k) plan?
- How many vacation days are there in the first year?
- Is there opportunity to move to other departments within the organization?

These questions might demonstrate to you a candidate's additional concerns or motivators, and, at the same time, could either strengthen or weaken your interest in her as the right fit for the job, assuming her questions go counter to the objective criteria you have in place for the position. After answering any questions and finding that there is still mutual interest by both parties, you will move on to the next area of the interview. Here is where the candidate will likely want to know what the company really has to offer him and if this is a place he could see himself working. Not at any time should you embellish or try to over glorify the job. The object is to reiterate the mutual benefit of the position for both the candidate and the company. At the same time, if as a manager you have handled the process well so far, you should know the applicant's key desires and motivators. By using this knowledge, you can explain the position and the opportunity in terms that are most relevant to the applicant.

Now you have reached the time for the more formal offer. In many circumstances the position will warrant a written offer. The formality of it will often depend on the position being filled. The procedure could also be governed by law or corporate policy. Furthermore, other parties might have a vested interest, such as a contingency search firm.

The Written Offer

The offer typically covers the total package and not just salary, including any and all of the other benefits that are being offered. In fact, it is important to show the total package as opposed to just salary, as it could further validate the benefits of the position versus another offer she may or may not be considering.

The Job Description

A complete and thorough review of the job should be reiterated at the offer, in order to be sure there are no last-minute surprises. Again, be careful not to try to oversell the position here. A major complaint of those who leave the job within the first ninety days is that if they would have known in advance about certain responsibilities of the job, they would likely not have accepted the position. You could end up losing what you felt was an ideal candidate at this point. However, if instead you hired this person and she then either chose to move on very quickly or just never did produce up to expectations, then much of the effort put into recruiting and hiring was for naught.

Furthermore, when factoring in the cost in time and money to hire and train an employee, mistakes like this can be very expensive. Also, even if the employee for whatever reason (lack of other opportunities, financial security, etc.) chooses to stay, low productivity and cynical, negative behavior could result, and will be a major issue for not only the new employee, but will affect you, others on your team and around the organization, and your customers.

Performance Forms

Some companies choose to give an example of their company's performance review, evaluation, and or other measurement documentation at this time. This form or forms are typically used to set objectives that the employee will be expected to achieve in a certain time frame, and then results will be matched up to track performance and evaluate their work.

OTHER IMPORTANT INTERVIEWING CONSIDERATIONS

MULTIPLE INTERVIEWERS

When others are involved in the interview process with you, be sure they understand the criteria you have in place and what you are looking for. All too often, they are not prepped and merely come back with a one- or two-word opinion on the candidate. Not only does this lead to inappropriate subjectivity but could even lead to unethical or unlawful consequences. Make sure that others in the process are a benefit, not a threat, to sound hiring practices.

EMBEDDING THE CANDIDATE

Some companies choose to test out the candidates either on a trial basis or through formal or informal interactions with the sales team in their working environment. While this is usually with good intentions and could help both the company and candidate get to know one another better and see if there is a fit, it can also raise additional legal concerns, as it is more difficult to ensure objectivity in the process. It is therefore also something that should not be implemented without sound human resources and legal consultation.

SCREENING TESTS/EXAMS

Testing candidates up front is becoming more and more common in the interview process. These tests take anywhere from a few minutes to even a full day. In fact, some companies even pay the interviewee because of the lengthiness of the process. There are many companies specializing in preemployment testing, and while they cannot gauge everything-like attitude, passion, and determination- they can help to weed out many candidates that do not possess the types of skills or even ethical standards that you are seeking. Like everything else in the interview process, be sure you are consistent, and if you implement a test, do so across the board for all applicants.

CHECKING REFERENCES AND CREDENTIALS

Diligent verification of references is typically in the domain of the human resources department. However, in certain companies it may be left up to the managers themselves. References are tricky in that personal ones, from friends and relatives, are typically not very useful. Also, certain employers are not able to give out any information that isn't strictly factual and are therefore not able to share any opinions about your applicant. In any case, you should do your best to verify the facts and ask some open-ended questions if allowed to try to get what you are able to. Furthermore, at the end of the reference check, ask if there is anything that was not covered that they would like to add about the candidate.

THE BASICS OF THE LAW

Always stay current on the law. This chapter is intended to give you many of the core skills and practices for recruiting, selecting, and hiring top candidates, but it is not intended to substitute in any way as legal advice nor for any company policies with which you must comply. It is your job to stay abreast of current law through your human resources department, company legal counsel, and any other governing bodies associated with your industry and business. It is typically the role of your human resources department (possibly in conjunction with the legal department) to educate you on the interview and hiring process. In fact, in many cases these departments are not just there for training but to work with you during the entire process, and they often take the lead in certain if not all parts of the process.

The law prohibits you from asking questions relating to certain topics such as:

- Race
- Age
- Religion
- Marital status
- Sexual orientation
- Physical disability (certain exceptions apply)
- Criminal history

- Country of origin
- Financial status
- Veteran status

Another important piece of advice worth reiterating is consistency. When participating in the interviewing and hiring process, it is critical to maintain a level of consistency so as not to bias or favour unjustly one candidate over the other. Each person should have a fair chance and be assessed according to the standards that your company has put in place. You would not want to show up for an interview and find that you are being judged according to a different set of standards and practices than another interviewee, and nor should anyone who you are interviewing. Not only is it just plain wrong but it could very well be illegal. So be sure to maintain consistency and act on objective standards as they relate directly to the position, not on any personal or other non-job-related predispositions, biases, or prejudices. You, your company, the new recruits, and your customers will all be the better for it.

FIRING IS INEVITABLE

Firing someone can be a traumatic experience for both parties involved. It is something that everyone fears, whichever side of the drama they fall on. Keep some core things in mind that might make the process somewhat easier and will hopefully put the inevitable into perspective. First of all, excluding the case of across-the-board layoffs, in most cases a termination should not come as a complete shock. Employers are asked to document problems along the way. In fact, documentation on all employees is important. This is twofold; it gives the company a record of any discipline issues and also it allows the employee a chance to improve or rectify the problem. Of course, there are issues that by law do not require either verbal or written warnings. Some of these categories are:

- Stealing
- Destruction of company property
- Criminal behavior
- Extensive absenteeism
- Gross insubordination
- Falsifying timekeeping records

However, most other problems require that the employee is given the benefit of the doubt and has sufficient time to comply with standards and/or improve performance. This could even be the case with "at will" employees (those that the company has hired and have less of a responsibility toward, should management wish to terminate them). Performance review forms often will contain pertinent information and maintain a record of performance or other issues as well.

Human resources and/or legal counsel should play a very active role if termination becomes necessary, not only to train you, but quite possibly to handle certain parts, if not all, of the process, depending on the situation or severity. Never engage in firing an employee without their direct involvement.

While firing may be extremely difficult as well as emotional, it is a necessary part of management. Also, keep in mind that it is being done for the good of the company and is intended to be of benefit to the entire team in the long run. In most cases, improved performance, productivity, and team morale are the result. Recruiting and hiring is a great challenge to managers. Yet if done correctly, it can be a very rewarding activity and one that you might even look forward to participating in. Always remember that you are working to bring on new talent, with the objective of improving productivity of both the individual contributors as well as the overall team. Later we will look at ways to ensure that both new and existing employees are trained and up to speed on all necessary aspects to perform their job at a high level. Now you will take a look at motivation and the critical role it plays in the success of you and your staff.

Note: ArvinMeritor is a global supplier of a broad range of integrated systems, modules and components serving commercial truck, light vehicle, trailer and specialty original equipment manufacturers and certain aftermarkets. The company primarily operates in the US, Canada, and Europe. It is headquartered in Troy, Michigan and employed about 19,800 people as on September 30, 2008. For a case study visit company's site www.arvinmeritor.com

13

Building the Environment for Motivation

One of the most challenging areas for managers is motivation of sales professionals in order for maximizing their performance. Also, since maximizing your team's performance is so key to your own success, it requires a great deal of attention. What makes it so challenging is that there is no one-size-fits-all formula to increase the motivation of your staff members. What motivates one person might not motivate someone else. If fact, it might do just the opposite. This chapter will take you through the theory of motivation and all the major ways to increase the chances of motivation.

Most important, it will give you insights as well as specifics that can be applied to your various team members. Keep in mind as we go through this section that you are not actually motivating someone else. Only that person can motivate himself. You, on the other hand, can provide an environment that will increase the odds of someone being motivated.

We will also look at the area of compensation and incentive planning and the importance that motivation has in the overall plan. Finally, you will learn more about core motivational techniques (monetary and nonmonetary) including the tremendous importance of recognition and rewards.

CLASSICAL MOTIVATION THEORY

Several different classic theories guide us today in terms of motivating, or setting up a motivational environment. Most are based on the notion that internal motivators need to be tapped into in order to bring out the best in people. Before delving into some of these internal motivators, it is necessary to look briefly at the works of two psychologists who you might already know something about.

HIERARCHY OF NEEDS

Back in 1943, in an article titled "A Theory of Human Motivation" in the Psychological Review, Abraham Maslow proposed a progressive, hierarchical, pyramid approach leading to the ultimate internal motivator: self-actualization. At the base of the pyramid, physiological needs are a priority. Here basic survival instincts such as the need for food and water are evident. These are what people will seek out in order to exist.

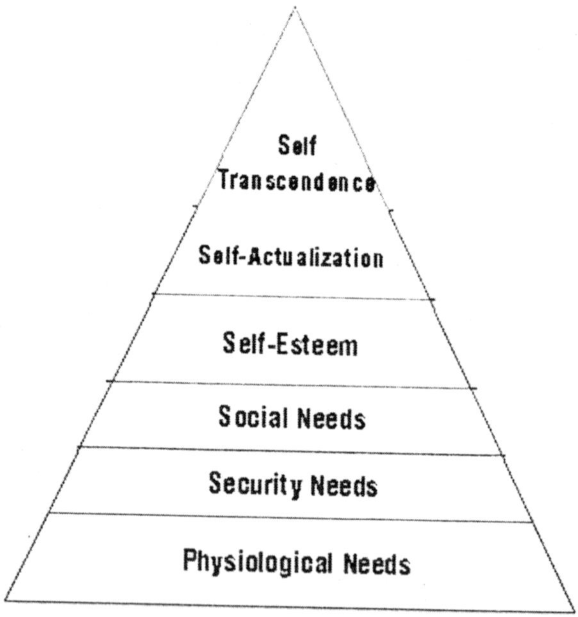

Maslow's Modified Hierarchy Of Needs Including Spiritual Needs

Figure: Abraham Maslow's hierarchy of needs.

The next level up the pyramid is safety and security needs. These include the need to protect oneself from the elements, enemies, or imminent danger. The third level from the base is belonging needs. With some exceptions, people are social animals, and they need others like family and friends to be a part of their life. The fourth level includes ego needs. This is the need to be distinguished from others. The formation of a personal identity is important to people because no one wants to be exactly the same as anyone else.

The top of the pyramid is self-actualization needs. This is the point in life at which people are fully satisfied and have "found themselves." It is said that this need is never actually fully satisfied but is actively pursued once the other needs have been met. When considering these categories in their purest sense, one needs to assume that the other elements of the hierarchy of needs have already been satisfied in order.

For example, without your basic survival needs being met, it is not likely that you will be looking to form social groups. If you then look at this from the top down, self-actualization can't not take place without the existence of the other preceding motivators. That said, one could say there are exceptions to that rule.

For example, someone might sacrifice her own safety or well-being for that of someone else, say a child or loved one. In this case, she is actually motivated by self-actualization before safety and security. While this hierarchy sheds some light on motivation, and stresses the importance of self-actualisation as a motivator, it has its limitations.

The research findings of Frederick Herzberg, published in the book The Motivation to Work in 1959, illustrated motivation from a somewhat different perspective, and considered motivation in tandem with what he referred to as hygiene factors. Hygiene factors include categories such as company policies, working conditions, working relationships, and salary and benefits.

Under motivation you have such categories as the work itself, achievement, growth opportunities, and recognition. In the absence of hygiene factors, the setting becomes demotivating, although the presence of these factors do not motivate in and of themselves. That is to say that categories such as salary and benefits are not considered motivators, whereas achievement and recognition are. Graphically, Herzberg's theory could be depicted as follows:

Hygiene Factors or Potential Demotivators	***Motivators***
Company Policy	Responsibility
Salary, Benefits Growth	Opportunities
Relationship with Boss	Recognition
Safety on the Job	Rewards

As you can see, the factors leading to satisfaction or that motivate employees are different than those that could lead to dissastisfaction or that demotivate someone. One other way to think of it is that the hygiene factors are the baseline in order for the motivational factors to be able to play their part. In essence, they are two very different yet important categories in their own right. With these two theories in mind, it is necessary to now look back in time a bit to the work of another psychologist, Eduard

Spranger. Back in the 1920s, Spranger's work helped to identify six core internal motivators:

Theoretical

Aesthetic

Social

Political

Structural

Economic

Two things to points out:

1. There is no particular order to these motivators.
2. You will see other similar words used in place of these over the years. For example, sometimes you will see order in place of structural or power in place of political.

Although originating before Maslow and Herzberg, these six motivators have some similarities and correlate to those later findings in certain ways. However, the body of knowledge around them and what has evolved over the years looks at motivation from a somewhat different perspective. You can think of these six motivators like behavioral styles or DISC in that they are very important and help you to identify ways to work with your team and others around you.

However, whereas DISC patterns guide you on how to work with others and look introspectively at yourself, motivators are based on the why or what that leads someone to act or react in a certain way. To a greater extent it takes into account your values and deep-seated beliefs-those that not only are represented through your behaviors but also those that guide them. So a primary focus of these motivators is on what people strive for or are seeking out of their work.

THEORETICAL

People that highly value the theoretical strive for knowledge. The more one knows, the stronger one is. Theoreticals have an insatiable appetite for knowing and understanding. They have an intellectual curiosity that is systematically satisfied. They constantly ask questions to fill in blanks. They are incisive, logical, objective, and unemotional in their pursuit of knowledge.

Probable Strengths of the Theoretical

- Likely to be an expert in their field
- Curious about a wide range of subjects
- Questions and challenges logic
- Patient
- Incisive

Potential Weaknesses of the Theoretical

- Methodical approach sometimes delays results
- Answers questions with questions
- May come across as too intellectual or a snob
- May be absentminded

MOTIVATING THE THEORETICAL

Theoreticals tend to move toward jobs that entail a lot of analysis or mental stimulation. In the absence of this, it is important to try to assign tasks that require research or investigation. When delegating, be extra conscious of providing measurable goals with specific deadlines. This will keep Theoreticals from wandering off the subject. Use their analytical ability to develop other uses for the information they gather. For example, a salesperson may need to turn in a monthly competitive pricing report. Writing the report may not be stimulating. If an additional challenge is given to look for patterns or investigate alternative pricing strategies, then the report becomes part of the knowledge motivation.

AESTHETIC

People who place a high value on the aesthetic seek balance and beauty. Aesthetics have a need to enjoy and respect objects of beauty. The beauty can be a great work of art or something in its natural setting. Aesthetics also seek balance, symmetry, and harmony. The Aesthetic person experiences each event separately and on its own merit. Experiences are not necessarily linked nor do they need to be relative to anything else in life. Aesthetics are sensitive people who are keen observers. Aesthetics tend to want to enthusiastically share their experiences, especially with those who appreciate the harmony and beauty in life. They tend to be or at least aspire to be in more creative roles. Money is not the prime motivator for Aesthetics. It is the enjoyment of creating something that brings them ultimate pleasure.

Probable Strengths of the Aesthetic

- Creative
- Artistic
- Excellent sense of symmetry
- Above-average spatial/visual intelligence
- Alert observer

Potential Weaknesses of the Aesthetic

- Perceived as a dreamer and not a doer
- Perceived to be on the edge of societal norms (dress, lifestyle, etc.)
- Temperamental
- Very sensitive

MOTIVATING THE AESTHETIC

Aesthetics work best in a hassle-free environment. Since they enjoy beauty, their physical surroundings need to be pleasant. They may not just want nice furniture and works of art on the walls, but also to work with "pleasant" people. Aesthetics function well when allowed to be creative with projects. Something as simple as being allowed to design a new format for a report makes the report a motivating task. Personalizing tasks are important to Aesthetics since to them each event is its own experience. Ill-mannered people, cluttered offices, and volatile circumstances will be depressing or can slow or impede Aesthetics' performance. And while Aesthetics may prefer room to work freely, a manager may need to follow up with a bit more frequency.

SOCIAL

A person who values being social tends to put others first. They delight in working with and assisting others. They do not typically seek gain or a great deal of recognition. They do not have hidden agendas. Socials will give time, talent, and money to further what they see as a worthwhile cause. Socials tend to be in jobs or aspire to work in places that allow them to fulfill their desire of helping others.

Probable Strengths of the Social Environment

- Charitable
- Benevolent
- Concern for others

- Empathy
- Team player
- Good teacher or educator

Potential Weaknesses of the Social Environment

- May be taken advantage of
- May neglect self for the sake of family and others
- Has difficulty saying no
- May be too trusting of others

TO MOTIVATE THE SOCIAL ENVIRONMENT

Put Socials in an environment where they can help. If their sales role does not always lend itself to this, assign projects that might accomplish the same goal. Encourage them to work on teams within your department and across the organization. Also, encourage any extracurriculars, such as volunteering in organizations outside of work. At the same time, you will need to keep an eye out that extra work does not cause productivity to drop. Give them time or support in their projects. Socials are usually pragmatic, so they can distinguish between outside activities and career. Socials also want to feel and actually be needed. Although this is true for everyone, it is especially important for Socials. Put them in a position where they can see that they have made a difference.

POLITICAL

Those who place a high value on the political seek out and desire power. Politicals look for a variety of ways to gain control. If there is a lull or gap in the leadership role, the Politicals want to step in and take charge. Although it is not always true, Politicals are often viewed as leaders. In some ways, Politicals want to be elevated over others. They enjoy center stage and public recognition. Titles, positions, and lofty status symbols are typically more important to them than to others. Politicals are usually self-centered and need that extra special attention. Politicals have been known to take positions with a lower income if it gives them more authority.

Politicals are very responsive to competition. The bonus money associated with winning a contest is secondary to the win itself. Of course, the caveat is that the money may allow them to attain more status symbols that demonstrate power or authority. Politicals move toward fast-track jobs. Upward mobility is important to them, and they either seek it within the organization or need to move on to another one.

Probable Strengths of the Political Environment

Industrious

Competitive

Accountable for actions

Desires to lead

Passionate

Potential Weaknesses of the Political Environment

- May appear superficial
- May be seen as egotistical
- Sometimes may be merciless
- Lack of patience

TO MOTIVATE THE POLITICAL

Place Politicals in leadership roles on projects or teams. Be aware of titles for job positions. Although not always feasible, a wording change in their title could increase motivation. Office position or workstation placement is also important to the Politicals. If possible, give them a prestigious place to work. This cannot be done in an arbitrary way. Performance must be associated with the work area or job title. The Politicals want glory, yet at the same time they are willing to earn it.

STRUCTURAL ENVIRONMENT

Those who highly value structure seek order from life. Organizational charts, strategic plans, measurable goals, and benchmarks are all motivators. Salespeople motivated by structure tend to have high moral and ethical standards. They also will rely heavily on standard operating procedures. Go by the book whenever possible. If the book's procedures require modification, make changes cautiously and respectfully. More than others, they will focus on the importance of SMART goals. In fact, achieving a goal in a sequential and orderly fashion is more motivating than what the goal achieved. They tend to pick up on superficial motivation or manipulation and will quickly reject it.

Probable Strengths of the Structural Environment

- Honest
- Direct
- Dedicated

- Hardworking
- Systematic

Potential Weaknesses of the Structural

- Overly strict
- Tunnel vision
- Limited comfort zone
- Overly zealous on minor points

TO MOTIVATE THE STRUCTURAL ENVIRONMENT

The Structural individual works best for someone who is honest and has a high degree of integrity. This person does not respond well to threats or false bravado. They are turned off by those who are overly enthusiastic and impetuous. Give the Structural person a working environment that requires order and systems. Training a person with this style to prospect requires a very specific approach. Do not expect them to cold-call impulsively; they will opt to be more methodical.

ECONOMIC ENVIRONMENT

People who place a high value on the economic strive for material rewards and practicality. They desire to accumulate wealth and possessions, not necessarily for just themselves but for their family and others as well. They strive to accumulate accomplishments in clearly identifiable forms.

Practicality leads to a concentrated concern for the bottom line. If an idea cannot bring a "tangible" return on investment, then the idea may be worthless to Economics. An Economic has little need for knowledge that cannot be readily used.

Economics are constantly comparing and contrasting, and measurement devices are consistently analyzed. Observation, desire, and acquisition are the processes Economics use in accumulating material rewards. Economics are not afraid to work for these possessions, and they believe others think likewise.

Probable Strengths of the Economic Environment

- Dedicated worker
- Competitive
- Goal-directed
- Profit-oriented

Potential Weaknesses of the Economic Environment

- May want to win at any cost
- Could be seen as greedy
- Workaholic
- May become overextended trying to keep up with societal standards

TO MOTIVATE THE ECONOMIC ENVIRONMENT

Provide them with opportunities to accumulate materialistically. Again, this is not always just in terms of money, but other possessions as well. The faster the accumulation, the greater the motivation; for example, a commission is more motivating than profit sharing. Therefore, Economics typically want rewards associated with a known quantifiable value. Economics expect to be paid for their skills. Once Economics have something, they tend to not want to lose it. They will be motivated to keep what they have and then continue to want more. Economics can sometimes move forward with fearless abandon. At the same time, managers must be careful not to push the Economics beyond their means.

A note here to try to clear up any confusion about financial rewards (primarily money) as it relates to motivation. As was theorized by Herzberg, the financial aspect (salary, benefits, etc.), while a core component of any organization's strategy, is really just to satisfy the core needs of your staff. Once these needs are met, it is necessary to find out what will motivate each individual salesperson. The confusion arises in that one of the six motivators identified by Spranger was Economic. So how can these two be justified? The answer is that they cannot. The theories and studies out there all take a look at motivation from a slightly different perspective. What is important to realize is that financial rewards do play a role in motivation, whether they are the motivator in and of themselves or whether they are more of a means to get to the true motivators; what is consistent is that they are not the sole or primary driver of motivation. Many other factors come into play, and it is incumbent upon you as a manager to try to tap into these other factors.

ADDITIONAL IDEAS ABOUT INTERNAL MOTIVATORS

Just as in the AMA DISC styles, internal motivators are prioritized. According to some of the work around this theory, everyone has all six. Some are just more important than others to the individual. Generally, people work with internal motivators two at a time- two that they are currently striving to satisfy, and two that are waiting in the background in case of or for when the first two get satisfied. Regarding the remaining two internal motivators, there is a limited desire to satisfy.

For example, an Economic who has already built great wealth may then set up trust funds for charities or provide scholarships for schools. Thus he is moving on to satisfy his Social need. It is important to recognize that no one actually reaches the top of the pyramid nor satisfies all needs. Everything is really about the quest for total satisfaction. Furthermore, each of the six internal motivators have different thresholds for different people. For the Economics, what amount of money or material possessions are enough? For the Aesthetics, when does beauty end? For Theoreticals, is there nothing left to learn? And once people reach one threshold, another is then generated.

It is fair to say that everyone wants utopia. Everyone wants to be self-actualized. Everyone wants to satisfy their particular needs. The good news for managers is that everyone wants something. The manager's job is to find out what that is. If this discovery can be made, managers can now help to motivate their people by guiding them in the right direction. There is a saying: "Help enough other people get what they want, and you will get what you want." The trick is to know what people want and, more important, why they want it. Now that you have much of this basic knowledge around the six internal motivators, it is important to do two things. First, identify the primary internal motivators of your team members. Second, lay the foundation for an environment that brings out the best in them.

IDENTIFYING MOTIVATORS

Of course, various instruments exist that seek to identify your internal motivators. They can also be identified through observation and questioning. For example, to determine an individual's internal motivator, you can ask a very basic, straightforward question, such as: "What would you do with the extra income from an increase that was above and beyond what you were anticipating?" Sample employee responses could be as follows:

- Theoretical. I have been looking to take some classes that the company reimbursement policy does not cover. The raise will cover my expenses.
- Aesthetic. I would like to buy a new piano. The more I play, the more I realize how bad my current one is. Also, I believe I

was brought in at the lower end of the salary range, and while I do not expect nor need to be the highest-paid in the department, it should help balance things.

- Social. I am thinking about adopting a pet from the local shelter. If the raise comes through, it will help offset some of those expenses. Either way, I still plan on making the commitment.
- Political. I am not sure yet, but what I can say is that this is long overdue. I deserve it, as I am one of if not the single largest contributor to the team.
- Structural. I am not yet decided, but I am glad this is taking place. I believe that company policy states that I am due for this type of increase.
- Economic. This extra money is necessary so that I can add to my investments. This will help to further compound my rate of return.

Remember that while the above responses will help clue you into likely internal motivators, you would still not want to rely on just one indicator, so additional questions, observation, and other assessments would help to give you a more accurate picture. For example, at first pass you might confuse the following Structural versus Social distinction:

A Structural person who has a real concern for the well-being of others would tend to think logically and long-term. A Social would be more focused on the here and now. The Social would therefore look to give a hungry person the fish, and a Structural would likely want to teach him how to fish.

To sum this up: What people do is behavior; why people do what they do is their internal motivator. Now that you see what types of things drive motivation, the balance of the chapter deals with actually creating the environment in which it can flourish.

SALES COMPENSATION AND INCENTIVES PLANS

The sales compensation and incentives plan is an integral part of the planning process. Like the core elements of the sales plan discussed in prior chapters, the comp plan needs to tie the sales department into the overall corporate strategy. A well-thought-out plan helps to measure, reward, and align the team. Also, while it can at times seem focused on mostly the financial aspects, it opens the doors to the vast category of nonmonetary rewards that can very much enhance the plan and fill in the gaps where necessary.

Since you are a new sales manager, you may not feel you have much say in this part of planning. You do, however, have a major stake in the behaviors driven by your departement's plan and the results that follow. Therefore, whatever level of involvement you have in preparing the plan, you can still find numerous ways, direct and indirect, to get involved. Some of the key benefits of a well-developed compensation and incentives plan are:

- A clear link to corporate and other departments' plans
- A defined role for sales in the organization
- A defined role for the salesperson
- A defined role for others compensated or incentivized under or tying into the plan
- The ability for the company as a whole to attract and retain some of the best employees
- The ability to encourage/discourage certain behaviors
- The image of the sales department, both internally and externally

You and your sales staff are operating in a larger environment that affects your level of motivation. This not only encompasses the culture surrounding you, but the policies, procedures, and business practices in place. Let's take a look at the three categories (corporate, departmental, and individual) and what can be affecting you and your staff in each of these areas. Then you will learn ways to address each category through an enhanced plan as well as rewards and recognition programs. The first level is "corporate." Corporate is responsible for things that reflect the general work environment and company image such as:

- Company Brand Name/Reputation. Do people on the outside speak highly of your company? Is reputation and the company missing something that affects your team's motivation and/or drive for success?
- Cross-Functional Teams. Is the culture interactive? Does your staff have the opportunity to work with people of other departments and levels across the organization?
- Benefits Package. Does your company offer a good health plan? Are there additional services offered such as gym membership, child care, etc.?

- Working Conditions. Is it a safe and clean environment to work? Is your human resources department and IT (help desk) very helpful in answering questions and resolving issues? Does your company provide food or beverages?

The next level is the department. The department level has many areas that cross over with corporate, but your department likely has its own nuances and cultural norms. While you might not have as much leeway with the corporate policies and areas affecting all employees, you should have a greater say in what affects your department, or at least your direct team members.

- Do you have sales contests, employee recognition programs, or other programs different from the rest of the organization?
- Is your dress code the same as corporate or is it more formal/ casual?
- How close or far apart does the motivation or level of ambition seem from one department to another?
- Is your sales staff expected to participate in general corporate meetings or are you more autonomous?
- How are the players in your department being compensated? Are there differences in the pay packages and what are some of the guidelines?

The third level is individual. As you saw, while you can work to have an environment that taps into the motivation of your team, it can never be all things to all people. This is where specific tailoring of rewards and recognition will come into play. Of course, you should not play favourites when it comes to rewards (monetary or nonmonetary), as this could be discriminatory and possibly even illegal, but as you now know, there are many different ways to engage different team members. A solid plan is meant to get the most out of your star performers and not carry the weaker players on their shoulders.

THE SALES COMPENSATION AND INCENTIVES PLAN: WHERE TO START

The "comp plan" needs a starting point, and what better way than by looking at the competition? As we mentioned before, benchmarking can be used to compare yourself to the competition. If you are in a start-up business or beginning a new category, you can look to similar industries for examples.

Before you can look to improve or enhance your current plan, it is critical that your plan be competitive with the industry. People within industries talk, and at times take a look at the competition, so it should be known industrywide that your company has a solid, if not the best, plan in place. That is not to say that you are directly sharing information with the competition but rather that when one of your staff shops around, they should not be surprised and find a significantly better compensation package with one of your key competitors.

You should, of course, only attempt to obtain competitor comp information through legal and ethical channels. This might include past salary information from new hires, studies on your industry by independent sources, trade association research, and so on. Also, your competitors might actually post their salary ranges directly on their job listings.

The competitor's compensation and incentives package would also include programs the competition engages in, such as sales contests. In this case you might have just heard that salesperson at X competitor won a trip to Aruba or that the top twenty producers at Y competitor went on an all-expenses-paid trip to a resort in Palm Springs. What is important to know is that word gets around on what is and what isn't a "good" place to work, and the comp plan is very much the foundation for this to happen.

THE ELEMENTS OF THE COMPENSATION PLAN

The compensation and incentives plan is meant for encouraging the right behaviors as well as discouraging the wrong ones. What those behaviors are needs to be determined. However, it is necessary that they take into account the salesperson, you, the department, and the company as a whole. The comp plan should also address both the short term and the long term. For example, while revenues and profits might be necessary on evergreen products and services you provide, certain new product launches (the future of many business strategies) might be a longer-range initiative without the immediate payback or return on investment. In this case, you would need to be sure that everything (not just revenues and profits) are spelled out in the plan, and compensated for as necessary. Salespeople more than anyone else in the company, will work for what they are getting paid for, and not much else.

This need to motivate salespeople to carry out nonrevenue/ profit tasks can be carried out through specific performance measures, which look at both volume measurements and other activities that are being carried out to reach what ends. In sales planning we looked at the various inputs needed to ensure SMART goals and objectives. Since the comp plan is an integral part of the larger sales plan, it should also spell out many of the expectations.

RELATIVE AND AMBIGIOUS TERMINOLOGY

One of the keys to measuring the success of a salesperson, or really any employee, is to be as specific as possible. If you are going out into the field and are told you are being paid X commissions on sales revenue, you have a clear understanding of what your pay will be. However, as mentioned, it might be other activities that are necessary for the long-term success of the sales department and the company as a whole, and those need to be accurately measured and compensated for.

For example, what happens if someone said that you are being paid for your "best efforts in thinking long-term for the company"? This rather farfetched example helps to give you a more clear idea of something that is impossible to measure. For example, what is meant by "best efforts," "thinking," and "long-term"? While these words might mean one thing to you, they could mean something entirely different to someone else. In addition, they do not live up to the SMART standards discussed. Since every business is different and has its strategic priorities, it is up to you, along with your management, to determine what activities are to be measured and rewarded. Following are some examples that companies commonly put in this category:

- Sales calls to defined national accounts
- Presentations to senior executives
- Prospecting calls to prequalified accounts
- Sampling of new products
- Proposals requested by customers

Unfortunately, it is typically only performance in terms of revenues and profits that companies are able to measure effectively. That is because they have not taken the time to set up a strategic comp plan, and even with some of the basics in place, that plan might still not be communicated or monitored effectively. Furthermore, even those companies that try to include important activities into the plan are likely not capturing one very key element-productivity. For example, you might find that one of your salespeople is completing everything ahead of deadline and even surpassing some of the numbers targeted in areas such as prospecting calls and national account visits. However, that person is falling far short of meeting her monthly sales quota and is falling behind on getting in her sales reports.

Therefore, she might be working "hard" but not "smart," or what is really happening here is that she doesn't know how much value to place on each area of her job. Three questions are important to answer here:

1. Which areas hold a greater weight in the compensation plan?
2. Does the salesperson understand the goals and objectives?
3. Is she qualified to achieve the stated goals?

The answer to this first question is what truly separates the good and bad sales organizations. Remember: Since salespeople are working for what they are being compensated for, it is up to you if you want to drive certain behaviors, making sure it is in the plan. If not, you will be left scratching your head, asking, "Why didn't they do X or Y?"

As you saw, besides revenues and profits, sales activities such as prospecting calls and sales proposals could be a part of the plan. However, consider measuring several other key areas, such as sales skills and product knowledge. All told, you can end up with several categories that are determined based on your strategic priorities, including:

- Revenue/Profits. Is the salesperson on course to meet quota for existing and/or new products?
- Sales Activities. Is he involved in the right activities that lead to the desired results?
- Sales Skills. Is he working as a solutions provider (partner) with the customer?
- Cross-Departmental Communications. Is he working well with others in your organization?
- Product Knowledge. Does he understand the ins and outs of the current product line and new product launches?
- Competitive Analysis. Does he understand what the competitors are offering?
- Financial Understanding. Does he understand the numbers side of the business?

You can break each one of these into subgroups as necessary as well. For example, under sales skills you might have:

- Presentation skills
- Closing skills (different from closing ratios, which could be an activities measurement)
- Discovery techniques or needs analysis

Another major category of measurement that has grown in importance over the years is customer satisfaction. After all, most sales today are not transactional in nature, they are long-term. Even the purchase of a consumer item like a suit, which might take only an hour or so, still has the potential to be that of a long-term customer.

Therefore, customer satisfaction is not only a measure of today but of the future as well.

You can then rate your team members against each of these categories and specific factors. For example, Salesperson X might rate a 7 out of a possible 10 in presentation skills, and 3 in product knowledge. Keep in mind that there is almost always a way to apply objective measurements to these. For example, with presentation skills you can monitor whether or not the salesperson completed a course on presentation skills. Also, it is an extremely useful tool for deciding how best to train and coach each team member when there is a deficiency.

You would then need to look at weights for each factor. While revenues and profits typically have the greatest weight, the others, especially in certain industries and with certain types of sales roles, might have as great or even greater weight than dollar figures. Whatever the determined weights are for each factor, they will likely tie into some type of performance management system.

Performance management has several purposes:

- To set goals and objectives
- To see where you meet, surpass, or fall short on agreed-upon goals and objectives
- To formalize (make official) the measurement process
- To have in writing areas mutually agreed to by the employee and employer

Note that performance management and performance reviews vary greatly from company to company. Sometimes the goal setting is part of the same process, while other times it is separate but ties into the process. Also, some companies have additional or other forms of reviews such as 360 and peer reviews, so that not only does a manager review her employee, but an employee also can review his manager, and/or multiple people are reviewing multiple people (customers can even be included in the process) to get a broader range of inputs. There are pros and cons to each, and you likely already have one in place with which to work and that is mandated by your human resources department.

HOW SALESPEOPLE ARE PAID

Since financial rewards are still always a core component of any plan, how salespeople are paid should take into account many factors. First off, what type of an organization are you? Are you a startup in a growth industry in need of attracting an entire new sales force or an established company in a more mature market with a great deal of existing talent and a cadre of new talent from which to choose? The reality is that there are many ways to set up a compensation package, and not any single package fits every company.

Some of the most common formats are:

Salary (Base) Only

This is when you pay only a salary to a salesperson and without variable pay (commission or bonus). This is typical of the "maintainer" (the person maintaining the account) and/or when the salesperson is more of a coordinator of a team and is not the initiator and closer of the sale. It is not very common to have a salary-only plan, as typically salespeople are involved to some extent in increasing business through opening new accounts or building existing ones, and would therefore require some form of variable pay based on their performance.

Commission (Variable or Incentive Pay) Only

This is the other extreme from a salary-only plan. Here the salesperson is paid a commission on the percentage of revenues generated. Also, the commission can be derived not just as a flat percentage of revenues but also might include other variables such as profit margins, number of units sold, or other factors. Furthermore, the payout can vary and have what are known as "accelerators" or "decelerators," whereby the percentage goes up or down with increased volume. It is important to pay commissions as frequently as possible in order to further drive results. Commission-only plans are more common when the salesperson acts very independently and the consummation of the sale relies on her almost entirely. "Gogetters," those salespeople who go out and get the new business, would often fit into this category. Typically this type of salesperson is willing to take on a great deal of risk with the intention of benefiting from a high upside potential. Like salary-only plans, commission-only plans are not the norm either.

Salary Plus Commission

Some type of mix between salary and commissions is typical in the sales arena today. Here the salesperson receives a base pay for his work in maintaining accounts and conducting other non-revenue generating activities, but he is also compensated through commissions for generating additional business. The mix can vary from anywhere from a high base with limited commission potential to a very low base with a very high commission potential.

Salary Plus Bonus

A salary-plus-bonus system is very similar to a salary-plus-commission type of comp strategy. The main delineation is that a bonus typically signifies a percentage of the salary (as opposed to a percentage of sales) that will be given based on achieving the predetermined objectives. The minor difference from that of the commission program is that the salesperson under most bonus plans typically has a lesser degree of influence on the sale. As in the commission program, the payout could accelerate or decelerate; however, it would be based on salary percentage and not revenue, profits, or other volume factors.

Draw

A draw is another form of salary. In this case the company loans or advances the employee the money, and the employee repays it out of future earnings. In most cases this is a legally binding loan owed to the company. There are other types of draw structures stipulating that if the employee does not earn enough to repay the loan, the loan is forgiven. They are often used to help ramp up a new employee where sales potential seems very likely.

Of course some plans combine all three of the major elements- base, commission, and bonus. Also, some plans start off with a higher base and then it is lowered over time as the salesperson gets up to speed and the higher commissions start to kick in. Whatever the specifics of the plan are, make sure it is clear to all parties involved. An overcomplicated plan can only detract from its original purpose. If goals and objectives are clear, your staff will know where they stand at any point.

A note about caps: Putting a cap on the payout to salespeople should generally be avoided. After all, a more driven salesperson can be to everyone's benefit. However, although it might sound somewhat harsh, the sales staff works for the company and not the other way around. So if there are certain controls that need to be put in place, in order to not give away the ranch should a major unexpected order come to fruition, then by all means do so. This is why some companies or industries favour a bonus over commission variable pay, as it helps to mitigate this type of risk. Besides growth versus mature industry, several other factors go into deciding on the best suited strategies for an organization:

Competition: What are they doing? How do they compensate their salespeople? Again, always strive to have the best comp package in your industry.

Consultative Sale Versus More Transactional: How much impact does each person have on the actual sale versus account maintenance and administrative duties? Typically the more involvement in the actual sales process, the higher the variable pay compared to straight salary.

Length of Sales Cycle: This can vary greatly by industry. For example, is your business selling airplanes (an extremely high-ticket, long-term sale) or are you a wholesaler of consumer products? In the case of the former, it is difficult to commission on such a long-term, complex sale with purchases in the hundreds of millions of dollars.

Type of Salesperson: Different people should be compensated in different ways depending on their involvement and direct ties to the sales process. For example, a sales coordinator should not have the same compensation structure as an account executive.

Length of Service: This is one of many specific factors relating to individual team members. A salesperson can have a more advantageous comp package due to their years with the company (or years of experience for a recently hired salesperson).

Size of Territory: The package can vary depending on the geographic area or other territory distribution. If it is a larger, more challenging territory, then compensate for it.

Type of Account: Some companies have a different set up for what they classify as major accounts, so the comp package for them can vary as well.

Team Selling: Even in a true team selling environment, it is likely that team members have very different roles. Again, the variable part of their pay should vary according to their closeness to the actual sale.

The Role of Other Departments: This is perhaps one of the trickiest parts of sales compensation planning. The best organizations tie compensation plans corporatewide.

Remember, "People will do what they are paid to do." Then, depending on how closely tied to the sales process they are, they should share in the rewards to some extent. One final note of clarification: If someone is doing the same thing as someone else with the same amount of experience, pay him accordingly. That is what differentiates them, and the one who performs better will then earn more. However, if circumstances are different and you decide that warrants a different approach, then change it. Keep in mind again that it cannot be discriminating in any way to one or more of the employees. You will find that while many companies have different structures for different employees, you must always err on the side of caution.

Again, there are many structures for the compensation plan to follow. The key is that whichever one your company has chosen or is in the process of working on, it needs to be administered effectively. The plan should always take into account both attracting and retaining the best salespeople. A good plan should get the best to rise to the top, and the weakest links will be exposed. It will also take into account both the veterans and the newbies.

Finally, make sure the plan is fair to all. A plan that plays favourites might benefit some and not others, thus only serving part of its purpose. This is not to mention the fact that certain parts of the plan could end up being not only unfavourable but also illegal.

BENEFITS AND THE TOTAL COMPENSATION PACKAGE

Remember that the total package does not only consist of salary, commissions, and bonuses. The benefits that your company offers can greatly enhance (or reduce) the total value of your comp plan. In fact, in many ways they all have a financial component to them. While you do not directly take advantage of all of them, those that the company does offer are costing the company money to service and administer. Some of the benefits companies make available are:

- Health Insurance. Medical, dental, eye care (typically at some cost to the employee).
- Life Insurance/Disability Insurance.
- 401(k) plan. Some companies will match up to a certain percentage of what you contribute.
- Stock Options.
- Vacation Pay/Sick Pay.
- Child Care. Some companies even have facilities on the premises.

- Company Vehicle/Auto Allowance. More common with salespeople and in certain industries.
- Flexible Health Care Spending/Commuter Reimbursement. These are where a portion of your salary is put aside before taxes for you to then get reimbursed upon usage.

NONFINANCIAL INCENTIVES-REWARDS AND RECOGNITION

As mentioned earlier, you can energize employees in countless ways. This can be either via monetary or nonmonetary rewards and incentives. The balance of this chapter deals with low- or no-cost ways to reward and recognize your employees. Keep in mind as you go through these ideas and examples that the only thing holding you back is your imagination. Nonfinancial compensation typically falls into two main categories-recognition and rewards. Due to the fact that there is so much crossover between the two, we will categorize them by cost and time to implement, starting with easy to implement, small-ticket ideas.

Praise (recognition) is the most undervalued reward. As the expression goes, "a little praise can go a long way." There are so many things to recognize someone for. It can be something as large as landing that big deal or as small as getting that first face-to-face appointment. It does not have to tie directly into sales results, either. For example, you can praise someone for helping you configure a report or making a nice internal presentation.

No-Cost Ways to Praise:

- A kind word/short note
- Congratulations in a team or corporate meeting
- Recognition as "Employee of the Month"
- Recognition on the corporate intranet or in a company newsletter

Low-Cost Rewards

- Give an achievement award.
- Award a certificate of excellence for something the employee accomplished.
- Award time off. This one can be tricky and should always be done in coordination with your human resources department, as company policy may dictate how this works and if it is even allowed.

Give a dinner for two at a nice restaurant, a Rs. 100 gift certificate to a department store, or tickets to a concert or other event.

WORK ITSELF AS A REWARD

As you have seen, some people feel recognized by just getting more new responsibilities. Of course, this needs to be new and exciting work. One way is to assign someone to a special cross-functional task force (one that high profile would be even better). Empowerment, or letting an employee take the lead in something, can be a great reward. This not only gets your team to notice her-making her feel good in the presence of her peers-but could also give her more visibility among others, including managers and senior management.

In many cases, promotion is the ultimate recognition for a job well done. Of course, this is usually coupled with financial benefits. Taking this one step further, not only is more responsibility and an actual promotion a motivator, but so is a career track. When allowing employees to see the future within the company, they can feel they are working toward something long-term. Provide training in the areas that not only you feel they need, but also that they want. In fact, to many, a training program in and of itself is a reward. This could hold especially true for the Theoreticals, who are constantly striving for more knowledge.

REWARD PROGRAMS REQUIRING MORE TIME, MONEY, AND PLANNING

Sales Contests

Sales contests are a great way to boost sales. They are especially useful when a particular type of product/service needs that extra push. The key to remember with sales contests is that they work best for short-term sales results. Also, don't implement them too frequently.

The prize for winning a sales contest can be anything from a small gift to an extravagant trip. Trips are typically in the form of a trip for the individual (or with a guest), or companies sometimes have more elaborate programs where multiple winners take part. For example, the winners go to a resort where they can network with their peers and enjoy the atmosphere and festivities.

Sales Meetings

Sales meetings are often used to build up your staff. There are two types of sales meetings. One is the sales update meeting (typically either biweekly or monthly), and the other is the large team meeting (usual either annual or semiannual). Both are great venues to recognize and reward individuals or the group. In the larger meeting, there is the added benefit of time (they can last anywhere from a day to a week) so that sales training sessions, team-building exercises, motivational speakers, and other activities can all be incorporated.

Expense Management

Since salespeople generally have a higher amount of expenses than many other business professionals, it can be important to help manage this. In fact, there are ways to actually reward salespeople for how well they keep expenses in check. Some companies have been so creative as to have set up contests to see who manages such expenses as airfares and dining the best.

Some additional considerations:

Think of the Individual: Remember, someone who places a high value on Social might be motivated by getting extra time off to volunteer. However, an Economic might be just looking for the financial reward and put less value, if not a negative value, on the other types of rewards.

No to Public Recognition: While not common with salespeople, it is possible that someone does not want to be recognized publicly. It could just plain embarrass him, and it would go a longer way to recognize him one-on-one. Again, take the person into account.

Teams Need Recognition, Too: Since your salespeople are probably not working in isolation and are often part of a larger group effort, team recognition and rewards could be desirable to many. After all, some people feel very comfortable in a team environment and want to see their colleagues shine as well.

Think Out of the Box: Since what energizes one person might demotivate another, it's all the more reason that when you are not exactly sure what is motivational to whom, you should mix things up. Besides, doing the same thing over and over will likely start to bore your staff. And by far the most creative way to determine what potentially helps motivate someone? Just ask him or her.

Don't Skimp: Whether it is a T-shirt or a free sales trip, the reward will lose its importance if you cut too many corners. For example, if it is a team trip to Orlando, make sure the expenses cover what is customary for such a trip. If you book in July and eliminate alcoholic beverages and any recreation, you could have more disappointment than if you had not offered the trip at all. So if cost containment is key, rethink the type of reward.

Don't Make a Reward a Punishment: Similarly, if your annual sales meeting is in a resort destination, let the staff enjoy some of it. Don't schedule meeting after meeting until all hours. There's nothing worse than looking out at a golf course all day and then having time to tee off only when it gets dark.

Consistency: Similar to compensation, rewards and recognition must not unfairly play favourites. Rather, it should be based on specific evidence of achievement, however small or grandiose that may be.

Make It Fun: If you give a gift, don't just buy something boring that's a safe bet. Think about what your team members might really like. It could be more interesting items like a new gadget, luxury goods, personal care items, and so on. After all, if you are trying to motivate, it is not always just "the thought that counts." You might even be able to inconspicuously poke around for ideas first. In the end it shows that you went that extra mile.

Tapping into internal motivators is one of the keys to success for any manager, both today and in the future. It is also a skill that you can carry with you wherever you are in your career. Remember, it is not about what inspires you, but what inspires them. In the next chapter (on training, coaching, and counselling), you will see many areas where motivation is important, and how this knowledge can make you a better manager. As a manager, it is in your hands to get the most out of your staff, and by following many of these techniques, what you will get in return is the best from them.

Note: Packaging Corporation of America (PCA) is a producer of containerboard and corrugated packaging products. It also produces special design application boxes used in the food and agriculture industry. The company operates primarily in the US. It is headquartered in Lake Forest, Illinois and employed 8,100 people. For further knowledge regarding this chapter reader can visit www.packagingcorp.com

14

Training, Coaching, and Counselling

The topics in this chapter are all paramount to the sales manager's career. In fact, similar to communication skills and motivation, these skills are applicable to any position in management, so they will benefit you as you advance up the management ranks. It is also important to realize that while certain theories, skills, and techniques apply specifically to training, coaching, or counselling, there is also a great deal of crossover. You will find that right off the bat you are charged with some of each, depending on the person and the circumstances.

You will begin by looking at the area of training, which then directly ties in to coaching. Then we'll cover the topic of counselling and special circumstances including legal issues.

METHODS OF TRAINING BASED ON LEARNING STYLES

Every one of us has the ability to acquire information, store information, and call on that knowledge at any time. This ability is generated by a combination of factors unique to each of us. In the past, many teachers and trainers had limited their instruction to a traditional method of telling you something and hoping that you then absorbed that information.

Today, training is a far cry from that old method. The days of sitting in long lectures are being replaced by an array of new adult learning techniques. Before delving into core training methods, it is important to understand how we learn.

THE FOUR LEVELS OF AWARENESS

The way we learn is a process of four stages: unconscious incompetent, conscious incompetent, conscious competent, and unconscious competent.

Unconscious Incompetent

This is when someone does not know that a particular behavior, piece of knowledge, or skill exists. For example, a child too young to write may not be aware that the writing skill, exists. You might not have the skill nor be aware of it, or it is possible that you might just deny its importance or usefulness.

Conscious Incompetent

This is when someone realizes that he does not possess a specific skill set. This person might then decide to seek out this knowledge or not. Assuming it is a necessary skill you will hopefully be inclined to learn the skill to improve yourself.

Conscious Competent

This is when someone knows a particular skill, but must think about that skill in order to accomplish the behavior or activity. She might not require assistance, but more repetition and practice are still necessary to fully develop the skill. This is often a difficult level to fully surpass, as certain skills require a great deal of time to master.

Unconscious Competent

This is when a person does not stop to think about a particular skill. She is able to do it automatically. It is what is often called "second nature." She may not even realize that she is doing it nor how to explain it to others. Each of these levels could pertain to any one of us at any given time, depending on the circumstances. At the same time you could be at the unconscious competence level and then a particular related skill is brought into the picture and throws you back a stage or two. As a new manager, you are learning certain skills that you did not even know existed, as well as handling tasks and accomplishing certain things with ease. While the topic of training is primarily about improving the skills of your staff, you must first understand the basic training methods, and how and when to apply them. It is also your responsibility to continually move your staff forward in the learning stages.

MULTIPLE LEARNING STYLES

The human brain has a tremendous capacity to multitask. Therefore, we are able to learn and be at different levels of awareness for different things all at the same time. The ways that we get people to learn will vary, and there are a plethora of tools to make this happen. Today, the emphasis is on the receiver of the information or a learner-focused environment. Learner intake can be done via stimulus impacting any of the five senses (hearing, feeling, sight, smell, taste). The three traditional learner intake styles are depicted in figure below:

- Auditory
- Kinesthetic
- Visual

The other two-olfactory (smell) and gustatory (taste)-are not as important in the types of training you will be involved in. As it relates to the primary styles, some learn by using auditory skills that enable them to process information that is heard. Others like being part of the experience, feeling, touching, or working with a product or service. Still others prefer to use their sight to process information being provided to them. Of course, we all can learn by using a combination, but typically one style of learning is most suited to us and provides the best environment for us to learn.

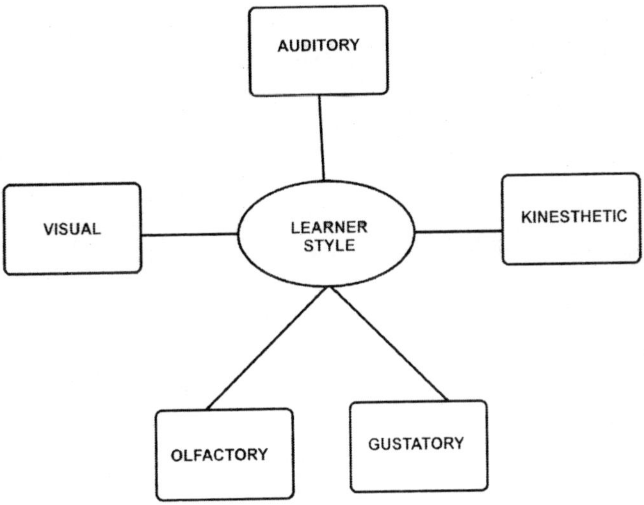

AUDITORY

Auditory learners gain knowledge through hearing. The interpersonal intelligence is extremely important since auditory learners like to have someone "talk them through it." They prefer listening to a tape instead of reading a book. The auditory learner will remember what is said over what was seen.

Auditory learners might expose their style by frequently saying things like "I am listening to you" or "That sounds good."

Ways to help train the Auditory:

- Converse with him often.
- Give presentations (more lecture style).
- Allow time for Q&A after a presentation.
- Ensure a conducive setting for open discussions and dialogue.
- Provide tapes or videos whenever possible.

KINESTHETIC

Kinesthetic learners are sometimes called tactile or physical learners. They absorb information through moving, doing, and touching. Kinesthetic learners will think best as they are pacing. They have a tendency to gesture frequently or have exaggerated facial expressions during conversations. Kinesthetic learners can remember subjects or locations best when they have had a lot of involvement with the subject and spent time at the subject's location. For example, the kinesthetic learner would tend to be field-dependent. They prefer to learn in the contextual environment. Field trips, hands-on experiments, and real-life applications are most important. Kinesthetic learners want to try it first, then read about what they just did. Textbooks and lectures are of limited value.

They might express their preferred style by asking to participate in a demonstration.

Ways to help train the Kinesthetic:

- Paint mental pictures.
- Use metaphors.
- Show videotaped demonstrations of a subject.
- Observe or participate in role-playing.
- Allow them to work on flipcharts.
- Ask them to imitate or practice something.

VISUAL

The visual learner processes information through seeing. Visuals like to follow the pictures and read the directions. They prefer art to music. They might memorize through visual associations. The visual learners tend to accept things for how they look. They may buy something based on how it looks, even if they don't fully understand its applications. Visual learners can learn in a flexible environment. Noise is usually not a distraction. The exception to their flexibility is someone in their space or blocking their view. Employees might offer clues as to their learning style by looking for more descriptive examples of the subject matter being presented. Ways to help train the Visual:

- Use colourful and visually appealing presentations.
- Handouts and overheads are desirable.
- Provide charts, learning maps, posters, etc.
- Have them take notes on a subject being taught (the act of writing it down can be useful).

The objective is to expose the new salesperson to as many of the techniques as possible to ensure that what you are training is compatible with the salesperson's learning style. You can also look for other clues in advance from the salesperson as well. For example, the better presenters and public speakers on your team will tend to be more auditory learners. And those that tend to explain things to others by allowing them to fully participate in the learning are likely more kinesthetic themselves.

It is also helpful to think in terms of personal styles (DISC) when training. For example, if the employee is a High "C" (Contemplative), it will be best to train him using concise, detailed data, attempting to fill in all of the pieces of the puzzle. A High "D" (Directive) might be more impatient and just want the core information, not all of the explanation around it.

Furthermore, some prefer a slower pace, allowing for more time to absorb all of the information; moving too fast could overwhelm them. Also, keep in mind that within each style of learning there are those who prefer to work independently and those who prefer to learn more in a group setting. Therefore, it is always good to mix up the amount of interaction (i.e., individual learning, group in pairs, team learning, and so on). Also, don't forget one of the best but most often underutilized ways of discovering a preferred style-to ask!

We have all been trained over the years, and many of us already know what style we prefer, at what pace we like to learn, and in what type of setting, so why fight it? If you are already training someone on something that is potentially a weakness, why make it that much more difficult? It can only lead to more frustration on the part of the learner. With this knowledge, it is up to you to try to work into your sales training various methods of the three learner intakes, deciding when and with whom to provide these different approaches-sight (visual), sound (auditory), or more hands-on (kinesthetic).

THE CORE CONCEPTS OF REINFORCEMENT

Now that you have some basis for how people learn best, it is important to couple this with behaviors that promote and support the training. Behavioralist B.F. Skinner (1904-1990) was a pioneer in the subject of reinforcement, and his theories form the basis of much of the work and techniques used today.

- Reinforcer. Any stimulus affecting the individual that he seeks to experience.
- Aversive Stimulus. Any stimulus affecting the individual that she seeks to avoid.

In the work setting, for most people, reinforcers and aversive stimuli usually come from the behavior of other people. Examples of this are as follows:

Reinforcer	*Aversive Stimuli*
Praise	Inconsiderate treatment
Recognition	Reprimands
Attention	Being ignored
Being liked	Being mocked
Understanding	Criticism

Also, what may be reinforcing to some people may indeed be an aversive stimulus to another. For example, as you recall from the topic of motivation, some people enjoy a great deal of public recognition. However, some find that type of recognition embarrassing. Supervision is another example. Oversupervision on a project may demoralize the individual attempting to complete a certain task. Remember some of those traits of a micromanager? On the other hand, there are those that prefer a certain amount of supervision, and it could be an aversive stimulus if they are not being paid attention to.

PAIRING

Any stimulus can become a reinforcer or aversive stimulus through pairing. By this we mean that something like praising can become aversive by pairing it with criticism. For example, "That was a good job you did creating that sales proposal, Fred, but why did it take so long to get the printing done?" As a manager, it is up to you to get to the bottom of what is affecting your salespeople, both negatively and positively. You may find that a salesperson has been avoiding a certain customer because that customer is aversive to the salesperson. Recognizing that information about the salesperson could help you think of certain areas of training that will hopefully offset the avoidance behavior.

For example, it could be that the person is always trying to present new products when a needs analysis has not even taken place yet, and this is turning the customer off. In this case, more training on how to probe and ask discovery questions to get to the customer's pain points might be helpful, and then the presentation can follow. You could also find that just by getting more involved with the salesperson and understanding his challenges, you are providing reinforcing stimuli.

Therefore, it is important to recognize on an individual basis what is reinforcing and what is aversive to that individual. Attention must be focused on the individual's action or reaction to any outside influences that seem to be affecting her in a reinforcing or aversive manner.

PRINCIPLES OF REINFORCEMENT

Any response followed by a reinforcer has a higher probability of occurrence in the near future.

This means that it is important to catch people doing things right and then recognizing that activity. When recognizing people for doing things right, be specific in describing the correct behavior. Tell them exactly what they did right and why it was right. Conversely to what some novice managers think, encouraging employees and telling them what a good job they did will not make them lazy or overconfident but rather sets the stage for them to continue with the positive behavior.

However, a negative action can also be reinforced. For example, consider the person in a meeting who complains about everything. That person is usually reinforced by attention. When you allow that person to dominate the floor or constantly recognize her, you have reinforced the complaining, and the behavior will continue. One option here is to just ignore it. Of course, a deeper behavioral issue might need to be addressed directly with her in a more appropriate setting. We discuss this in greater detail later in the section "Coaching and Counselling."

Any response not followed by a reinforcer has a lower probability of occurrence in the future.

Assuming for a moment, that a certain salesperson has excellent presentation skills. When observing him making sales presentations, the manager forms a positive impression but for whatever reason says nothing about the positive behavior (as in complimenting or congratulating him on a job well done). After a while, there will probably be a slight drop in the efficiency of that salesperson's presentation skills. This could be because the salesperson feels that either his presentation skills are not important or his skills are not actually very good. Neither assumption by the salesperson is accurate, but could, unfortunately, be the end result. Again, holding back on praise is not the answer.

Any behavior followed by an aversive stimulus has a lower probability of occurrence in the future.

In one example, a salesperson who complains constantly about other employees can be told that talking about others behind their backs is not constructive, and, in turn, he takes on a more positive outlook. Another example would be ideas that are given to management that are completely ignored, which could reduce the odds of additional new ideas being presented-two completely different stimuli, the latter of course being a result that was not intended.

To decrease the probability of a behavior controlled by a reinforcer, pair the reinforced behavior with an aversive stimulus.

Let's return to the example whereby a salesperson likes to be center stage because he finds recognition in meetings reinforcing. On a one-on-one basis, the person is told that other people in the group find this to be disruptive and unproductive and that if he continues in this fashion that he will not be included in future meetings. An aversive stimulus (taking away recognition) was paired to what that person considered a reinforcer (attention in meetings, even though the attention was negative). In turn, that threat of no attention at all will decrease the probability of the disruptive behavior occurring in the future.

Now consider the salesperson who reaches 150 percent of his quota only to be told that the quota "must have been too soft." The odds of that salesperson reaching this high a percentage of his quota again will be reduced. Here the unintended result could be taking away some of the motivation or foundation previously built up.

To decrease the response controlled by an aversive stimulus, pair that aversive stimulus with a reinforcer.

Because many managers have been programmed to catch people doing things wrong, those managers have a tendency to become an aversive stimulus to the salespeople. In order to provide reinforcing stimulus to these people, managers must focus their attention on reinforcing behaviors. Again, the simplest way to do this is to not only catch people doing things right, but also by make it known at the right moment.

Here it is important to note that timing of the response (or lack of a response) is critical to reinforcement theory. As you know, something can lose its affect with the passing of time. For example, when you find that your salesperson has just done something well, it is better to commend her right after the occurrence as opposed to waiting some time. Also, not just the length of time, but the amount of times, can affect this as well. Reinforcing someone one time and then not doing so on subsequent instances can turn into an aversive stimuli.

Giving feedback or criticism is one of the more challenging areas for a manager. However, keep in mind that when criticism is presented in what is perceived to be a positive way, it can actually become constructive and productive.

Take the following example:

Manager: On that last call, you positioned the third benefit in a negative way. If you reword your approach, it will be even more effective. I know you can do that because the rest of the presentation was done very well. Similar to this, remember that you hold the keys to turning around a negative sentiment and making it something more positive.

For example:

Salesperson: Boy, I really messed up that contract with the XYZ account.

Manager: Do you mean the XYZ account in New York? I think they've kept up business well with us, even with the price increases we were forced to pass on to them due to our rising costs in raw materals.

THE PROBLEMS WITH USING AVERSIVE STIMULI

- When people constantly pair themselves with aversive stimuli, they eventually become aversive by reputation.
- Employees withhold information from aversive managers.
- Using aversive stimuli to reduce the probability of an undesirable behavior does not necessarily increase the probability of desirable behavior.

As managers and leaders, it is vital to utilize the correct reinforcers at every possible opportunity. Again, pay attention to when your staff is doing things right, and reinforce that positive behavior. Positive reinforcment can help to improve the environment for the individual to be motivated from within.

REINFORCEMENT IN TRAINING

The rule when training new salespeople is simple: Always use positive reinforcement on positive behaviors. Looking at it another way, never think of punishing someone for something they do not know how to do. Even when making corrections, always finish with a positive.

This gets the salesperson focused on making the correction instead of dwelling on your feedback. In the long run, a series of small positives will add up to a larger positive, and the result will be better performance.

The Development of Winners

Training sometimes appears to be more complicated than what it really is. In fact, training follows a very basic cycle. The objective is always to get to a specific goal of development.

The Training Cycle

- Tell: The first part of the cycle is to tell the individual what should be done and what will be expected, based on a specific standard of performance.
- Show: Demonstrate the procedure or process to them.
- Try: After the demonstration, allow the trainee to try the procedure while being observed.
- Evaluate: While observing performance to evaluate what was learned, focus on functionality and not personality. Evaluate based on the goals.
- Correct: Get the trainee's opinion of the performance. If the trainee did not perform properly but knows it, learning has still taken place. Practice will now improve performance.

Keep in mind that the norm is to start with "Tell." If, however, there is uncertainty as to the trainee's capabilities, it is best to start with "Try." For example, if a person goes to a golf instructor to take golf lessons, one of the first things the instructor will do is to ask the person to hit a few balls on the driving range. Once the instructor has observed and evaluated the person, she can now correct, and the cycle continues.

The New Team Member

Rarely is any direct stair-step approach or system found in dealing with human behavior, Developing winners will still follow a very distinct pattern. Some people will move faster than others, but all go through certain phases. Of course, a new hire will have his own distinct challenges, which could include the following:

- Learning about the products/services
- Learning about the organization
- Getting to know his colleagues
- Learning about and getting to know the customers
- Learning about the competition
- Learning new systems (CRM, Sales Force Management software, etc.)
- Understanding the business processes and working relationships
- Other

This is a time to really step up as a manager and get involved to make a new hire's training and acclimation to the work environment as smooth as possible. A few suggestions would be:

- Have a plan for her (first day, week, month, quarter, etc.). This doesn't have to necessarily cover all the details of her job, but it should hit most of the core areas.
- Networking. Let him get to know the people he is going to work closest with in a stress-free environment. No need to have someone start in a "trial by fire" atmosphere if it is not necessary. Again, training is tough enough for most people.
- Rotate her about the core departments. If at all possible, let her spend some of those first few weeks meeting and talking about the roles, responsibilities, and challenges in other departments.
- Give him time. While you might operate in a very aggressive sales atmosphere, realize that some people are ready to pound the pavement on day one and others need more time to grasp things. That does not necessarily mean the latter has less potential; it could be just the opposite.

Your Existing Team Players

It is time to look at the level of competency and skills of each individual salesperson. This is where many managers categorize their staff as A, B, and C players (or something similarly straightforward). In a perfect world you would have a team of all A's. However, as you probably realize, that is not the case. You likely have a staff that fits into a classic type of curve:

A Players-Low Percentage

B Players-High Percentage

C Players-Low Percentage

If your systems are properly in place (especially the sales and comp plan), it should be easy to identify where your team members fall. If not, your job is a bit more challenging. However, you still have the ability and insights to identify those who shine in the field and those who seem to be setting everyone back. Whatever the percentage of each (A, B, C breakdown), the task is the same, to maximize overall productivity. So the critical question is: Where do you spend your time?

If you think back to the basics of time management and prioritizing, it seems intuitive that you would want to focus on the A tasks (then B and, only if time permits, C). This same idea holds true for training your team, with certain exceptions. Another way to think of this is like the 80/20 rule in account management. With your team, you can easily fall into the trap of spending 80 percent of your time with the players that show the least upside potential. Meaning, the incremental gain to focusing on C players is often minimal, whereas the gain by enhanced training of the A ones could be exponential.

The following are some of the common reasons why new managers spend too much time with the C's:

- Productivity is down with the C's.
- The C's are always at your door.
- The A's are rarely at your door.
- The star players intimidate you.
- If it isn't broke, don't fix it (A's).
- Poor time management.

All of these reasons in a way lend themselves to why you should spend more time with your stars and less with those that are tying up all of your time with little gain. Now that you have some tools in place to better manage your time and ways to increase motivation in your team, it is time to focus your attention on those who will benefit you the most. Sure, training your best producer might seem awkward at first, and you will likely get some resistance, but it could be more advantageous than focusing on all those C players combined. Here is an example the typical A verses C upside potential.

Revenues/Past 3 Years	*3 Years Ago*	*2 Years Ago*	*1 Year Ago*	*This Year*
Top	1,350,000	1,300,000	1,275,000	1,400,000
C Producers	1,000,000	975,000	1,110,000	1,220,000

In this not so uncommon example, by providing the right training to your star, you have increased her sales by 10 percent. While working with the few C players you manage, sure you have also increased sales by 10 percent, but it took up a significantly greater piece of your time compared to working on maybe one or two extra skill enhancements your star player was missing. Also, you will notice in this scenario that the top producers' performance (or at least revenues) was deteriorating slightly year over year. This could relate back to the reinforcement examples discussed; a lack of the right stimuli under the right circumstances will only set them back. Even someone who by all appearances wants to be left alone has internal motivators that can be tapped into and deficiencies in certain skills.

One particular situation you might find is that your A players give off the impression that they are very engaged and eager to learn and participate. While this might be the case, it can actually be a smokescreen. For example, they might be eager to communicate with you and others and flex their own muscles or brag about their successes. Their confidence can put a new manager on the defensive, feeling uncomfortable approaching them for training. Well, you will at some point need to approach these top performers, similar to colleagues who have been your friends. And just like in these other unique situations, if you do so in as objective a manner as possible, focusing on goals (theirs, yours, and the organization's), you will be able to make these breakthroughs.

Now for an important caveat. While there are certainly those A's who deserve your attention, there are going to be B's and even some C's that have a great deal of upside potential as well. This is where your job can get even more intricate, identifying the right internal motivators and types of training necessary and then getting a sense of how valuable this could prove to be. This is where you need to be sure to identify all the strengths and weaknesses of each of your team members. You can then conduct a gap analysis and see where your most likely benefits can come from. For example, if you determine a weakness in a solid B performer getting referrals, you can determine how far off he is from really grasping this art and then map out the appropriate training to get him there. Or if more praise or recognition is what a C player needs, you might find that this alone can dramatically change her eagerness to perform. The golden rule-like they say about picking stocks in the market, "the upside gains need to outweigh the downside potential." As you can imagine, an eager salesperson is still just a starting point. In order to take her to the next level, she needs skills, and training is the way to make this happen. Also, keep in mind that you can train in many areas, but the primary ones that will impact performance relate back to those skills that make up the exceptional sales professional-communication skills, business acumen, technical knowledge, and market experience.

Through your efforts, a salesperson needs to possess two things:

- The necessary skills and knowledge (four categories)
- A motivational foundation that will drive her forward

If she is low in both, she will of course require more guidance in both. If she is high in one-say, skills and knowledge-but the motivational factors are not there, then you will need to work on the environmental ones.

If he has the motivational factors but not the skills and knowledge, then of course you will need to work on the latter. However, keep in mind that, as we have been discussing, they can both go very much hand in hand. For example, how can you expect someone to be eager to receive more training when he is demotivated? Also, as you have seen, it does not have to be a broad-based motivational issue, but rather one that touches on a particular area that is posing a challenge to the salesperson. In this case, be careful not to push too hard in that area, as the problem could get worse. This is a very difficult level of learning, especially for a new hire. An extreme example is when responsibility after responsibility seem to compound themselves, and then the realization strikes that the job or position is far more complicated than originally thought. All the information that has been given during the earlier learning phases has now become scrambled. The employee's confidence level drops. He questions his own ability to handle what he thought looked very attainable in the interview.

This is when you need to slow down the information flow while at the same time building esteem and self-assurance. One useful way to build up confidence without overwhelming the salesperson is to get her more involved in the decision making. If the salesperson can do just a small piece of a project or new task well, let her do it. While something may seem insignificant to you, it could actually be significant to the trainee.

For example, if an important report is due immediately, let the trainee help with the design. Although the content of that report may be significant, the design or outline (although an integral part) is probably not as significant. Even if the salesperson's input into the design is small, if it is remotely close to something you can use, you should consider it. This will allow him to feel part of the report and at the same time have his confidence bolstered by your willingness to give him credit.

The trainee will be able to learn about the report more quickly because he is involved and because he feels appreciated and that his input is valued. Also, how a salesperson responds to a particular activity is typically based on her past training as well as other, sometimes tricky to identify, factors. Your staff might avoid activities for several reasons:

- It could be a behavior conflict- high D's don't like paperwork.
- It could be a value conflict-learning a computer spreadsheet program doesn't relate directly to selling.
- It could also be a lack of proper reinforcement on the manager's part. A particular report may sit on the your desk for several weeks before being read, and therefore the salesperson assumes it's not important to you. Here you could be inadvertently reinforcing a laissez-faire attitude. After all, why should the salesperson care about the report if you don't seem to?

This can only be compounded if you were the one to initially ask for the report and stress its importance. While some of these examples have demonstrated subtle ways of changing behaviors, reprimands are often more direct. An important note regarding reprimands: Always remember that reprimands must be saved for people who absolutely know what they are doing, but who are not doing it or not doing it well. Do not use reprimands for people who do not know what their job is or how to do a specific function of that job. Even if they know how to do it, make sure you have tried to motivate them and that you have worked through the training process carefully before you resort to reprimands.

A final level where a sale person could be is both high in motivation and strong in the necessary skills. Time to let him coast, right? Wrong. If you are working with someone who possesses both the eagerness to produce as well as the skills and knowledge, then your challenge is to keep making both stronger. One caution as it relates to your star players: If as a manager you turn to your thoroughbreds more often, knowing they are the ones to usually come through, the results could ultimately turn into a "piling on" or "dumping" syndrome.

If the workload gets too high, the winners will begin to prioritize their work. That prioritized schedule may or may not be the same priority as yours. If it is not the same-the wrong reinforcers, aversive stimuli-ultimately reprimands often become the result. As the frustration grows in both camps, the high achievers now become less motivated and less eager to perform. The object is to let the winners stay winners. This does not mean that winners are to be ignored. It means to set short-term and long-term objectives, add parameters to any goals, and let the winners take it from there.

Keep in mind that winners, like all of your team members, will always need to improve upon existing skills and learn new ones. It is often a veteran salesperson that is used to the systems in place and prefers the status quo. This new level of training could set her back in this area. The trick is to not let it affect other areas of her work. Remember that if you can keep her moving in the right direction, nothing could be better than a star player exemplifying positive behaviors.

THE CATCH TO TRAINING

There are two distinct challenges with training. The first is recognizing the speed that people take in learning. The second is the fact that one person will be in all four training stages at the same time depending on the skill.

Some people will move faster than others through the training cycle. Again, much of this depends on past experiences. In other words, if people can relate to something, they will absorb it faster. If a job or project is not relative to a past experience, the brain has to search for a place to store or connect that information. That search for relativity takes longer. The answer is to take the time to understand all team members in the interview or goal-setting process. Know what they relate to and give them information during the training cycle that is conducive to their thought process.

The second problem, being in different stages of development at the same time, further complicates your role as trainer. This is a problem eventually because of the negative effect it can have on the salesperson over all.

Let's look at using sales automation software again as a skill. Someone may be excellent with a specific contact management program; however, if a new one is introduced that is mandatory to use, this person will automatically move a step backward. The desire may be there, but the understanding of the new program may not. The new program will not work just like the older one, and if the salesperson is not introduced to it properly, getting to the next stage could be very frustrating. Even worse, the salesperson may develop contempt for it, and maybe even for you. Clearly something that if gone unchecked can hurt you and the rest of the team. At this point, a good idea would be to relate the old program as much as possible to the newer version, highlighting the like features as well as the differences.

As the person relates specific functions old and new, the new program becomes less complicated and the person becomes more comfortable. The salesperson is now accomplished with the new program. It is now time to raise the bar and introduce him to the more advanced features that it offers. Of course, this means going back to the beginning in this area, so you need to start all over with tying in something that will help to motivate him. Happily, the process works. Almost every training demand or problem has a solution. As a sales manager, you take responsibility for the training in order to move all people in the direction of your star performers.

Just imagine an entire staff of winners in all categories. It is now time to focus specifically on one of the major functions of the sales manager: on-the-job training.

JOINT SALES CALLS

As a sales manager, you will likely have to be out in the field making joint sales calls with your salespeople. While your amount of time in the field may vary, the idea is to have your planning and reporting done in such a way that will still provide you with a great deal of time to be out on the road. Many argue over the optimal percentage- 15 percent, 25 percent, 50 percent, or even up to 80 percent of your time-but it is really more dependent on your industry, your specific role, the type of sale, and your staff 's capabilities.

No matter what the target for your time on the road, you will need to look back at the territory plan with your sales team members and make sure that you interweave your own plan, accounting for how your time will be spent. For example, if X sales rep is scheduled to see Q, R, S, and T accounts, then you need to plan accordingly if you are making any or all of these calls jointly. Some of the factors to consider when deciding on whether or not to make a joint sales call are:

- Distance. Is there major travel involved (by rail, cross-country, overseas)?

- Organization of Territory. Is it by geography, where there is a more systematic approach to the visits, or is it more piecemeal, where a route needs to be developed from scratch?
- Rank of Account. What is the overall value of the account (e.g., are they a must-visit or a nice-to-visit only if there is extra time to spare)?
- Importance of the Sales Call. At what stage is the customer in the sales cycle?
- Players Involved. Will the account have multiple contacts at the meeting, and are there other players from your company that are needed (e.g., technical specialist, financial specialist, etc.)?
- Extenuating Circumstance. Is the salesperson having big problems with a key account or has a recent development just lifted an account from a Low to a High Value status?

Once you have laid out your own plan, there are several rules (do's and don'ts) to follow when making the joint sales call. Far too often, the problem that many sales managers have is the urge to take over the sales call. When a manager sees a salesperson starting to lose ground, jumping in to try and save the day is what most managers believe is their role; however, it is often the worst thing you can do.

The rule in field sales training is to train during the "routine" calls. Do not set up on-the-job-training for must-get orders, dropin/ unannounced calls, or even emergencies (which may be necessary but are not part of training). Give the salesperson plenty of warning that you will be riding along. One argument for short notification is that you can catch her off guard and see what she is really doing when you are not looking.

The problem with that argument is twofold:

- If she does not perform well, you cannot be sure if the reason is because of your unexpected presence or not.
- It sets up a level of distrust or unnecessary anxiety in the salesperson.

Others might still argue that if you give the salesperson plenty of notice, a "milk run" of the best customers could be set up. In other words, he knows the accounts where he has the soundest relationships and could steer you toward making joint calls to those accounts. Keep in mind that if the salesperson takes you to what he considers to be his best accounts, issues will still surface, especially with a B or C performer. They may not be glaring, but they will exist.

Therefore, if you give the salesperson plenty of notice and the performance is lacking or subpar, you will now be able to specifically target areas for improvement.

CHOREOGRAPHING THE JOINT SALES CALL

Each call should be well planned. According to the experience level of the salesperson and the particular circumstances of the call, establish a leadership role. The general rule is that the salesperson should be the leader whenever possible. This can only help her confidence and increase her credibility with the customer in the long run. Of course, as a sales manager, you will inevitably have those really struggling team members where a routine sales call is never routine. This could also be the case with a new hire, who at some point needs to get his feet wet. Barring these two cases, the leader's job is also to decide who is going to do what during the call. For example, the leader can decide who will handle the product features part of the call versus the pricing and terms.

As a sales manager, once your plan is determined, you must stick to it. Do not jump in or interrupt unexpectedly, do not correct (unless, of course, a critical error was made), do not let the salesperson give it back to you, and do not take over the call. If the salesperson falters, you can train after the call. Again, the idea is that together you have selected accounts and situations where the out-come is not highly at risk. By trying to take over the sales call, you not only lose out on valuable training needs, but it could possibly end up hurting the customer relationship with you and/or the salesperson.

If, as part of the plan, you have already established that you can step in from time to time to clarify information, a great way to be in sync is to establish subtle signals. By tapping on his notepad, for example, the salesperson could indicate to the manager that her help is needed here, or, in the event that you have already stepped in, that it is time to give back the floor to the salesperson. Another approach is for the salesperson to finish whatever he is saying and then turn to you to ask, "Is there anything you want to add?" Again, after adding or clarifying anything, turn the call back over to the salesperson.

After the call (yet before the next call on your schedule), coach the salesperson using the reinforcement techniques and techniques given based on the training stage she is in. If you find that the training points you wish to discuss will require a great deal of time and effort, you could wait until the end of the day to review. However, if at all possible, never wait longer than that. Remember, delayed feedback can only increase anxiety on the part of the salesperson. As soon as you can, reinforce what the salesperson did right first. Then you can seek to correct what the person did wrong. After that, always finish up with another positive. You will also want to establish a follow-up time to ride with the salesperson again. Here you might want to have the salesperson plan accounts that will allow practice and demonstration of what was learned and hopefully improved on from the previous call. Again, this can only help to set her up for success.

To summarize, before training people, managers need to know how to transfer information in an efficient manner. Knowing a person's learning style allows you to take into account where he is in the learning cycle and apply the training accordingly. Reinforcement must be properly used to help bolster confidence and self-esteem. The learner must also be eager to learn (motivational environment) and then will need to possess those skills and knowledge necessary for success. Always remember that people can be in different stages based on different skills and activities, and it is your job to go at the appropriate pace with each individual to ensure that they are moving in the right direction.

Some key ideas to keep in mind:

- Train based on the learning styles.
- Always reinforce positive behavior.
- Train at a level and pace where transference can take place.
- Work through the learning cycle; do not skip steps.
- Guide your staff through stages of training.
- Ultimately you will generate winners.
- End the day with a stronger team than you began with.

COACHING AND COUNSELLING

While we have separated much of the theory and practice of training from coaching and counselling, there is also a great deal of crossover. In fact, the whole category of on-the-job training (making joint sales calls) is often called "sales coaching." One way to think of it is that during the entire process you are acting as a sales coach, whereas the specific skills that are taught before, during, and after the sales call is the training.

Furthermore, there is also a fine line between coaching and counselling. The line here is between functionality and motivation. If a person has no knowledge or only partial knowledge of a particular job function, then that person needs to be coached toward competency. On the other hand, if that same person knows how to perform a particular job function and is just not doing so, there is another issue. This issue could range from a simple motivational one to a more complex one where counselling needs to take place.

Another way to look at it is that coaching has to do with the performance and the standards set, and counselling has to do with a problem that is affecting the employee and that could be affecting others as well.

For the most part, they can both be looked at through the process of goal-setting. Because, as you have seen, in the absence of goals, you have nothing to be working toward.

GOAL-SETTING SESSIONS

There are six basic steps to developing specific goals for your team members.

1. Set your own goals.
2. Set the stage.
3. Get opinions and facts.
4. Relate your opinion and facts.
5. Develop specific goals with specific plans (together).
6. Follow up.

Understanding the importance of these steps is key to being able to carry them out effectively. In both motivation and training you learned that it is necessary to develop salespeople in a way that will allow them to be motivated from within, thus maximizing their capabilities. Goal setting is often a core building block in this process.

Goal-setting sessions are a key component to coaching your team. They should be positive and growth-oriented. Design them to help people develop in areas of weakness in a win-win environment. Therefore, be sure to not use these sessions to reprimand people, as this will defeat the purpose. As you learned, reprimands do not work when training; save them for those who already have task knowledge and skills and refuse to use that ability to develop the territory or to help the team.

It is your job as a manager to help salespeople develop specific goals with specific plans to achieve them. Many people do not succeed because they do not have a specific goal nor the necessary direction. If you assist your team members in identifying and achieving what they want, in turn you will get what you want.

THE PROCESS

With this purpose in mind, the steps are as follows:

1. Set Your Own Goals

This is the point to develop a strategic direction for the session. The situation may be dealing with a weakness in someone that needs to be strengthened. Another scenario may be to work more with someone who could be developed for a promotion. The goal could be as simple as showing someone how to develop better habits, or the goal may be as complex as helping the salesperson control outbursts of anger.

Whatever the reason, have a specific direction in mind before entering the goal-setting session. However, do not get so locked into your own goals that the individual's needs end up being ignored. In setting your own goals, eliminate personality and deal with functionality. A good way to think of this is to always ask yourself the question of how the goal relates to the job, rather than what is your personal opinion of the individual. It is helpful to keep in mind the person's DISC style and his internal motivators, as you will need to communicate effectively as well as tap into the right motivators along the way.

Plan a meeting date in advance with a mutually convenient time and place so there can be no interruptions. By not allowing interruptions, you're establishing the importance of the session.

Prior to the meeting, review any materials appropriate to the session, including previous meeting information, job description, articles, books, growth areas, etc. Take into account everyone's time. As you know, experienced managers realize the importance of both their time and their sales team's. Often having the goal-setting sessions back-to-back with several people is not the best use of anyone's time. Pick the number of goal-setting sessions per month that you feel comfortable with. For example, if you have a core of six people, you could set time aside for one-hour sessions with each of them. You could then schedule one session every two weeks for twelve weeks in a row. The other benefit to doing this is that managers will get constant feedback from their people. Managers can develop their own coaching skills, and get better at goal setting and planning.

2. Set the Stage

Since these are meant to be growth sessions, the environment should be friendly and non-threatening. The physical surroundings should be professional. Inform the person as to the purpose behind goal setting and how the session will be conducted. Also, stress the importance of the session itself. At the end of the session, put a plan in writing. Taking notes during the discussion has its pros and cons. If you feel you need to take notes in order to keep track of key points, then do so, but keep in mind that it can be distracting and for some might add a level of anxiety.

The first meeting will be slightly different than the subsequent meetings. The first meeting will involve a lot of discussion about goals and performance. Subsequent meetings will likely involve clarification of goals and interim checks.

It is not always necessary to prepare a detailed agenda for each meeting. In fact, in some cases you may not know in advance which skills the employee needs coaching in.

3. Get Opinions and Facts

Find out what the other person is thinking first. This is a two-way conversation that requires reciprocity. In order to know which way to take the goal-setting session, it is important to get further direction relative to the employee. Therefore, often the agenda for the second session will be established at the first, the third session agenda from the second, and so on. Coaching is similar in some ways to the interviewing process. You want to extract a great deal of information from the salesperson.

Ask questions that are open-ended and not leading:

- What do you like about your job?
- Is there anything you would like to change?
- What do you think you do best in your job?
- Where do you feel you would like to develop?
- Ideally, what would you like to be doing?

Generally speaking, the last question will directly relate to what you planned during the first part when setting your own goals for the session. If it doesn't, you need to ask more probing questions. Here again are a few of those core interviewing tips to apply:

- Do not interrupt.
- Do not jump to conclusions.

- Keep an open mind.
- Listen, listen, and listen.

You will find out everything from "I hate to do paperwork" and "I am having trouble with certain customers" to more complex situations like "I don't know if I am cut out for sales" and "I do not like working with X, and something needs to change."

4. Relate Your Opinions and Facts

Review what the person's perception is about personal strengths and weaknesses. Reinforce the positives first. Agreement and recognition of the strong points will aid in the dialogue. On the items where there is no agreement, you need to ask more questions for clarification. Determine whether there's a discrepancy in your perceptions versus the employee's-for example, if the person thinks he does the job well when, according to preestablished standards, he is not doing the job appropriately. You might then need to provide clarification and once again relate everything back to the job description and performance standard in place.

Explain yourself. Any agreement or disagreement should be completely discussed. An honest discussion could reduce a very complicated subject to a simple one. It could also surface much larger, unknown problems that need to be solved immediately. Break the large problems down into smaller ones if necessary. During the explanation, mentally get on the other person's side. Do not attack or try to put someone in the hot seat. On items of disagreement, be direct. Spending too much time posturing will dilute any message and distract from the subject at hand. By being direct you must also be explicit. For example, the word attitude is an example of a term that has a variety of definitions and is used way too liberally by inexperienced managers. In dealing with someone that you feel has an "attitude problem," the first step is to define the behavior that is taking place that is causing that attitude. Definable problems have a much greater chance of being solved than those that are vague. By using more concrete terms and having specific examples or supporting evidence, you'll help to center the discussion around facts and objectivity rather than personality. This will avoid putting someone on the defensive or provoking anxiety, resentment, or even anger.

5. Develop Specific Goals with Specific Plans (Together)

A SMART goal now must be established for the salesperson. And the only way to reach that goal is with a plan. Also, when identifying goals, they could relate to corporate, departmental, and/or personal-level goals. Be sure again to avoid relative terminology. If you ask someone to "communicate better and be more cooperative," you do not have a SMART goal in place. If that salesperson comes back the next day and says a big "good morning" to everyone, who is to say that that does not constitute improved communications?

Most important is the need for the session outcomes to be agreed to jointly. Both parties should know what the objective is and how it relates to job performance. If you cannot do anything to help the salesperson reach that goal, then you might be doing just the opposite. Remember, problems do not typically go away by themselves. Have the salesperson write down the plan that was jointly developed and keep it in a place accessible for her. Then track the daily, weekly, or monthly activities as needed to see that what is being done as it relates to the goals that have been set.

Inspect What Is Expected-Periodic Check-Ins

Be sure to check in as needed, especially on any specific milestones. It shows that you care, and, at the same time, if you don't follow up, it gives the impression that you do not care, or even worse, that it just doesn't matter. Again, keep in mind the balance between checking in and micromanaging. Also, the profoundness of the goal and the employee behavioral pattern may vary, so you may need to act accordingly. For example, checking in on very minor activities can be seen as belittling or condescending to many people. Also, unless you have reason to believe otherwise, there is no reason to not give your staff the benefit of the doubt.

6. Follow Up

The official follow-up should have everything to do with what was done in steps one through five. The major difference is that the first session starts with questions such as: "How do you think you are doing in your job?" and the main question to address in the follow up session is "How did you do against your plan?" Responsibility is directly on the employee's shoulders.

Follow-Up Scenarios

There are three scenarios that can happen at the follow-up session:

1. The employee completed everything to complete satisfaction.
2. The employee partially completed the goals.
3. The employee did nothing.

In the first scenario, the manager should reinforce the success and then move on to the next set of goals. In the second case, the manager needs to probe and investigate. Why did the person not perform to satisfaction? The answers could be:

- Lack of knowledge that would require more training
- Lack of time created by other projects
- Lack of motivation or another more serious problem that might require counselling along with potential consequences

Whatever the reason is, the employee needs to be accountable at some level. Unless you were informed in advance of something unforeseen that impeded her completing the goal (and it was a legitimate reason) or you did not follow through on something that you said that you would do, then it still should be addressed. After all, two-way communication is key, and, assuming you are doing your part, it is incumbent upon the salesperson to communicate openly and accurately as well.

The third scenario mentioned above could be lack of motivation or plain insubordination. This is where the process turns from coaching functionality to counselling motivation. While the six steps could still generally apply as well, they require extra care, and you need to determine how and what your role should be. Some problems are sensitive subjects that you might need to address, such as absenteeism, tardiness, and rude behavior, whereas others can go beyond the scope of your responsibilities and include more than just motivation and minor behavioral issues. No matter how severe you feel the problem might or might not be, it is necessary to first check with your legal and/or human resources department and get their input on how to proceed.

If the problem even remotely seems of a more serious nature, such as some type of psychological dysfunction, the manager's duty is to turn the employee over to a professional at once. These categories would include areas such as:

- Drug or alcohol problems
- Physical threats
- Harassment of any kind
- Signs of abuse

ADDITIONAL LEGAL CONSIDERATIONS

Remember, when in doubt or when something seems like a fine line, err on the side of caution. The information in this book is meant to be a guide and give you many of the core tools to help you succeed. However, it cannot delve into all of the specifics, nor can it stay current nor substitute for the law or your company's policies. Remember, as a sales manager, you have many new responsibilities, and one of them includes getting help when needed.

Of all of the job functions and skills needed as a manager, training and coaching through goal setting are some of the most important and widely used. They are not only something that you should not avoid, but something that you should embrace. Like other skills, they require a great deal of practice, so give yourself some time to allow them to build. This will increase your confidence as well. Also, as you have seen, they rely on many of the theories and techniques that you have been exposed to thus far. For example, they comprise a great deal of what was learned in interviewing, communications, planning, and motivation. In the long run, training, coaching, and counselling can be one of the most rewarding areas of sales management.

Note: Boise Cascade Holdings (BCH) is a diversified holding company engaged in manufacturing of engineered wood products, plywood, lumber, and particleboard and distributes a broad line of building materials. The company primarily operates in the US, where it is headquartered in Boise, Idaho and employs 4,600 people. For a very good case study regarding this topic, reader can visit company's website www.bc.com

15

Steps in Becoming a True Leader

It is only after having developed many of the fundamentals of management that you can begin to become a true leader. Managers help to bring out the best in others; leaders do so as well. However, leaders will, in turn, possess not only the tools of a great manager, but other characteristics as well. It is the combination of factors that encourages others to follow. Why leaders need to possess the principles of management first is because the skills and techniques are so intertwined. Communication skills form much of the foundation, and as you have seen are critical in planning, hiring, motivating, training, coaching, and counselling.

Above and beyond this, a leader needs to exhibit certain core values that inspire others and help garner respect from staff, peers, and customers. As we mentioned earlier, you are now on two teams-that of a team player, working in tandem with other managers; and a team leader, developing your team for the long run. With respect to your customers, you might find yourself on either one of the two teams, depending on the circumstances of the sale. As a sales manager, you may need to be a team player during a conversion project within the customer's operation and then the team leader, ensuring that the training is implemented in order to get the customer's operation fully up and running. Also, while you are often leading individuals to higher performance and productivity, you are also very often leading teams, small and large. Before looking at various types of teams, it is important to first understand what teams are all about.

THE CHARACTERISTICS OF A TEAM

We have all been involved in teams from a very young age. This might have been in school, on the playing field, at home with family, or with friends. No matter what the team, the successful ones have certain commonalities.

Team definition: Groups of people with common skills working together toward a set of common goals, whose members communicate with and trust one another.

TYPES OF TEAMS

There are two types of teams that need to be considered: the relationship team and the transactional one. The relationship team is the one concerned with the ongoing responsibility for the project. This team is program-oriented and is consistently communicating potential solutions and improvements. A relationship team does not typically have a specific timetable associated with it, but rather it is a long-term team with an indefinite end point.

The transactional team typically has a start and stop point for an identifiable projects. Like a relationship team's goals are specific, measurable, attainable, relevant, and timely; however, once the project is complete, this type of team will often disband.

TEAMS AND PLANNING

The foundation for establishing teams often comes out of the planning process. That is, it can be a strategy used to achieve an objective or goal. At the same time, just like in planning, a preassessment is necessary, in this case to see what type of team it should be and who should be the members.

Assessment-Where Are You Now?

Assessing the strengths and weaknesses of the individual team members is key to putting a team together. It then allows you to assess the strengths and weaknesses of the team as a whole.

Some questions on a micro (individual) level to consider are:

- What are the DISC patterns of the individuals?
- What are the probable strengths and potential weaknesses associated with those patterns?
- Have the individuals offset those potential weaknesses through a conscious effort?
- Based on job function, where are the salespeople in relationship to the training cycle?

- What training is needed to move the salespeople through the cycle?
- What is their level of eagerness (motivation) and knowledge and skills (four areas that make up the exceptional sales professional: communication skills, business acumen, technical knowledge, and market experience)?
- What coaching goals are already in place for the potential team members? What will the next set of goals require?

Other macro (team-level) areas to consider are:

- What strengths need to be brought to the team?
- Are the territories properly aligned?
- Are there any gaps where new hires or recruiting efforts need to focus?
- What team training needs to be implemented?

MISSION

Because you have established a mission statement for your department or area of responsibility, the direction for the team has a baseline from which to work.

SMART Goals

To move everyone toward the mission, you will need to set goals for the individual salesperson as well as the team. The goals must move the team toward the mission's completion.

Responsibility

Each team member has been assigned responsibility and accountability for the tasks and functions needed to make the team successful. Of course, involving people from other departments within the company is also important to enhancing many sales teams. Manufacturing, finance, distribution, IT, and other departments could easily play a part on a team. In general, people from outside of one area (cross-functional) work especially well on transactional teams.

Tracking

All goals and action items need to be tracked properly, including time frames associated with them that are tied to the responsible parties. This allows everyone on the team to know when the deliverables are due and who is the primary responsible person for any particular project or task. It also should include checkpoints and/or progress reports along the way.

Action Items

Again, responsibility needs to be assigned to each action item the team needs to complete along the way in order to reach the goal(s). Each action item needs to be clearly understood and communicated to all involved.

Flexibility

Finally, establish contingencies, not only just in case, but also because change is inevitable. Being too rigid can only stifle growth. The process around internal team planning has now been identified. However, teams can also include others outside of your organization, and, as you know in selling, it is critical to team up with your customer. This is how true long-term partnerships are formed.

Matching Customer's Team

Teaming up with customers is a process that helps establish joint goals and strategies. Many of the same concepts for developing your internal team apply to developing a partnership with your customers. Before creating external teams, determining what the customer considers important will ensure the success of the team relationship. The planning stage is the best time to do an assessment and establish the foundation and the customer's expectations. Some questions to consider are:

- What is the political climate of the customer's business?
- Who in the customer's organization wants to be a team player? Who does not?
- Who is best for the relationship team?
- Who is best for the transactional team?
- How deep in the customer's organization are you going to be allowed to go?
- How high up in the organization are you going to be allowed to go?
- Will you have access to certain internal customer meetings on related projects?
- Are there backup or substitute team members?

Answers to these and other related questions will help establish the structure and operation of each team. Once the customer's environment has been established, the next step is to pick the relationship and transactional teams. Keep in mind that usually the transactional teams cannot be created until the project has begun. This is because transactional teams often are designed to solve a current problem or offset a known future problem. An initial step in deciding on team members is to brainstorm all of the departments that are involved.

As we have seen in earlier chapter on planning, the more aligned you become with the customers, the stronger the relationship can be. Remember to think "out of the box" here, as you might find that a department that you least expected is actually a primary stakeholder. IT, for example, is key in so many new initiatives, as technology plays such a pivotal role in analyzing, managing and communicating information and data. Here are some of the main corporate departments or functions to look to team up with as it relates to both organizations-yours and your customer's:

- Sales
- Marketing
- Purchasing
- Legal
- Finance
- Engineering
- Corporate executives
- Operations
- IT
- Customer Service
- Manufacturing
- R&D

Once this has been identified, the next step is to create crossfunctional teams. A note of caution for teams in general: In the beginning managers tend to establish a "committee of one" versus team approach. In this case, the manager tries to become the hub for all communications. This centralized control can generate departmental barriers, which tend to hurt the team. Again, keep in mind the team definition: Groups of people with common skills working together toward a set of common goals, whose members communicate and trust one another. This means that while you may be taking on a leadership role, you should not make yourself the centerpiece of the team, whereby everyone is either relying on or resenting your authority. Rather, you should communicate that you are still a member of the team and have the same goals as everyone else.

Selecting the Team Players for Cross-Functional Teams

This type of relationship team will be made up of key players, not necessarily management, from the predetermined departments. The objective is to get a team that is closest to the issue, product, or operation. The players selected need to:

- Be a knowledgeable representative of the respective department or area.
- Meet the motivation requirements from the earlier set of questions.
- Be willing to work with or even lead transactional teams.
- Be solution-oriented.

Once the players are determined, each player needs to be assigned a specific function as a team member based on expertise. It is also important early on that each team player describe to the other members her respective job function and responsibilities. In other words, do not assume that everyone knows what everyone else does. The more understanding that team members have of one another and the roles they play within their organizations, the more solutions-oriented the team will be.

Also, by assigning specific tasks along with accountability to each team player, buy-in for the project is created for the players as a whole. The more team members understand the importance that they have for the team, the more motivated those team members will be. In addition, it tends to be best that one person is ultimately responsible for the completion of an action item. This does not mean that others do not have their say, nor that their involvement is not expected. Rather, it is difficult to spread accountability too thin. When this happens, everyone tends to point fingers.

Influencing the Customer's Team

The best way to influence the customer's team and to become a partner is to find the common denominators between the two. Although most of this would have been done in the planning stage, reminding the customer of the common elements is significant in convincing him to become, and stay, a partner. For example:

1. Both partners have certain common objectives (e.g., profit improvement, improved quality, cost containment, etc.).

2. Both have an equal risk, which includes something to gain and something to lose.
3. Both add value to one another.
4. Both are supportive of the other instead of being competitive or territorial.
5. Both are reliable and straightforward.
6. Both enjoy the relationship and work at making it even stronger.

Sometimes companies choose to keep a progress or feedback form that encompasses all of the updated information on work being done with the customer. The feedback form helps to keep your plan, your team players, and the customer's team players on track. The written document could be distributed at regular intervals, for example, weekly, biweekly, or monthly.

THE EVOLUTION OF A TEAM

Remember, teams can be of different sizes and types and can take on a personality of their own. The one unifying factor is the progression that they follow:

STAGES IN TEAM DEVELOPMENT

In 1965, Dr. Bruce Tuckman developed a theory based on the four stages of team development as a way to look at the process that teams go through when working together. Then, in the mid 1970s, he refined the theory, identifying a fifth stage to team development. The stages in team development are as follows:

1. Forming
2. Storming
3. Norming
4. Performing
5. Adjourning

In the Forming stage, team members are introduced and become acquainted with one another. They often share information about themselves, and some of their strengths and weaknesses are either shared or become visible. The second stage, Storming, is often the most difficult. Team members find out, not just through information sharing but also by actual actions and behaviors, who is willing to contribute and at what level. Any preconceived notions members had about one another become amplified or altered (positive or negative) as they become more familiar with one another.

In the Norming stage, team members have worked through some of the initial challenges and differences and begin to set up processes to complete the tasks and project. A consensus is reached as to who is responsible for which deliverable and how and when it is to be accomplished.

In the Performing stage, the strategies and tactics are carried out in pursuit of the objectives and goals. Relationship issues are, for the most part, cleared up, and every member begins to carry out his or her duties as they relate to the role they play on the team. In the final stage, Adjourning, the team will share their results with others and formulate the next steps. Those next steps could be that the team applies the knowledge or action and then moves into the next round of activities, or that the outcomes are transferred to or used by others not relating directly to the team and the team disbands.

As you look at these five stages today, keep in mind that they can actually relate to anything from a short-term transaction team to a long-term relationship-oriented team. It is the amount of time and intensity you spend in each stage that will vary. The key is that from all of the planning already done to be able to limit the extremes in order to save more time for productive team involvement as opposed to spending too much time in the "storming" stage, which is often the case when teams are not well thought-out and expectations and goals are vague or unclear.

While teams do not always have a specific team leader-that role may rotate among different team members-there will be times now and certainly going forward as you progress in your career as a manager that you will need to step up and answer the call of leadership.

Time to Lead

Now that you have an understanding of what it takes to develop a team, it is critical to exhibit the leadership qualities that will allow you as a team leader to thrive.

Leaders are Made, Not Born

While there has been a long-standing debate about this, there is no denying that leadership is a skill that needs to be cultivated. While some more than others grow up showing a propensity to lead at an earlier age, circumstances can also greatly affect leadership growth, and factors will come into play that push many in the right direction. For those that argue that people are born with innate talents, it is true that there are "natural athletes" or prodigies. On the other hand, if a natural talent is not developed or fostered, that talent will atrophy. Also, it is often those who show the greatest potential who work the hardest. These are the ones who progress to the next level of their sport or career. Eventually some of those that exhibit the greatest talents can become legends.

By believing that there is no such thing as "pure" born leaders, the paradigm shifts to believing that skills, confidence, and self-image will determine leadership performance. Those who have the desire to achieve their mission in life, and who can use strengths to offset weaknesses, can have unlimited leadership potential.

Power of a Manager

There are generally three categories of power: fear-generated, gaingenerated, and sincerity-generated. Leaders that use fear-generated power are interested in control. Their followers are afraid that they may lose out spiritually, emotionally, physically, or mentally if they do not follow the leader. Losing the sense of belonging is a significant fear generator. Followers are intimidated by the consequences of not following. "Go along to get along" is the motto. Do not question their authority because the consequences might cause some measure of pain. Leaders that use gain-generated power are also interested in control. Followers look to the leader to provide for them if they do something for the leader. "Do A and B for me, and I will do X and Y in return for you." Similar to a fear-generating leader, this type might even tap into a specific area such as an emotional or spiritual desire or some weakness in the person that they know they can't resist. Therefore, they are really deceiving or coercing the person into doing something as opposed to getting authentic buy-in. People will follow leaders that use sincerity-generated power, because this type of leader allows the followers to make an educated commitment to the mission. Followers believe in the leader's vision because it is communicated clearly and openly. They are not being manipulated by the leader, as is the case in the other power styles. Leaders that use sincerity-generated power build long-lasting relationships with their followers. This type of leader is service-oriented, trustworthy, and inspiring.

Leaders that use sincerity-generated power are, in effect, aspiring to as well as teaching the corporate values and providing guidance as it relates to them. They bring people together for open discussion of these values, which in turn fosters a sincere desire to move in the right direction. It is really the true leader that uses sincerity-generated as her only power style. Other leaders are short-term and will not create any long-lasting devotion nor trust and respect from others. The following are some core examples of what a leader is, including some common traits and characteristics, along with some ways you can continue in the direction of becoming a strong leader.

Visionary

Leaders have a vision of what can be. They go beyond themselves to consider possibilities that others cannot see. Often they have a desire to be the best, which generates excitement and enthusiasm for the people who are following them. This sense of purpose and direction unites the team and maximizes the team's capabilities. Part of the reason many leaders are so successful is because they provide a safe environment that allows the people to be motivated from within. It is what some call the "passionate workplace." You now have the ability to develop the vision for your team as well as marshal your staff around it. It is a surefire way to get both you and your team moving in the right direction-together.

Strategist

A vision without a plan is merely a dream. Leaders are constantly thinking through and planning the next move. What are the consequences? What are the rewards? What changes can be made to strengthen the team? They constantly question strategies and tactics and strive to improve upon the past. Leaders also know that a strategy without action is the same as having no plan at all. They realize that execution or implementation is key to making any strategy come alive. Leaders innately feel a sense of urgency and then react expeditiously to the opportunities as they take shape. Leaders will stay in the offensive mode at all times with the strategy. Even when their plans are criticized or uncertainty begins to present itself, leaders have the patience to stay the course because they are confident in themselves and their team.

You are a leader in setting the strategy for your team going forward. If you waver, then they will too. Trust in them, and you will get the same in return.

Mentor

Whether you realize it or not, you are not just a manager and coach, but also a mentor. Remember that a real leader is constantly encouraging and empowering his people. This inspires trust, confidence, and commitment to achieve the stated goals. A sense of loyalty is developed toward the leader and the leader's mission because of her willingness to involve her followers. Leaders believe in the potential of others. In fact, leaders are not afraid to loosen the reins and allow their team to shine. Far too often a manager tries try to take credit for the work being done by his staff. A true leader deflects much of the credit and places it where it belongs, with the team members. The more a leader looks out for the well-being of his employees, the more the commitment will be returned.

Remember that being a mentor comes with your new role. Think about the great mentors you have had over your lifetime. It is your time to step into that role yourself. So don't forget, your staff is looking to you for your input, guidance, and reassurance. Treat them right, and they will not only be looking at you, but beginning to look up to you.

Honesty

Honesty is at the core of management and leadership. If a leader demonstrates her commitment to being truthful and forthright, it can become contagious. Honesty in a leader is always a sign of strength. Believing it is a weakness is actually a character flaw in an insecure person, who will remain a follower at best. Also, remember that it can take just one lie or deceptive act to lose the trust of your staff forever.

But honesty is not just about telling the truth; it is about being candid and up front with your team. This is more important than ever because, in the face of rapid change and uncertainty, people long for truthful and full disclosure of information. That is not to say that there might not be certain information that is not appropriate to share at any particular moment, but whenever possible, provide the maximum rather than "just enough" information. Furthermore, lack of open sharing of information can also be a demotivator, and people are very perceptive and will see through mixed messages.

The more you express yourself-your concerns, desires, and expectations-the more you will get openness from your team in return. So if you feel your team needs to know something that could affect them, address it, even if you don't have all of the answers. If not, the uncertainty and fear will only build, making a problem that much more difficult to handle later on. Your team will surely respect you more in the long run, and you will all reap the rewards of closer working relationships.

Work/Life Balance

Another age-old question that has garnered a great deal of discussion and debate by thought leaders in the area of leadership: "What is the quintessential balance between work and free time?" Typically we think of great leaders as working seventy-hour weeks, on weekends, and so on. However, these are not necessarily great leaders. A true leader knows how to weigh the various aspects of her life, including what is most important to her, and then set her own priorities and stick to them.

Therefore, some leaders will inevitably fit into the category of "workaholic," putting his career and the business first and foremost, while others value their family and downtime as much as or more than their work. Great leaders know how and where their energy and time needs to be spent in order to achieve this balance and, in return, they as well as those around them all benefit. Again, no right or exact prescription works for everyone. Both types of values have culminated in excellent leaders. So think about the balance you want in your life, and stay true to it. Also, at the same time remember that your staff has their own set of needs and values, so be sure to respect them as well.

Innovative Thinkers

Leaders ask themselves, "Where can we go from here?" They look at roadblocks and hurdles merely as challenges in the course ahead. They are also able to use creativity and imagination to overcome the obstacles. In fact, by surpassing a barrier, you are one step closer to achieving a goal. Some have even gone as far as calling leaders paranoid, meaning they are not only looking ahead at the road in front of them, but over their shoulders to be sure that competition and other influences (both external and internal) are playing to their favour. If something is off course, they look to themselves as well as others for ways to get back on track, never saying, "But this is the way it has always been done."

You should always look for the new, better approach, and ask that your team does the same. Also, know that progress comes from unexpected places. Therefore, look out for the unexpected from your competitors, and encourage new ideas from your staff. Another way to look at creativity and innovation is to not only encourage debate but even disagreement. The mark of a confident person is one who can accept the differences of opinion of others. You are building a team of high performers. Don't just ask for their input when you feel it is in line with yours. Challenge them to challenge your thinking. No one has all of the answers, let alone all of the right ones. Value this way of thinking, and then look for ways to reward it as well.

Committed to a Win-Win Mentality

Because their focus is constantly on winning, leaders never look backward. They do not waste their time looking for someone to blame.

Leaders are dedicated to excellence and quality. This means that they do not look for ways to break people down, but rather, constantly look for ways to build people up. They also have the ability to be introspective. They recognize their capabilities and limitations.

Through their positive energy they are able attract compatible competencies. Their team then feels this energy, and they are uplifted by it, especially during difficult and trying times. A leader should always give her people the benefit of the doubt. First challenge them and then trust in them. Anything else would be stifling them and, in turn, yourself. It is commonly believed that your team members can only live up to the expectations that you have for them. If you have low expectations, you will get that in return. You'll be pleasantly surprised at what your team is capable of when you set the bar high and allow some freedom for them to reach their goals. Have confidence in your team; it will be returned in spades.

Excellent Communicators

You have already looked in depth at the importance of communication in building your careers in management. Leaders exemplify the best in communication, with all, not just select, business relationships. Leaders can articulate their vision at will. Furthermore, the goals and direction that they have put in place are made clear and understandable. They constantly communicate their standards, ideals, and values, and relate them to every task and accomplishment. This is because they have put their goals in definable terminology.

Leaders are also considered very approachable. They realize the importance of being highly visible to their staff and readily available to those who need them. Some of the greatest leaders spend a major portion of their time on interpersonal skills. It is their people-development focus that in turn opens others to them. Because of this style of consistent interaction, leaders get regular, timely, and applicable information.

By being a great communicator, you can then encourage open communication among others. When you communicate, remember that all of the players on a team, including yourself, are equals; you just each have different roles and responsibilities.

Excellent Listeners

You have also learned the importance of listening in order to be a great communicator. Great leaders have the uncanny ability to actively listen, focusing not just on the person with whom they are speaking, but also on absorbing the commonality of messages that are coming from their staff. Because of their listening skills, leaders have a tendency to learn a great deal about what is going on with people at all levels of the organization, as opposed to just the thoughts of a few. This allows them to make adjustments through consensus.

You will need to practice the skill and art of actively listening. It will be evident to your staff, showing that you care, and it will also help you to make sound decisions. After all, you need to gain the trust of others in order to get the necessary input and cooperation from them. The more you listen, the more you can expect others to listen to you.

Self-Awareness

Leaders not only analyze the abilities of others, but are constantly reviewing their own strengths and weaknesses. They know their own abilities, and they strive to constantly build on them. Leaders are honest with themselves, and they are not afraid to look to others with specific strengths to offset any of their own weaknesses. A leader is able to analyze those areas that cause self-doubt, and work to improve themselves.

Leaders are at the same time sensitive to others who act out or react based on their own insecurities or fears; they attempt to help those people find direction and purpose. Remember that just like your staff, you are not perfect either Sometimes the more you feel you are running up against a wall, the more the solution is with you and not with others. Don't overdemand, but instead realize that the best way to address the shortcomings of others is to be in touch with your own.

Leadership by Example-Walk the Talk

Leaders inspire the team by showing their willingness to pitch in. True leaders do not live exclusively in an ivory tower, but rather spend a great deal of time at all levels of the organization, getting to know the staff and letting the input of others carry substantial weight, as opposed to just paying lip service to their staff. They realize that the foundation of the organization is not the corner office but rather the people on the front lines who develop the products and services, interact with customers, and ensure that the processes run smoothly along the way.

Show your team that you care by talking with not just them but all stakeholders in all areas in your organization and at the customer sites as well. Show that you are not afraid to roll up your sleeves and get your hands dirty. People want a leader they can respect and who understands things from their point of view, not someone who is out of touch with their needs. So be the first in line to take part in a training program or a team-building exercise that involves your staff and others.

Also, in setting the right example, hold yourself responsible first and foremost. The sign of a true leader is someone who can stand up and take the credit when something went right and take the blame when something went wrong. Businesses without leadership have a plethora of finger pointers. Before you look at who did what wrong and why, look at who did what right and how.

Risk Takers

If an organization is to grow, it needs to accept failures as a distinct possibility. A leader does this and asks others to not fear it either. In fact, leaders go by the philosophy that a failure or mistake can only help get you that much closer to a success. When Thomas Edison was asked how it felt to have failed more than 10,000 times in attempting to invent the light bulb, his reply was that he never failed; instead he successfully figured out 10,000 ways not to make a light bulb.

You need to show your team that you are willing to take risks, and that you have the ability to ask the right questions to mitigate them. When someone comes to you with a new, unproven idea, don't brush it off. Allow him to think it through and see if it really seems to make sense. If it does, look for ways to make it happen, rather than excuses to not take on something new. And if it is not a complete success, latch on to the good that came out of the experience and the learning for the next time. You will then be encouraging more risk going forward.

Ethical

While all of the above are central to being a great leader, being ethical is perhaps the most important characteristic of our greatest leaders. A lack of high ethical standards is why some of those who we thought were at the top for good came tumbling down. The leadership role is first and foremost based on a foundation of trust and credibility. Leaders are not afraid to voice what they believe in. At the same time, they keep their promises to both their followers and to everyone they touch. Leaders set very high standards of integrity for themselves and their organization. They always err on the side of fairness, which could, at times, seem like it is holding the company back. Yet in the long run the organization will be that much stronger for it.

As a leader, you will have to make some very tough decisions. Realize that it is impossible to make everyone happy all the time, but it is possible to be fair to all concerned. While business is very competitive and difficult decisions will need to be made, the decisions you make will stay with you and your team for a long time, so make them ones that you can be proud of.

Positive Attitude

One cannot say enough about the importance of attitude. Great leaders have a positive attitude that is infectious. They exude confidence and have the ability to bounce back in the face of adversity. The more it seems that the odds are stacked against them, the more they are able to rise to the occasion. In fact, many of the greatest leaders have made a name for themselves by being resilient during the toughest of times. People sometimes describe them as unwavering or unflappable. This does not mean that they are putting on an act and not being truc to themselves. A great leader, more than others, can ask for help when something is wrong or they are in need. This is only the more proof that they are continually committed to the betterment of themselves and those that surround them. Also, your attitude is evident in everything you do. Your team is always looking to you to see how you react. Even when everything is not moving on all cylinders, be the first one to build them up, to congratulate the team and the individual contributors on a job well done.

One great way of maintaining a great attitude is through the use of positive visualization. See yourself as someone who can take the lead and address challenges that will inevitably cross your path. You already possess many of the core characteristics of a great leader. It is now only a matter of time and commitment.

Steps Toward Leadership

- Decision. You must make the decision to do what it takes to move into a leadership position. This means to start embracing the characteristics of great leaders now. This can only help you to grow in your new role as a sales manager.
- Determination. Accept the responsibility of leadership and feel the driving need to want to experience that leadership role. Be tenacious when others attempt to question your desire. Passion and drive are not only the mark of a true leader, but the mark of a person who endeavors to become one.
- Study. Become a student of leadership. Read about the subject, listen to tapes and speeches, and take classes on leadership. There is an array of learning tools on the market. Take the

best ideas out of each and begin incorporating them into your daily activities and way of thinking.

- Role Model. Select your favourite leaders. They could be modern-day leaders or figures from history, or both. Then begin to work with the combination of styles that fits you best. You may also have mentors that you know personally and can learn from them along the way. Listen and observe; while they will approach leadership in different ways, they all have something valuable to share.
- Discipline. Becoming a leader requires a change of habits that were acquired as a follower. Self-control and constant effort are needed to implement leadership characteristics. Don't try to exhibit every characteristic so dramatically that it comes across as superficial. As you saw, leadership is based on sincerity; give it time, and it will come.
- Practice. Learn the basics and then consistently work until you begin to master them, adding some new element or level of consciousness all the time. Eventually, not only will you come to master the art of leadership, but you can teach others how to better lead as well. You yourself will ultimately become that role model that others will want to emulate.

All of this leads you back to the first statement about leaders being made, not born. It might not always seem so easy, nor loads of fun, but it is well within your reach. This book will hopefully prove to be one of many great tools you utilize as you continue through this journey. You will certainly be assisted by other people and resources along the way as well.

Some say that it is not the end result but rather the journey that contains all of the rewards. You should be commended on taking the time to reward yourself. It is with this proactive attitude that you are already exemplifying your ability to lead. Above all else, be patient with yourself and others. Managers, new and old, all face similar challenges and have the same horizon full of boundless opportunities. You have already proven that you are a success, and you are well on your way to even greater accomplishments.

Note: Yahoo! (Yahoo) is an internet and media communications company, offering internet services such as search and email. The company provides a range of services to individuals, including search, yellow pages, shopping, information, entertainment and communication. Its major websites include Yahoo! Mail, Yahoo! Jobs, Yahoo! Search, Yahoo! Answers, Yahoo! Videos and Flickr, among others. The company provides services in more than 30 languages and in more than 30 countries, regions, and territories. For a case study visit company's site www.yahoo.com

16

Sales Promotion

Marketing communications is one of the four major elements of the company's marketing mix. Marketers must know how to use advertising, sales promotion, direct marketing, public relations, and personal selling to communicate the product's existence and value to the target customers.

The communication process itself consists of nine elements: sender, receiver, encoding, decoding, message, media, response, feedback, and noise. Marketers must know how to get through to the target audience in the face of the audience's tendencies toward selective attention, distortion, and recall.

Developing the promotion program involves eight steps. The communicator must first identify the target audience and its characteristics, including the image it carries of the product. Next the communicator has to define the communication objective, whether it is to create awareness, knowledge, liking, preference, conviction, or purchase. A message must be designed containing an effective content, structure, format, and source.

Then communication channels both personal and non-personal must be selected. Next, the total promotion budget must be established. Four common methods are the affordable method, the percentage-of-sales method, the competitive-parity method, and the objective-and task method.

The promotion budget should be divided among the main promotional tools, as affected by such factors as push-versus-pull strategy, buyer readiness stage, product life-cycle stage and company market rank. The marketer should then monitor to see how much of the market becomes aware of the product, tries it, and is satisfied in the process. Finally, all of the communications effort must be managed and coordinated for consistency, good timing, and cost effectiveness.

Introduction-the five major modes of communication (advertising, sales promotion, public relations, personal selling, and direct marketing)

The communication process-communications as the management of customer buying processes over time, the nine elements of the communications model, reasons why message may not get through the receiver (selective attention, selective distortion, and selective recall)

Developing effective communications

A. Identify the target audience

Image analysis is a major part of audience analysis that entails assessing the audience's current image of the company, its products, and its competitors

First step is to measure target audience's knowledge of the subject using a familiarity scale

Second step is to determine feelings toward the product using a favorability scale

Specific content of a product's image is best determined with use of semantic differential (relevant dimensions, reducing set of relevant dimensions, administering to a sampıe, averaging the results, checking on the image variance)

B. Determine the communication objectives

1. Based on seeking of a cognitive, affective, or behavioural response
2. Assuming the buyer has high involvement with the product category and perceives high differentiation within the category, base objectives on the hierarchy-of-effects model (hierarchy: awareness, knowledge, liking, preference, conviction, purchase)

C. Design the message (AIDA model)

Message content-choosing an appeal (rational appeal to audience's self interest, emotional appeal attempt to stir up either positive or negative emotions, moral appeals are directed to the audience's sense of what is right and proper)

Message structure-one-sided presentation versus two-sided argument

Message format-must be strong, based on headline, copy, "sound," nonverbal clues, color, expression, dress, etc.

Message source -expertise, trustworthiness and liability

D. Select the communication channels
   1. Personal communication channels-direct (advocate, expert and social)
   2. Non-personal communication channels-indirect (media, atmospheres, events)
E. Establish the total marketing communications budget
   1. Affordable method
   2. Percentage-of-sales method
   3. Competitive-parity method
   4. Objective-and-task method

IV. Deciding on the marketing communications mix
- Promotional tools-benefits of each tool (advertising, sales promotion, public relations and publicity, personal selling, direct marketing)
- Factors in setting the marketing communications mix (type of product market, buyer-readiness stage, product-life-cycle stage)
- Measure the communications' results

V. Managing the integrated marketing communications process
A. A concept of marketing communications planning that recognizes the added value of a comprehensive plan
   - Evaluates the strategic roles of a variety of communications disciplines
   - Combines these disciplines to provide clarity, consistency and maximum communications impact through the seamless integration of discrete messages

ADVERTISING

Advertising-the use of paid media by a seller to communicate persuasive information about its products, services, or organization-is a potent promotional tool. Advertising takes on many forms (national, regional, local, consumer, industrial, retail, product, brand, institutional, etc.) designed to achieve a variety of objectives (awareness, interest, preference, brand recognition, brand insistence).

Advertising decision-making consists of objectives setting, budget decision, message decision, media decision, and ad effectiveness evaluation. Advertisers should establish clear goals as to whether the advertising is supposed to inform, persuade, or remind buyers. The factors to consider when setting the advertising budget are: stage in the product life cycle, market share, competition and clutter, needed frequency, and product substitutability.

The advertising budget can be established based on what is affordable, as a percentage budget of sales, based on competitors' expenditures, or based on objectives and tasks, and based on more advanced decision models that are available. The message decision calls for generating messages, evaluating and selecting between them, and executing them effectively and responsibly.

The media decision calls for defining the reach, frequency, and impact goals; choosing among major media types; selecting specific media vehicles; deciding on media timing; geographical allocation of media. Finally, campaign evaluation calls for evaluating the communication and sales effects of advertising, before, during, and after the advertising. Sales promotion and public relations are two tools of growing importance in marketing planning. Sales promotion covers a wide variety of short-term incentive tools designed to stimulate consumer markets, the trade, and the organization's own sales force. Sales promotion expenditures now exceed advertising expenditures and are growing at a faster rate.

Consumer promotion tools include samples, coupons, cash refund offers, price packs, premiums, prizes, patronage rewards, free trials, product warranties, tie-in promotions, and point-of-purchase displays and demonstrations. Trade promotion tools include price-off, advertising and display allowances, free goods, push money, and specialty-advertising items. Business promotion tools include conventions, trade shows, contests, sweepstakes, and games. Sales promotion planning calls for establishing the sales promotion objectives, selecting the tools, developing, pretesting, and implementing the sales promotion program, and evaluating the results.

Marketing public relations (MPR) is another important communication/promotion tool. Traditionally, it has been the least utilized tool but is now recognized for its ability in building awareness and preference in the marketplace, repositioning products, and defending them. Broadly, MPR is those activities that support the ultimate sale of a product or service. Some of the major marketing public relations tools are news, speeches, events, public service activities, written material, audio-visual material, corporate identity, and telephone information services. MPR planning involves establishing the MPR objectives, choosing the appropriate messages and vehicles, and evaluating the MPR results.

ADVERTISING DECISION

Modern marketing calls for more than developing a good product, pricing it attractively and making it accessible to the target consumer. Companies must also communicate with the present and potential customers. In this respect, advertising is a potent promotion tool of marketing communication mix, while the rest four are:

- Sales Promotion
- Direct Marketing
- Public Relations and Publicity
- Personal Selling

Various marketing Gurus have defined advertising according to their own views: "Advertising Consists of all the activities involved in presenting to a group a non - personal, oral or visual openly - sponsored, identified message regarding a product, service or idea. This message, called an advertisement, is disseminated through one or more media and paid for by the identified sponsor". — W.Z. Stanton

"To give public notice or to announce publicly".

"Advertising is mass communication of information intended to persuade buyers so as to maximize profits". — J.E. Littlefield

To summarise, advertising means any paid form of non - personal presentation and promotion or ideas, goods or services by an identified sponsor.

It is just not enough to manufacture a product. People must be informed of its existence and should be given good reasons to buy it. This is a job which is sought to be done by advertising. Without advertising, people would not be aware of the attributes of the product nor of its price. Let us now discuss the role and importance of advertising.

i. Way of Informing: Advertising is a way of communicating information to the consumer -information which enables him to compare and choose from the products and services available. Advertising enables consumbers to exercise their right of free choice " Encyclopedia Bitannica" such diverse media as handbills, newspapers, magazines, billboards, letters, radio and television broadcasts and motion pictures.

ii. Manufacturer's concerns: Advertising is the most economical means by which a manufacturer or an institution can communicate to an audience either to sell a product or to promote a cause of social welfare, such as, civic drive, or an immunization programme. This includes the process of mass communication which is different from ordinary communication. Here a macro level mass communication is between manufacturer and his mass audience. This is also connected through new sources. Mass audience gives various reactions as responses. Here audience is interconnected as a group within groups.

iii. Fundamental Right of Freedom of Speech: Advertising being a necessary means of communication is an inseparable part of free speech. Any restriction on the right to recommend legitimate services or ideas in public will diminish the fundamental right of freedom of speech.

iv. Improving productivity: Advertising can help in improving the economies of developed and developing countries. There is ample evidence to support this view. Advertising stimulates production and consequently generates more employment. It can help stabilize prices and leads to wider distribution and greater availability of goods an services.

v. Economic Growth of Country: Advertising is an essential and integral part of the marketing system. It is sometimes maintained that the marketing system is nothing but requirement of a country's social and economic growth. Advertising stimulates sales and compels the firm to improve its productivity and contributes substantially to the growth of the economy. Thus marketing and advertising are key tools used to aid a country's growth. Even though advertising costs a lot of money, and the costs are increasing day by day, a skillfully used advertising campaign can be the cheapest means of reaching the market and commutating with the consumers effectively. Advertising is wasteful if it fails to produce sales.

Advertisement leads to an increase in sales and market share. Pepsi came to India with a zero market share. By December, 1995, it had captured 40 per cent of Indian market. Promise, a toothpaste manufactured by a small -scale unit, was able to snatch a 15 per cent share of the market by strong customer -oriented advertisement. People feel safe in purchasing products they know of. Advertising makes them aware of the products and their attributes. In promoting a product or a brand, the manufacturer/ advertiser stakes his reputation. No manufacturer/ Advertiser would be foolish enough to risk his reputation by making misleading claims in his advertisements. Hence advertised goods are trusted the world over and India is no exception.

ADVERTISEMENT AND SALES PROMOTION

Advertising is a message which promotes ideas, good or services communicated through one or more media by an identified sponsor while sales promotion consists of short - terms incentives provided by the identified sponsors to consumers and traders to persuade them to purchase and stock his products

It is difficult to make an all - embracing generalization about distinctive qualities of advertising mainly because of its many forms and uses. Various companies do their advertising in different ways. In a small company advertising is handled by someone in the sales or marketing department who coordinates with an advertising agency. On the other side, large companies setup their own advertising departments, where Marketing Manager reports to the Vice -President, Marketing. The advertising department's job is to develop the total budget, help and develop advertising strategy and approach an advertising agency for advertising and designing a campaign. Most of the companies use an outside agency to help them design an advertising campaign and to select the media and decide about the timings and booking space.

In developing an advertising programme, marketing managers must always start by identifying their target market and the buyers involved. Thereafter, they have to make five major decisions in the programme development process known as the five Ms.

ADVERTISING AIMS

If an organization is spending crores of rupees on advertisement, then as managers we must attempt and be able to measure its effectiveness and delivery to find out whether we are receiving the value for money. However, advertising is only one part of marketing mix and the final delivery in rupees terms would involve the various marketing variables. The tragedy of advertising is that if it does not lead to an increase in sales of the product, the entire blame is put on advertising. Hence a clear definition of advertising goals in required. A successful advertising campaign can be compared with a military campaign where goal is set as "capture the army post No. 11" and the goal is achieved. Advertising goal can be defined as a clear and concise description of exactly what advertising is intended to accomplish, i.e.,

- To increase sales,
- To establish brand equity, and
- To enter the target market.

Sometimes these objectives are considered as marketing objectives instead of advertising objectives.

Need to set Advertising Objectives

Some of the possible objectives that are stressed are:

- Return on Investment (R.O.I) Advertising involves an investment of funds. Hence, it should produce a measurable return on the said investment in order to assess the desirability and profitability of advertising.
- Selection of media. The most effective advertising tool should be chosen in order to get the most profitable result.
- Coordination An appropriate co-ordination and integration of marketing and advertising efforts is imperative. Otherwise objectives of advertising are superimposed on objectives of marketing.

Various Approaches for Setting Advertising Objectives

i. DAGMAR Approach

This is the most popular method of setting advertising goals and was proposed by Russel M. Colley. DAGMAR stands for - Defining advertising Goals for Measured Advertising Results.

Colley outlined this method for turning advertising objectives into specific measurable goals. He lists 52 possible advertising objectives under the same approach.

The theory is based on the following: " The consumer passes through a hierarchy of stages between the time when the first ideas about the product comes to his mind and when he actually buys it" For example, an advertisement of a Generator should highlight fuel efficiency, easy start, after -sales service and ready availability of spares.

Initially it would inform us and we shall become aware of such a product. Then through product endorsement and trial we shall develop a favourable attitude and ultimately, we shall buy the product.

To set advertising objectives, we shall need to identify the stage in which the product is available and then we can set the objective.

Example:

A detergent manufacturing company wanted to position its product as the most powerful cloth cleaner and as a low cost detergent.

They worked out a campaign targeted to 3 crore households who own automatic washers.

Prior to the campaign release, they did an attitude survey on brand perception. After the campaign was over, they repeated the attitude survey.

The questions were focused on three areas:

i. Which brand is the most effective in removing the spots?

ii. Which brand will you buy when you go to the market next?

Specific advertising objectives could have been:

- Increase awareness from 38 per cent to 52 per cent
- Top image ranking to 24 per cent than 9 per cent
- Increase preference to 21 per cent.

ii. Product Life Cycle Approach

Advertising effectiveness varies according to the different stages of product life cycle.

iii. Primary and Selective Demand Theory

According to this approach the advertising objective is categorized into two ways Informative Advertising and Persuasive Advertising.

a. Informative Advertising. This advertising is important when the product is in the pioneering stage and the objective is to build Primary demand. Primary demand is sought to be created especially by concept selling for a category of products. Some particular conditions are required necessarily to advertise for creating a primary demand. The existence of a strong and basic consumer need is the most important prerequisite as advertising cannot create demand for a new product. It can only stimulate an existing demand. There must be strong buying motives in existence. Besides this, social trends, design, price, etc. also play a crucial rate at this stage. For example, the manufacturer of "VIM" initially had to inform potential consumers of VIM Bar's economic benefits and many other advantages.

b. Persuasive Advertising. This becomes important in the competitive stage, where a company's objective is to build selective demand for a particular brand. Most advertising falls in this category. Persuasive advertising is undertaken when a strong primary demand is in existence. The product should be distinctive, its benefits should be visible and also a strong brand consciousness must be generated.

Media Profile for Advertising

Role of Media. Media has a vital role in the process of advertising communication.

Effective advertising is possible only if suitable media are available.

The appropriateness of media used vis - a -vis the target audience and their reach are also of crucial importance. A substantial portion of the advertising budget allocation to the mass media is spent on buying space and time. Therefore media decisions assume a considerable importance when financial implications come to the force.

Media Planning. Advertisement becomes effective only when it reaches the desired audience. The value of the advertisement is determined by the number of persons seeing it, reading it and thus becoming aware of the product or the service.

Media Selection. Each media has a specific function to perform and its selection depends upon the requirements of the job. Media can be divided into two categories:

Main Media -- also called "above the line" media, e.g., newspapers, T.V. Radio, Magazines, etc.

Secondary Media- also called " below the line" media, e.g., hoarding, direct mail, point of purchase, etc. These are also known as reminder media.

Media Planning Process. The steps involved in media planning are:

i. Media planning and buying space is the financial side of advertising.

ii. It interacts with the creative process to form an important part of the overall marketing process.

iii. Whereas the creative process is a descriptive process, the media process is one of transforming their description to the public, i.e., a vehicle of communication.

iv. The primary responsibility of media practitioners is to ensure that the advertising message is seen, heard, read or recognized by the target audience. We believe this is a crucial role as there is no point in having the best advertising if nobody sees the advertisement.

Role of Media in the Advertising Process

Media Selection for Rural Marketing. The following points have to be considered while selecting the media for the rural markets:

- The total number of literates in the rural market and their reading habits.
- The extent and type of contribution of the product.
- The number of cinemas and video parlours, panchayat viewing and listening facilities and the type of audience.
- The number of publications which are circulated in the area concerned, the number of readers and their categories, whether casual, regular or headline readers.
- Whether the publications circulated in the area concerned are issued locally or are obtained fro the neighboring areas?

Media Selection Decisions

While selecting the advertising media the following factors should be borne in mind:

- Cost of advertisement,
- Nature of the product,
- Comparison of the medium selected with other media,
- Popularity of the media,
- Characteristics of customers, and
- Competition in the market.

Types of Media for Advertising

Print Media	Electronic Media	Outdoor Media	Direct Mail
Newspapers	TV	Billboards	Price Lists
Direct Mail	Video	Hoardings	Catalogues
Folders	Radio	Balloons	Personal letters
Product Literature	Voice mail	Advertising on transport means	Circulars
Journals	Cinema	Electric Display	

ADVERTISING AGENCY

An advertising agency acts as a consultant to the client, the advertiser, in formulating the advertising plans and translating them into an advertising campaign. Another role of the agency is placing the advertisement in the media, since it has a traditional association with the media. The placement aspect has assumed considerable importance owing to media boom and the resultant complexities.

An advertising agency can be defined as an independent organization of creative business people who develop, prepare and release the advertisements for the sellers seeking to find customers for their goods and services.

In India, there are about 7,000 advertising agencies out of which 700 ad agencies are recognized by the Indian Newspapers Society (INS). INS is a regulatory organization regulating ad agencies for:

- National Income Accounting
- Annual Billing
- Creditworthiness

The relationship between an advertiser and its advertising agency represents professionalism to the core. At the same time, capability in terms in culture and style of the two parties and the concerned persons is highly facilitatory for a fruitful relationship. Courage and candidness on the part of the agency can contribute much towards getting the client to appreciate the constructive use of a creative approach. It is in the interest of the client to provide the required reassurance to the agency so that communication is inhibited. The selection of an agency by a potential client has a degree of mutuality. A well considered and wise selection can pave the way for a productive relationship.

FUNCTIONS OF AD AGENCIES

Ad agency will be in a position to take an objective view of the advertiser's plan and proposals and thus venture to put forward its opinions and comments. Creativem qualified and trained personnel are required for an advertising agency. It may not be worthwhile for an advertiser to have on its permanent staff all the variety of skill required to produce appropriate advertisements. An agency provides an opportunity as well as flexibility for various combinations of agency personnel from different departments to form a team to work as per the specific requirements of their varied clients.

Advertising agency has regular contacts with various support systems required for the production of appropriate ad material. A major advantage of an agency is its regular dealing with the media and the expertise in developing advertisements to suit the requirements of its clients. The ad agency's skills can also be useful in the preparation of campaigns where the risks involved are high such as in the introduction of new products.

Clients' Expectations

Account Service: Responsive - prompt - accessible - listens - economical.

Creativity Review: Provide innovative proposals - ideas - visuals.

Production Review: Quality - timeliness - accuracy - economical.

Media Planning: Innovative media strategy - capable of coping with the budget changes - provide media trends update.

Buying Media Space: Explore cost effective alternatives - ability to negotiate attractive terms.

Market Research: Relate existing studies to the specific situation of the client - organize timely and meaningful research.

Retail Advertising and Sales Promotion: Innovative ideas - POP material, creative events - timeliness - economical.

Financial Control: Detailed estimates - accuracy in billing - reasonable rates - mutual trust.

Agency Education Parameters

- Knowledge of Client's Business
- Contribution to Market Planning
- Responsiveness to brief
- Listen, understand pro-act (be responsive)
- Develop Strategies and Plan Creativity
- Ability to involve Key Agency Resources
- Readily Accessible
- Cost Consciousness
- Effective Event Planning

MEASURING ADVERTISING EFFECTIVENESS

Good planning and control of advertising depend critically on measurement of advertising effectiveness. A lot of effort is, therefore, spent on fundamental research on advertising effectiveness. The most important measurement of advertising effectiveness is of an applied nature, dealing with specific ads and campaigns. Most of the money is spent by ad agencies on pre-testing ads, and much less is spent on post-evaluation of their effects. Many companies develop an advertising campaign, put it on the national market and then evaluate its effectiveness. It would be better for them to limit their campaign to one or a few cities first and evaluate its impact before rolling the campaign throughout the country with a very large budget. Measuring advertising effectiveness could be of two types according to the objectives of the advertisers:

- Communication Effect Research.
- Sales Effect Research.

COMMUNICATION EFFECT RESEARCH

The study seeks to discover if advertising is achieving the intended communication effect. This method is also known as "Copy Testing". The objective of this research is an improvement in the present system.

- The testing can be categorized into two types:
- Pre-testing of advertising campaign, and
- Post-testing of advertising campaign.

Three major methods of ad pre-testing are:

- Direct Rating
- Portfolio Test
- Laboratory Test

DIRECT RATING

In this type, respondents are asked questions to rate the alternative ads. These ratings are used to evaluate an ad's attention, read through, cognitive, effective and behavioural strengths.

The following steps can be adopted.

Evaluate ad's

- Attention strength
- Read through strength
- Cognitive strength
- Effective strength
- Behavioural strength

Method of evaluation through rating scale.

Primarily helps in screening out poor ads rather than identifying great ads.

Note: Chevron Corporation (Chevron) is one of the largest integrated energy companies in the world. The company is engaged in every aspect of the oil and natural gas industry, including exploration and production, refining, marketing and transportation, chemicals manufacturing and sales, geothermal, mining operations, and power generation. It has operations in more than 100 countries including the US. Chevron is headquartered in San Ramon, California and employs about 67,000 people. For a detailed example in "Sales Promotion" visit *www.chevron.com*

17

Retail Selling

An increasingly competitive market means that retail selling is growing in importance for all retailers, not just retailers of high-value, complex products. Retailing is a service, and retail selling is as essential a function as customer service. Indeed, the two are interlinked, not just because both functions are undertaken by the same staff in many retail organizations, but also because both customer service and sales staff have the prime role as interfacers between the retail organization and its customers. The customers' interpretation of the organization's image and ethos are affected by the nature of their relationship and encounters with retail staff.

Retailers, operating market-focused service businesses, need to tailor their retail selling to the customers' requirements with a regard to the type of product being bought and the type of purchase decision. They also need to take into consideration their customers' shopping motives and their stage in the process of making the buying decision.

Retail selling requires, therefore, a good knowledge of the products being sold, an understanding of the profile of target customers, and further, comprehension of customers' needs, in terms of both merchandise being sold and the shopping experience.

The nature and depth of retail selling is related to the variety of factors, including type of product, the customer's understanding of its qualities, uses and attributes, the complexity and value of the product, brand loyalty, and the extent to which the customer desires involvement in the buying process.

Retail selling, as only one element of the retail promotional mix, depends upon successful deployment of selected other elements, and should be integrated into a full promotional programme in order to nurture customer satisfaction.

PRODUCT CLASSIFICATION

The amount and quality of time a retail salesperson will spend actively selling depends firstly on the type of merchandise stocked by the retail organization. Merchandise can be classified as follows:

- Convenience goods – relatively inexpensive goods which are bought on a regular basis, without much thought going into the purchase, as customers are confident in product qualities, uses and attributes. Examples of convenience goods include items such as milk, eggs, bread, toilet rolls, clingfilm, floor cleaner and other 'everyday' items for which buyers tend to have low brand loyalty. The customer usually buys convenience goods at a supermarket or convenience store and needs little help to buy from the retail salesperson, although they can be encouraged to buy extra or associated items through suggestion and reminder. For example, cakes or pies can be suggested with bread, cream or cheese with milk; or the customer can be reminded of a special promotion on a larger size, or on two-for-one in a non-pressurizing manner.
- Preference goods – relatively inexpensive goods which are bought without much thought on a regular basis, for which the customer may have a reasonable amount of brand loyalty, but is less certain about desired product attributes. Goods such as tea, coffee, cigarettes, soft drinks and shampoos tend to fall into this category, and they are normally bought in grocery or convenience stores. Brand preference may have been established over time through other promotional activities such as advertising and sales promotion, and branding makes such stock highly visible within the store. Again, little help is required from the salesperson, although brand extensions and associated items can be suggested or new alternatives demonstrated.
- Shopping goods – more expensive and normally more complex goods which the customer wants to compare and contrast with competing or complementing goods within and outside the store. The customer is normally relatively confident about the attributes, qualities and uses of these goods, but is not strongly brand loyal and therefore wants to 'shop around' to compare quality, price and features. Although customers are willing to spend time shopping for these goods, they are not always keen to travel to make comparisons. These goods are

often bought from small specialist retailers. Goods such as clothes, shoes, accessories and cards often fall into this category. Salespeople can help customers to make a decision by giving information on comparative features, benefits and qualities for the price.

- Speciality goods – more expensive and complex goods, for example many electronic goods, in which customers experience uncertainty regarding attributes, qualities and uses, but for which they are willing to spend time and effort in shopping, including willingness to travel to buy from specialist retailers. Salespeople have an important role in helping customers to make a selection and come to a buy decision.
- Unsought goods – normally more expensive and complex goods which the customer would not necessarily think of buying, and therefore for which there is both uncertainty regarding attributes and low brand loyalty. Many unsought goods are sold door-to-door, although increasingly they are offered through traditional retail outlets. Examples are insurance, windows, conservatories and kitchens. Salespeople have a relatively important role in helping customers to make a buy decision. However, unlikely items which are occasionally juxtaposed with convenience and preference items also could be said to fall into the 'unsought' category. In this case the buy decision can be encouraged through strong promotional pricing or by information given to the customer through the sales process. In both cases the decision process will be aided by assurance through guarantee/ returns policy.

The classification above is general and retail sellers need to understand how their target customers regard the products which they are selling, something which is influenced by factors such as age, income, wealth and buying experience. Some buyers will have strong preferences for some convenience items for example, and others will regard some shopping goods as speciality goods. Direct communication between customer and salesperson allows rapid determination of the amount of help needed.

TYPES OF BUYING DECISION

The complexity of the buying decision is related to the variety of factors introduced in the sections above. The range of buying decisions can be classified as follows:

- Routine decision making – tends to be associated with repeat buying of convenience or preference products, either because of habit, low involvement in the purchase or because a strong preference for brand has been established, which aids decision making.
- Limited problem solving – in this situation the customer tends to have a higher level of involvement with the decision and will take more time to buy. Some information or incentive is needed to help make the buy decision. For example, a new brand or brand extension may have entered the market, or for a relatively simple, inexpensive item, the buyer may be new to the product category.
- Extensive problem solving – here the customer is willing to spend time and effort in shopping, either because the product is complex or new to the market, is expensive, has high value to the customer in some other way, or the customer has little experience in the product category.

The role of the retail salesperson is closely related to the complexity of the buying process. The complexity of the process can vary for individual customers and a knowledge of the target segment customer profile will help to determine the degree of personal selling needed. For example, a computer is a complex and expensive product for which many customers will need help to buy. However, many people are now computer literate, confident of buying and have established strong brand preference.

SHOPPING MOTIVES

People have a wide variety of motives for shopping:

- Necessity.
- Recreation.
- Fun/entertainment.
- Stimulation.
- Social.
- Exercise.

This is why, though the merchandise being bought is the main reason for the shopping experience, for most customers the total shopping experience will affect customer satisfaction. The total shopping experience includes peripheral aspects such as atmospherics, display, price, location, assortment and the dynamics of shopping, which will vary from customer to customer and on each shopping occasion. In addition to the variation of peripheral elements across shopping occasions there will exist differences in mood, staff encounters, number of other shoppers and so on. Even where the motive for shopping is necessity, it is widely recognized that the total shopping experience, rather than the merchandise itself, influences sales levels. Where shopping is for motives such as entertainment, recreation or social interaction, the dynamics of the shopping experience are more important, and the creation of a fun, exciting, interesting and diverting shopping environment are even more important.

Shopping motives vary from person to person and from occasion to occasion. Again, from a retail sales perspective, this illustrates the necessity to profile target customer groups. Almost every person who enters a store is a potential customer, however, and the role of selling in contributing to the total shopping experience should not be overlooked. Retail salespeople can quickly gauge shopping motives and respond accordingly. They can also help to create an 'exciting' shopping experience by exhibiting products or offering merchandise to customers to sample. Even if they only help in redirecting the customer to another store or destination, then they are contributing to the image of the organization as customer friendly – which may bring in future custom.

THE BUYING PROCESS

Two models illustrate the buying process. The AIDA model is the simplest to remember and is useful to consider here because it is widely used in developing promotional campaigns that include selling as one contributory element.

The constituents of the AIDA model is as follows:

- Awarness.
- Interest.
- Desire
- Action

Potential buyers first become of aware that they have the need for a specific product, brand or product group. Awareness can be stimulated by immediate lack of the product – running out of milk, for example – or by a growing awareness, such as a large car bill which heralds the onset of the need to start looking for another. Awareness means that the potential buyer consciously or subconsciously begins the search for a particular product.

The next phase is growing interest in finding the product required and is characterized by the search for and collection of information on the product. The type and extent of information looked for varies with product classification, with the type of buy decision, and even with the nature, confidence, experience and intelligence of the potential buyer. However, more information will be collected for shopping and speciality goods, which may include items such as product attributes, competing brands, competing outlets, prices, features and sources of finance. The potential buyer will collect information from the media, outlets, friends and family.

Studying the information and refining the data collected leads the potential buyer to gain a clearer picture cut of the product or brand required. One of the ways in which consumers reduce and refine the desired data from the plethora of information available is illustrated by a concept known as the 'evoked set'. For each product category, consumers will develop over time a set of brands from which they are most likely to choose an alternative. Hence, for example, a consumer in the biscuit aisle of the supermarket may decide between McVitie's Ginger Snaps, Rich Tea Biscuits, Hob Nobs, Nestl´e's KitKats and Traidcraft Geobars, automatically filtering out supermarket own-brands and other varieties. Further, for each member of the evoked set, customers learn and compare the various features and benefits (price, calories, taste, size) so that choice of alternative is facilitated. Desire has been defined as need plus ability to buy – so for expensive products, sources of finance will have been found. This customer is ready to buy. There may still be some doubts regarding brand, model, alternative finance sources and product features.

Action is when the potential customer makes the buy decision. Payment methods, terms and contracts need to be settled, but the decision has been made.

The weakness of the AIDA model is that it does not recognize what happens after the buy decision. The consumer buying process addresses this by dividing the process into five steps, the first four of which are comparable with the AIDA model:

1. Problem recognition.
2. Informaton search.
3. Alternative evaluation.

4. Alternative choice.
5. Post-purchase evaluation.

Post-purchase evaluation is the phase after the buyer has committed to buy decision and seeks reassurance that the right decision was made through continuing to scan for alternatives, asking friends, checking items out in other shops and so on. Post-purchase dissonance is the term used for the vague unease regarding whether the right decision has been made, and post-purchase evaluation helps to reduce the dissonance until the buyer is certain that the buy decision was, if not correct, good enough in the circumstances.

Table: Salesperson Activities in Relation to the Buying Decision Process

Problem recognition	Introduce new models or forthcoming product developments, can contact previous buyers to indicate current model is ageing or out of date; approach in-store customers to assess needs.
Information search	Give information on alternative models, outlets; indicate sources of information.
Alternative evaluation	Highlight particular features and benefits of alternative models, illustrations of satisfied customers.
Alternative choice	Indicate special offers, finance, guarantees to help the decision to buy
Post-purchase	Telephone or write to check satisfaction; can invite back to evaluation exhibitions, previews and other special events; can remind the customer it is time to buy again.

One of the benefits of retail selling is the potential of the seller to take the potential buyer through all the steps of the buying decision process, sometimes in a single visit, speeding and facilitating the decision to buy. Depending, of course, on the type of merchandise being sold and the type of buying decision, the retail salesperson has a role to play at every stage of the buying process.

However, because retail selling is primarily a one-to-one activity, and therefore is expensive, the most effective use of the salesperson's time is during the alternative evaluation and alternative choice stages. In many selling situations the successful deployment of the other promotional mix elements can abbreviate the sales time spent on customers in the other stages of the buying process.

RETAIL SALES ROLES

Retail salespeople have a major role to play in facilitating and enhancing the process of purchase decision making. Additionally, they can represent and reinforce store image, provide a dynamic shopping experience and build immediate relations with customers and potential customers.

There are two main roles which a retail salespeople undertake:

- Order taking.
- Order getting.

Many retail salespeople are order takers. That is, they process customers' decisions on products bought, at the very simplest merely running the item through checkout. This tends to happen with convenience and preference goods, and in shopping situations where routine decision making is the norm. These staff, nevertheless, have an important role in maintaining processing speed, and can influence sales through efficiency (or lack of it). Other order takers may show customers the location of goods, get them from stock, and give some limited information to aid evaluation and choice.

Stores which stock shopping and comparison goods, but which specialize in providing value at the expense of customer service, often operate staffing levels which preclude any but the most basic order-processing sales activities. These retailers rely on discounting, price, sales promotions and value to stimulate the decision to buy.

Increasingly, order takers will be encouraged to increase sales through means such as suggesting additional items to buy at the checkout, offering delivery service, or passing on information on deals and offers.

Order getters are retail salespeople who deal primarily with shopping and speciality goods where the decision to buy is not a routine work. The great benefit of salespeople in this role is their capability for direct customer communication, gauging shopping motive, relationship with merchandise and stage in the buying process. These sellers will engage potential customers in the selling process, informing them, guiding them and helping them make the decision to buy on the spot, or at some time in the future. Sometimes termed sales associates, order getters may be paid partly (or even wholly) in commission, which can lead to a pressurized selling environment that can conflict with customer preferences. One way round this is to relate commission not only to sales but to the value of returned products. Customer-orientated selling places customer focus at the heart of the selling process and aims at building a long-term customer relationship, which increases satisfaction with the product bought, salesperson, retailer and manufacturer. Due to their more extensive involvement in directly communicating with customers, order getters have a prime role in influencing customer perceptions of the retail organization and levels of customer satisfaction.

RETAIL SALES PROCESS

The selling process includes the stages summarized in Table below. Although stages of the selling process are most actively engaged by 'order-getting' retail salespeople, they also form a useful checklist for core retail activities.

Table: The Selling Process (and the Buying Process)

Buying Process Stages	Selling Process Stages	Salesperson Activities
Problem recognition	Prospecting	Developing a list of prospective customers
	Preparing	Learning customer profiles; learning features/benefits of products and other relevant information; matching to profiles
Information search	Approach	Approaching customer to determine shopping motives and needs; finding out desired product(s), benefits
Alternative evaluation	Presentation	Presenting information on product or products under consideration; showing demonstrating features and benefits
	Overcoming objections	Finding out reservations and or reservations barriers to the buy decision for products under consideration; answering questions
Alternative choice	Close	Asking for a buy decision
Post-purchase evaluation	Follow-up	Suggesting additional or complementary items; checking the customer's satisfaction with the product

A 'prospect' can be defined as any person who has the potential to purchase your goods or services. Sources of the prospects are as follows:

- Previous customers.
- Customer and employee referrals.
- Lapsed customers.
- Direct mail and other promotional methods.
- Exhibitions and demonstrations.
- Centre of influence method – use of local/regional/national celebrities to endorse store/organization.

Preparation includes learning about the target customer group, and how to handle different types of customer, including difficult customers. It also includes learning about the merchandise, its makeup, uses, performance, care, background and associated services. Retail salespeople also need to know about store policies on opening hours, payment, returns and delivery.

Customers who ask for help, try to catch the eye, or who are inspecting merchandise closely are the salesperson's best prospects, and a friendly outgoing approach with a direct greeting is recommended. The salesperson has to quickly determine the customer's needs through open questioning, but should remember to allow the customer time to talk freely, while listening, understanding, responding and summarizing. During the approach the salesperson has to indicate extensive product knowledge, show a genuine desire to meet the customer's needs and show a positive service attitude.

Once the customer's needs and price range have been defined, the salesperson presents the merchandise. The AIDA model (Awareness, Interest, Desire, Action) can serve as a structure for the presentation, as the salesperson outlines or demonstrates merchandise features, advantages and benefits to the prospect, relating these to the customer's specific needs. Allowing the customer to try or handle the merchandise helps to build desire, as does showing that a particular product will save money or exceed customer needs. Open questions allow the customer to express reservations or further needs, and closed questions allow the salesperson to determine understanding, facts and level of interest. The aim is not to 'sell' the customer, but to help the customer buy the merchandise which will give most satisfaction.

Reservations and objections are barriers to the buy decision and, if they are genuinely important to the customer, they have to be overcome to make a sale. It is best to anticipate common objections early in the presentation to prevent negativity later in the process. Other means of handling reservations include:

- Pass up the objection – skirt around the issue. If it comes up again it is important and needs to be addressed.
- Ask questions – find out the prospect's concerns.
- Rephrase the objection – summarize understanding of the customer's reservation. This buys thinking time.
- Compensate for the objection – outline the features and benefits which make the product worth buying.

- Deny the objection – where the customer reservation is based on a misconception, acknowledge their views and concern, then explain the correct situation.
- Use a testimony or third party – explain or demonstrate an instance in which the objection was previously made and the customer subsequently satisfied.

As each objection is answered, the salesperson should check that it has been overcome, using a closed question to determine the customer's agreement. This is sometimes called a 'trial close'. Where the objection cannot be overcome, this has to be acknowledged, followed by an indication of how the benefits of the product outweigh the disadvantages, or if appropriate, presentation of an alternative product.

Closing the sale is the point at which the customer is directly asked whether they want to buy. Buying signals are those behaviours which indicate genuine interest in purchase, such as reading the warranty or user manual, trying the product, examining the item in detail, asking questions about colours, styles, delivery, accessories, and making positive comments about the product. If the buying signals have been misinterpreted and the customer refuses to close, it is possible that there is a further reservation which requires to be determined and met. Alternatively, there may be another product or model which will meet their needs. It is, however, important not to pressurize the customer into buying.

Following up the sale can lead to extra sales in a number of ways, such as: supplementary and complementary items can be suggested to the buyer; a discount can be offered for the next purchase, or for a referral; the buyer can be added to a list of future prospects. It is good practice to enquire by telephone or card about customer satisfaction with any expensive or complex purchase.

RETAIL SELLING AND THE PROMOTIONAL MIX

Retail selling should form part of an integrated promotional plan, encompassing a variety of promotional mix elements and clear promotional objectives, which need to be communicated to those undertaking sales roles. Integration is required due to the nature of the consumer buying process. Consumers engaged in the 'information search' and 'alternative evaluation' stages of the buying process will be consciously or unconsciously acquiring and absorbing information put out by the retailer in the form of advertising, publicity, sales promotions and/or sponsorship (in addition to information from other agencies such as the media, competitors and friends). This information feeds into their expectations regarding the product(s) sought, the retail experience and the sales experience. Where there is a divergence between expectation and actuality, there is likely to be dissatisfaction.

For example, where an advertisement indicates a price reduction, the buyer will expect the salesperson to know about it, and to be offered it. Where a retailer advertises certain products for sale, the buyer will expect them to be in stock. When a retailer advertises in a magazine associated with high-quality, high-price merchandise, the buyer will expect an equally polished retail and sales experience.

The other promotional tools act together to form the foundation of the sales experience – they will bring to the potential customers, and the more successful they are, the less 'selling' will be required. However, the sales role undertaken by staff, the selling process itself, has to be tailored to accommodate the customer expectations raised through other promotional efforts. The knowledge salespeople have, their sales targets, the way they dress, the way they act and how they sell have all to be related to the other elements of the promotional mix and to the overall promotional objectives of the retailer.

SUMMARY

There is a strong relationship between retail selling, customer service and customer satisfaction. Retailers, operating market-focused service businesses, need to tailor their retail selling to customers' requirements with regard to:

- The type of product being bought;
- The type of purchase decision;
- Customers' shopping motives;
- Stages in the process of making the buying decision.

The nature and depth of retail selling required are related to the type, complexity and value of the product, the customer's understanding of its qualities, uses and attributes, brand loyalty and the extent to which the customer desires involvement in the buying process.

Merchandise can be categorized into convenience, preference, shopping, speciality and unsought goods, although the category for any one product may vary according to the customer's attributes, such as age, wealth and buying experience. The role of retail salespeople and the nature of the selling process will vary according to merchandise category and target customer profile. The nature of retail selling also varies according to the extensiveness of the customer decision-making process. Less involvement is required in selling convenience items, or those for which a strong brand preference has been established. More extensive selling is required for complex and expensive products which engage customers in extended problem solving.

The role and activities of retail salespeople also depend on the shopping motives of customers; where shopping is for social reasons, or for fun and entertainment, salespeople can contribute to a dynamic and changing retail experience. The customer buying process can be summarized within the Awareness, Interest, Desire, Action (AIDA) model, or more commonly within the five stages of the buying process.

The speed at which customers proceed through the stages depends on individual characteristics such as age and background, merchandise category and type of buying decision. The role of retail salespeople as direct communicators with customers allows them unique capability in rapidly determining, through simple questioning, which stage any individual customer has reached. The activities of retail salespeople will vary according to each stage of the buying process, but the most effective use of salespeople's time is to contribute to alternative evaluation and choice.

Most retail salespeople have an order-taking role – processing customers' orders once they have selected the merchandise. However, these staff can increase sales through their own efficiency and by suggesting supplementary and complementary merchandise to customers. Order getters have a more extensive sales role, usually associated with more complex and expensive merchandise, and these salespeople will engage potential customers in the selling process, informing them and helping them make the decision to buy. The sales process undertaken by order getters includes seven stages: prospecting, preparing, approach, presentation, overcoming objections, close, and post-purchase evaluation and follow-up. These can be linked to the stages of the buying process so that the salesperson has a more informed basis for the activities to be undertaken during each stage.

Retail selling is one element of the promotional mix and contributes to the achievement of promotional objectives. The integration of selling and other promotional mix elements is required to meet in-store customer expectations built through promotional activities during the information search of the buying process.

Note: Avocent designs, manufactures, licenses, and sells software and hardware products, which provides connectivity and centralized management of information technology (IT) infrastructure. The company primarily operates in the US. It is headquartered in Alabama, United States and employs 1,099 people. For further knowledge regarding this chapter reader can visit www.avocent.com

Bibliography

A. Birritteri, "Realizing the Benefits of an All-inclusive Employee Base," *New Jersey Business,* November, 2005.

A. Prayag, "All Work and More Play," *Business Line* (The Hindu), June, 2005.

A.G. Dawson, "Administrators Settle into New Digs," *Delaware Coast Press,* July, 2003.

A.H. Maslow, *Maslow on Management*, New York: John Wiley &Sons, 1998.

A.H. Maslow, "A Theory of Human Motivation," *Psychological Review*, 1943.

A.P. Hare, "Types of Roles in Small Groups: A Bit of History and a Current Perspective," *Small Group Research*, 1994.

B. Nussbaum, "Get Creative! How to Build Creative Companies," *Business Week,* August, 2005.

B.W. Tuckman and M.A.C. Jensen, "Stages of Small-Group Development Revisited," *Group and Organization Studies,* 1977.

C. Goforth, "Still Recruiting Staff," *Akron Beacon Journal,* July, 2001.

C. Lachnit, "The Young and the Dispirited," *Workforce*, August, 2002.

C. Smith, "Finding The 'Right People' Just Got Easier," *Franchising World*, November, 2005.

C.A. Beatty and B.A. Barker, *Building Smart Teams: Roadmap to High Performance*, Thousand Oaks, CA: Sage Publications, 2004.

C.C. Pinder, *Work Motivation in Organizational Behavior*, Upper Saddle River, NJ: Prentice-Hall, 1997.

C.K.W. De Dreu et al., "A Theory-Based Measure of Conflict Management Strategies in the Workplace," *Journal of Organizational Behavior*, 2001.

C.T. Crumpley, "Skill-Based Pay Replaces Traditional Ranking," *Kansas City Star,* June , 1997.

C.T. Kulik and M.L. Ambrose, "Personal and Situational Determinants of Referent Choice," *Academy of Management Review*, 1992.

D. Brady, "Will Jeff Immelt's New Push Pay Off for GE?" *Business-Week,* October, 2003.

D. Brown, "Success Begins in the Middle," *Canadian HR Reporter,* June, 2003.

D. Creelman, "Interview: Bob Catell & Kenny Moore," *HR.com,* February, 2005.

D. Hopewell, "Credit Union Keeps Productivity up with Friendly Competition," *Silicon Valley/San Jose Business Journal,* December, 2002.

D. Robb, "Global Workgroups," *Computerworld,* August, 2005.

D. Robey, H.M. Khoo, and C. Powers, "Situated Learning in Cross-Functional Virtual Teams," *Technical Communication,* February, 2000.

D. Ulrich and N. Smallwood, *Why the Bottom Line Isn't*, Hoboken, NJ: John Wiley & Sons, 2003

D.A. Harrison et al., "Time, Teams, and Task Performance: Changing Effects of Surface- and Deep-Level Diversity on Group Functioning," *Academy of Management Journal*, 2002.

D.C. Feldman, "The Development and Enforcement of Group Norms," *Academy of Management Review,* 1984.

D.C. McClelland, *The Achieving Society*, New York: Van Nostrand Re-inhold, 1961.

D.L. Miller, "The Stages of Group Development: A Retrospective Study of Dynamic Team Processes," *Canadian Journal of Administra-tive Sciences*, 2003.

D.M. Figart, "Equal Pay for Equal Work: The Role of Job Evaluation in an Evolving Social Norm," *Journal of Economic Issues*, March, 2000.

E. Hart, "Manager of the Year: John Mang," *Iron & Steelmaker,* June, 2003.

E. Horwitt, "Knowledge, Knowledge, Who's Got the Knowledge," *Computerworld,* April, 1996.

E. Silverman, "Making Your Mark," *Human Resource* Executive, November, 2004.

E. Ulich and W.G. Weber, "Dimensions, Criteria, and Evaluation of Work Group Autonomy," in *Handbook of Work Group Psychology,* ed. M.A. West, Chichester, UK: John Wiley and Sons, 1996.

E.B. Peach and D.A. Wren, "Pay for Performance from Antiquity to the 1950s," *Journal of Organizational Behavior Management*, 1992.

E.E. Lawler III, "From Job-Based to Competency-Based Organiza-tions," *Journal of Organizational Behavior*, 1994.

E.E. Lawler III, *Rewarding Excellence: Pay Strategies for the New Economy*, San Francisco: Jossey-Bass, 2000.

F. Piccolo, "Brownie Points," *Atlantic Business,* October-November 2004.

F.L. Schmidt and R.D. Zimmerman, "A Counterintuitive Hypothesis about Employment Interview Validity and Some Supporting Evidence," *Journal of Applied Psychology,* 2004.

G. Johns, "Absenteeism Estimates by Employees and Managers: Divergent Perspectives and Self-Serving Perceptions," *Journal of Applied Psychology*, 1994.

G. Buckler, "Staking One for the Team," *Computing Canada,* October, 2004.

G.H. Harel, A. Arditi-Vogel, and T. Janz, "Comparing the Validity and Utility of Behavior Description Interview versus Assessment Center Ratings," *Journal of Managerial Psychology*, 2003.

G.P. Latham and C.C. Pinder, "Work Motivation Theory and Research at the Dawn of the Twenty-First Century," *Annual Review of Psychology*, 2005.

G.P. Latham, "Goal Setting: A Five-Step Approach to Behavior Change," *Organizational Dynamics*, 2003.

G.S. Crystal, In *Search of Excess: The Overcompensation of American Executives*, New York: W.W. Norton & Co., 1991.

G.T. Milkovich, J.M. Newman, and C. Milkovich, *Compensation*, Burr Ridge, IL: McGraw-Hill/Irwin, 2002.

H. Das, "The Four Faces of Pay: An Investigation into How Canadian Managers View Pay," *International Journal of Commerce & Management*, 2002.

H. Fayol, *General and Industrial Management,* trans. C. Storrs, London: Pitman, 1949.

H.J. Bernardin, C.L. Tyler, and D.S. Wiese, "A Reconsideration of Strategies for Rater Training," in *Research in Personnel and Human Resources Management*, Stamford, CT: JAI Press, 2001.

I. Teotonio, "Rescuers Pull 'Victims' from Rubble," *Toronto Star,* April, 2005.

I.D. Steiner, *Group Process and Productivity*, New York: Academic Press, 1972.

J. Becker and L. Layton, "Safety Warnings Often Ignored at Metro," *Washington Post,* June, 2005.

J. Chelius and R.S. Smith, "Profit Sharing and Employment Stability," *Industrial and Labor Relations Review*, 1990.

J. Gordon, "Do Your Virtual Teams Deliver Only Virtual Performance?" *Training,* June, 2005.

J. Larson, "Temps Are Here to Stay," *American Demographics*, February, 1996.

J. Pellet, "Driving Diversity," *Chief Executive,* May, 2004.

J. Pfeffer, *New Directions in Organizational Theory*, New York: Oxford University Press, 1997.

J. Pfeffer, *The Human Equation*, Boston: Harvard Business School Press, 1998.

J. Yang and K.W Mossholder, "Decoupling Task and Relationship Conflict: The Role of Intergroup Emotional Processing," *Journal of Organizational Behavior,* 2004.

J.A. Breaugh, *Recruitment: Science and Practice*, Boston: PWS-Kent, 1992.

J.A. Breaugh, *Recruitment: Science and Practice*, Boston: PWS-Kent, 1992.

J.B. Miner, "The Rated Importance, Scientific Validity, and Practical Usefulness of Organizational Behavior Theories: A Quantitative Review," *Academy of Management Learning and Education*, 2003.

J.J. Dose and R.J. Klimoski, "The Diversity of Diversity: Work Values Effects on Formative Team Processes," *Human Resource Management Review,* Spring 1999.

J.J. Higuera, "Willcox, Ariz., Greenhouse Tomato Grower, Union Reach Contract Deals," *Arizona Daily Star,* November, 2002.

J.R. Hackman and G. Oldham, *Work Redesign*, Reading, MA: Addi-son-Wesley, 1980.

J.S. Adams, "Toward an Understanding of Inequity," *Journal of Abnormal and Social Psychology*, 1963.

K. Jelin, "A Multimethod Examination of the Benefits and Detriments of Intra-group Conflict," *Administrative Science Quarterly*, 1995.

K. Tyler, "Train for Smarter Hiring," *HR Magazine,* May, 2005.

K. Walters, "Dream Team," *Business Review Weekly,* October, 2005.

K.J. Dunham, "Career Journal: The Jungle," *The Wall Street Journal,* October, 2003.

K.N. Wexley and G.P. Latham, *Developing and Training Human Resources in Organizations,* 2nd ed., New York: HarperCollins, 1991.

K.T. Dirks and D.L. Ferrin, "The Role of Trust in Organizations," *Organization Science*, July-August, 2004.

L. Adams, "Medrad Works and Wins as a Team," *Quality Magazine,* October, 2004.

L. Coch and J. French, J.P..R, "Overcoming Resistance to Change," *Human Relations*, 1948.

M. Muckian, "Irreverent Heritage," *The Business Journal*, Milwaukee, March, 2003.

M.J. Frank, "Justifiable Discrimination in the News and Entertainment Industries: Does Title VII Need a Race or Color BFOQ?" *University of San Francisco Law Review*, Spring, 2001.

N.L. Kerr and S.R. Tindale, "Group Performance and Decision Making," *Annual Review of Psychology,* 2004.

N.R. Lockwood, "Workplace Diversity: Leveraging the Power of Difference for Competitive Advantage," *HR Magazine,* June, 2005.

O.E. Williamson, "Calculativeness, Trust, and Economic Organization," *Journal of Law and Economics*, 1993.

P. Drucker, *Peter Drucker on the Profession of Management*, Boston: Harvard Business School Press, 1998.

P. Dvorak, "Out of Tune," *The Wall Street Journal,* June, 2005.

P. Haw, "Learning from Lean Principles," *Business Day,* July, 2003.

P. Kershaw, "Happy Days," *Sydney Morning Herald,* August, 2005.

P. Siekman, "This Is Not a BMW Plant" *Fortune,* April, 2005.

P. Sullivan, J. and D.L. Feltz, "The Relationship between Intrateam Conflict and Cohesion within Hockey Teams," *Small Group Research,* June, 2001.

P.P. Wernimont and J.P. Campbell, "Signs, Samples, and Criteria," *Journal of Applied Psychology*, October, 1968.

PR. Lawrence and N. Nohria, *Driven: How Human Nature Shapes Our Choices*, San Francisco: Jossey-Bass, 2002.

R. Cross, "Looking before You Leap: Assessing the Jump to Teams in Knowledge-Based Work," *Business Horizons,* September, 2000.

R. Hallowell, D. Bowen, and C.-I. Knoop, "Four Seasons Goes to Paris," *Academy of Management Executive*, November 2002.

R. Mullins, "Verizon Goes to Great Lengths," *Tampa Tribune,* February, 2006.

R. Romell, "Sharp Focus on Employee Satisfaction Pays Off for ACUITY," *Milwaukee Journal Sentinel,* June, 2004.

R.C. Lee, "Keeping Up with Growth," *Houston Chronicle,* August, 2005.

R.C. Liden et al., "Social Loafing: A Field Investigation," *Journal of Management*, 2004.

R.E. Baumeister and M.R. Leary, "The Need to Belong: Desire for Interpersonal Attachments as a Fundamental Human Motivation," *Psychological Bulletin*, 1995.

R.F. Mager and P. Pipe, *Analyzing Performance Problems*, Belmont, CA: Lake Publishing, 1984.

R.J. Lowry, *The Journals of A.H. Maslow*, Monterey, CA: Brooks/Cole, 1979.

R.M. Belbin, *Team Roles at Work*, Oxford, UK: Butterworth-Heine-mann, 1993.

S. Beatty, "Bass Talk: Plotting Plaid's Future," *The Wall Street Journal,* September, 2004.

S. Prashad, "Building Trust Tricky for 'Virtual' Teams," *Toronto Star,* October, 2003.

S. Prestegard, "From Heritage to Acuity," *Marketplace Magazine,* March, 2001.

S. Rajagopalan, "Bangalore to Hawaii, an All-Paid Holiday," *Hindustan Times,* May, 2005.

S. Theil, "The New Old Age," *Newsweek.* January, 2006.

S.E. Jackson and R.S. Schuler, "Human Resource Planning," *American Psychologist*, 1990.

S.E. Nedleman, "Recruiters Repeal Their Top Interview Questions," *Financial News Online,* February, 2005.

S.F. Matusik and C.W.L. Hill, "The Utilization of Contingent Work, knowledge Creation, and Competitive Advantage," *Academy of Management Review,* October, 1998.

S.J. Karau and K.D. Williams, "Social Loafing: A Meta-Analytic Review and Theoretical Integration," *Journal of Personality and Social Psychology*, 1993.

S.S. Webber and L.M. Donahue, "Impact of Highly and Less Job-Related Diversity on Work Group Cohesion and Performance: A Meta-Analysis," *Journal of Management*, 2001.

T. Janz, "Manipulating Subjective Expectancy through Feedback: A Laboratory Study of the Expectancy-Performance Relationship," *Journal of Applied Psychology*, 1982.

T. Matthews, "Ohio-Area Companies Turn to 'Evaluation Hiring' to Pick Best Employees," *Columbus Dispatch,* May, 2005.

T. Weiss, *Coaching Competencies and Corporate Leadership,* Boca Raton, FL: St. Lucie Press, 2003.

V. Gait, "Kid-Glove Approach Woos New Grads," *Globe & Mail,* March, 2005.

W.B. Scott, "Blue Angels," *Aviation Week & Space Technology,* March,. 2005.

W.G. Dyer, *Team Building: Current Issues and New Alternatives,* 3rd ed., Reading, MA: Addison-Wesley, 1995.

Y. Cohen-Charash and P.E. Spector, "The Role of Justice in Organizations: A Meta-Analysis," *Organizational Behavior and Human Decision Processes*, November, 2001.

Index

A

Accounts, 29, 143, 145

Achievement, 61

Action, 48, 58, 59, 60, 127, 239, 275, 276, 280, 283

Adjourning, 243, 244

Advancement, 61

Advertising, 72, 165, 257, 258, 259, 260, 261, 262, 263, 264, 265, 266, 267

Aesthetic, 186, 187, 188, 193

Agencies, 165, 266

Agreement, 140, 232

Approaches, 2, 262

Attention, 5, 215, 268

Attitude, 252

B

Business, 9, 10, 12, 65, 67, 128, 258, 267, 285, 286, 287, 288, 289, 290

C

Cambridge, 9

Campus, 160, 161

Candidate, 174, 178

Catalogues, 265

Categorization, 59

Change, 2, 4, 79, 287, 289

Cinema, 265

Climate, 28, 61, 240

Commission, 56, 201

Communication, 72, 76, 78, 83, 85, 86, 91, 93, 95, 97, 237, 268, 286

Company, 54, 60, 160, 163, 164, 166, 195, 204

Compensation, 61, 194, 196, 197, 204, 287

Competent, 210

Concepts, 55, 214

Conditions, 1, 35, 51, 60, 99, 100, 144, 159, 185, 263

Conscious, 210

Contingent, 160, 161, 162, 291

Controlling, 6

Courses, 51

Creditworthiness, 266

Criteria, 156, 287, 290

Customer, 1, 14, 17, 21, 35, 58, 59, 112, 120, 131, 135, 146, 241, 278, 279

D

Dangers, 17

Delegated, 139, 140

Description, 177, 287

Detail, 5

Developing, 6, 31, 68, 156, 218, 255, 256, 289

Difficulty, 27

Dimension, 17, 24, 25, 89

Director, 67

Distibution, 47, 54

E

Economic, 186, 191, 192, 193, 194, 207, 260, 286, 289

Electronic, 17, 24, 163, 265

Employment, 165, 287, 288

Engineering, 241

Enlargement, 138

Exams, 178

Excellent, 52, 188, 249

Exercise, 274

Expectations, 267

Experience, 118, 158

Export, 25, 26

F

Finance, 241

Fires, 136

Firms, 165, 166

Forecasting, 133, 150, 152

Forming, 20, 243

Foundation, 72

Four-Quadrant, 88

Frederick, 41, 60, 185

G

Global, 25, 143, 286

Group, 7, 39, 62, 67, 71, 95, 153, 285, 286, 287, 288, 289, 290, 291

Growth, 61, 152, 159, 260, 290

H

Herzberg, 41, 60, 185, 186, 192

Honesty, 247

Huthwaite, 12, 62

I

Idea, 52

Incompetent, 210

Innovation, 5

Interest, 129, 141, 275, 280, 283

International, 25, 27, 287

Interview, 168, 170, 286, 287, 291

Introduction, 1, 256

Issues, 34, 286, 291

J

Job, 71, 138, 160, 162, 163, 164, 169, 177, 286, 287, 291

Journals, 65, 66, 265, 290

K

Key, 2, 13, 34, 44, 55, 60, 62, 63, 65, 267

L

Legal, 234, 241

Licensing, 27

Literature, 265

M

Management, 2, 4, 9, 11, 14, 21, 28, 31, 43, 58, 60, 67, 72, 80, 133, 137, 166, 207, 219, 285, 286, 287, 288, 289, 290, 291

Manufacturing, 239, 241

Market, 4, 25, 72, 73, 118, 131, 267

Marketing, 17, 25, 27, 67, 71, 72, 115, 116, 117, 121, 152, 166, 241, 255, 258, 259, 261, 265

Massachusetts, 9

Maximizing, 161, 162, 164, 165, 166

Mentality, 248

Mentor, 246

Mission, 123, 124, 125, 239

Motivating, 6, 31, 41, 61, 187, 188

Motives, 263, 271, 274, 275. 282, 283

N

Necessity, 274

Newspaper, 160, 165

Norming, 243

O

Objectives, 32, 127, 262

Online, 162, 291

Operations, 241

Opportunities, 19, 117, 159

Options, 25, 204

Origins, 86

Overview, 90, 92, 94, 96

P

Performing, 243, 244

Plan, 33, 106, 110, 122, 123, 196, 197, 230, 267

Players, 219, 220, 226, 241

Political, 186, 189, 190, 194

Practice, 9, 22, 29, 47, 54, 105, 218, 253, 288

Presence, 26

Professional, 65, 67, 71

Profile, 57, 86, 87, 264

Projects, 137

Purchasing, 241

R

Radio, 264, 265

Recognition, 61, 79, 205, 207

Recreation, 274

Recruiting, 36, 155, 160, 161, 165, 166, 168, 181, 285

Reinforcement, 214, 215, 218, 228

Relationship, 244

Research, 20, 22, 29, 38, 41, 49, 62, 65, 120, 267, 268, 285, 287, 288, 290

Resources, 65, 81, 267, 288, 289

Responsibility, 4, 61, 233, 239

Resume, 169, 174

Rewards, 141, 205

Round, 9

Rule, 168

S

Salary, 60, 159, 201, 202

Sales, 1, 2, 3, 6, 9, 11, 12, 13, 14, 18, 25, 26, 27, 31, 32, 33, 34, 36, 47, 48, 54, 56, 57, 58, 59, 61, 62, 66, 67, 71, 72, 73, 74, 75, 76, 77, 78, 79, 80, 109, 110, 111, 115, 116, 117, 120, 133, 142, 149, 150, 152, 157, 162, 166, 194, 196, 198, 199, 203, 206, 219, 225, 226, 227, 241, 255, 258, 259, 261, 267, 268, 269, 277, 279

Screening, 164, 178

Searching, 5

Security, 61

Selection, 156, 262, 264, 265

Sites, 162, 164

Situation, 47

Skills, 75, 83, 105, 199

Social, 92, 186, 188, 189, 193, 194, 207, 274, 286, 289, 290, 291

Staff, 68, 115, 161, 162, 285

Staffing, 6, 31, 36

Standards, 57, 140

Statement, 123, 124

Status, 60

Stimulation, 274

Storming, 243

Strengths, 90, 92, 94, 96, 117, 187, 188, 190, 191

Structural, 186, 190, 191, 194

Supervision, 60, 214

System, 88

T

Tactics, 127

Team, 74, 75, 94, 109, 143, 152, 155, 189, 203, 218, 219, 237, 238, 240, 241, 242, 243, 286, 287, 288, 289, 290, 291

Temperature, 61, 103

Terminology, 55, 57, 126, 232, 249

Territory, 57, 133, 142, 203, 225

Theoretical, 186, 187, 193, 291

Theory, 85, 86, 101, 183, 184, 263, 285, 287, 288

Thinkers, 55, 60, 65, 248

U

Unconscious, 210

V

Video, 265

Vision, 72, 123

W

Winning, 62, 65, 67